COLLECTIVE ENCOUNTERS:

DOCUMENTARY THEATRE IN ENGLISH CANADA

Alternative theatre has been one of Canada's strongest cultural institutions over the past twenty years. Coinciding with a major revival of nationalism in Canadian culture during the late 1960s, this strength was in evidence throughout the country, and provided fertile ground for the growth of an important dramatic genre: the collectively created documentary play. Typically inspired by a distinctive community or a political issue, these plays are created through a process that begins with a group of actors researching a specific issue or community and ends with a performance aimed at a specific audience. Some of the works thus created represent the most popular plays ever staged in Canada.

In this study of the genre as it has developed nationally, Alan Filewod examines six landmark examples in terms of their impact on their respective theatres and their role in Canada's cultural development generally. The plays include Theatre Passe Muraille's *The Farm Show*, Toronto Workshop Production's *Ten Lost Years*, Globe Theatre's *No. 1 Hard*, 25th Street Theatre's *Paper Wheat*, The Mummers Troupe's *Buchans: A Mining Town*, and Catalyst Theatre's *It's About Time*.

Each of these six plays represents an aspect of the documentary genre. Together they evoke a period of unprecedented activity in Canadian theatre and the wide range of social, political, and cultural issues that have driven it.

ALAN FILEWOD is assistant professor in the Department of Drama, University of Guelph, and editor of *Canadian Theatre Review*.

ALAN FILEWOD

Collective Encounters: Documentary Theatre in English Canada

UNIVERSITY OF TORONTO PRESS
Toronto Buffalo London

© University of Toronto Press 1987
Toronto Buffalo London
Printed in Canada

ISBN 0-8020-2633-8 (cloth)
ISBN 0-8020-6669-0 (paper)

Canadian Cataloguing in Publication Data

Filewod, Alan D. (Alan Douglas), 1952–
   Collective encounters
   Bibliography: p.
   Includes index.
   ISBN 0-8020-2633-8 (bound) ISBN 0-8020-6669-0 (pbk.)
   1. Experimental theater – Canada – History.
   2. Historical drama, Canadian (English) – History
   and criticism. 3. Canadian drama (English) – 20th
   century – History and criticism. I. Title.
   PN2304.F55 1987   792.1'4'0971   C87-094126-7

Cover photo: A scene from *Ten Lost Years*, 1975, courtesy of Toronto Workshop Productions.

Photos courtesy of Catalyst Theatre, Chris Brookes, Globe Theatre, Theatre Passe Muraille, Toronto Workshop Productions, 25th Street Theatre.

This book has been published with the help of a grant from the Canadian Federation for the Humanities, using funds provided by the Social Sciences and Humanities Research Council of Canada.

Contents

Preface

In this book I have attempted to define in historical and critical terms one of the most important developments of modern English Canadian theatre. In Canada, as in the rest of the western world, the 1960s and 1970s saw a widespread revival of political and experimental theatre. In little more than a decade Canadian theatre experienced an unprecedented revolution as hundreds of new troupes emerged, introducing new playwrights who legitimized Canadian drama. In 1965 there were fewer than a dozen professional theatres in English Canada; ten years later there were well over a hundred (and as many again in Quebec). This development was the result of a complex intersection of historical forces, among them the revival of nationalism that was so crucial in all sectors of Canadian life in the 1970s; the large scale injection of government funding into the arts; the maturing of the post-war generation and its rejection of traditional artistic conventions; and a world-wide revival of experimental theatre that challenged traditional forms of theatrical production.

These factors came together in what critics called the 'alternative theatre movement' because it was perceived to oppose the system of publicly subsidized civic theatres established across Canada in the late 1950s and early 1960s. The development of the alternative theatre was an important stage in the evolution of Canadian culture from colonialism to cultural autonomy. For that reason I refer to the alternative theatre as 'post-colonial,' not in the constitutional sense but because of its explicit rejection of foreign models and standards. A colonized culture is one that defines itself in terms absorbed from a dominating power. In that sense, the experience of theatre reversed the historical evolution of colonialism in Canadian society. If English Canada in general moved from a colonial allegiance to the British connection in the early years of this century to an increasing assimilation into American cultural hegemony in the post-war decades, in the theatre the reverse was the case.

At the turn of the century almost every theatre in Canada was owned or contracted to the giant American touring syndicates. Fearing (correctly, as it turned out) that this would retard the growth of independent Canadian theatre and drama, critics of the day argued for a 'theatrical declaration of independence' from the United States. They advocated instead the new British idea of subsidized civic theatres. It was this vision, promoted initially by men whose artistic sensibilities and cultural loyalties were those of a British Canada, that was realized in the regional theatre system established after the Second World War. Not suprisingly, these new theatres looked towards Britain for expertise, artistic standards, and repertoire. Consequently, to the emerging, fiercely nationalistic generation of the 1960s, the regional theatres exemplified what came to be criticised as a colonial dependence on Britain. This attack on established theatre as colonial was fuelled by the disproportionate number of British directors in the large theatres and by the extreme caution and frequent scepticism with which they greeted Canadian plays.

In its repudiation of 'colonial' structures of thought and methods of theatrical creation, the alternative theatre sought to discover authentic, indigenous Canadian dramatic forms. The quest was successful: one of the major results of the movement was the introduction of a unique dramatic genre in the collectively created documentary play. From the late 1960s to the present, Canadian theatres have produced hundreds of collective creations, created by the actors through research and improvisation, and documentary plays, compiled from research into communities and historical issues. Typically these two features overlapped: collective creation was the most common means of creating documentary theatre, and documentary plays were usually created collectively. There was, however, enough of a divergence to suggest that the two cannot be understood as synonymous. Consequently it is necessary to consider collective creation as a process, and documentary theatre as its most common result. It is because documentary theatre can be analysed as both an historical phenomenon and a genre of performance with its unique formal characteristics that I have chosen it as the focus of this study.

Because it investigates the documentary theatre in both of these terms, this book is at once theatre history and dramatic criticism. An understanding of the conditions out of which the documentary plays emerged, the methods used to create them, and their subsequent effect on the theatre as an institution is necessary to an appreciation of their dramatic form. Unlike the literary drama, which I suggest is essentially antithetical to documentary theatre, the documentary play rarely survives as a 'final' text.

The decision to examine the documentary theatre in both historical and analytical contexts was necessitated in part by the fact that this is the first in-depth study of the theatrical forms emerging out of the English Canadian alternative theatre. Instead of attempting a broad survey, I have looked at six representative plays, of which only three have been published. Most of the documentary plays produced in Canada have already disappeared; those that survive do so as typescripts or tape recordings to be found in theatre files, private homes, or, more rarely, in archival collections. Consequently any discussion of the form must contain enough description to acquaint the reader with the plays even as they are analysed.

The plays discussed in this book have been selected for their representative value, providing a cross-section of the range of Canadian documentary, and as individual models of specific aspects of the form. They include some of the most celebrated of Canadian plays as well as some of the least known. I have included Theatre Passe Muraille's *The Farm Show* because it was the prototype of the most common form of Canadian documentary; it also raises the issue of documentary form and collective creation. *Ten Lost Years* by Toronto Workshop Productions provides the opportunity to examine the relation of documentary structure and original source material. To accommodate the regional impulse behind much of Canadian documentary, I have included plays from the prairies and Newfoundland. In the first case, a comparison of two plays about the Saskatchewan grain industry, Globe Theatre's *No. 1 Hard* and 25th Street Theatre's *Paper Wheat*, examines the apparent authenticity of documentary theatre and the collectively created revue. In the second case, the Mummers Troupe's *Buchans: A Mining Town* exemplifies the political documentary devised as an active intervention in a community struggle. Finally, Catalyst Theatre's *It's About Time*, an interactive 'theatre forum,' questions the limits of the documentary idea.

My analyses of these plays rest on the critical assumption that the documentary theatre must be considered a genre of performance rather than a form of literary drama. For that reason I have chosen to examine these plays as they were performed in their historical contexts. The descriptive analyses of the plays are contained within more general discussions of their place in the development of their respective theatres. I hope that this approach will lead to a fuller understanding of the relation of dramatic form and performance structure to the society upon which both reflect. As 'non-fiction'plays, they also deserve to be considered in terms of their subjects. In the course of such discussions I have tried to refrain, not always as successfully as I might wish, from passing judgment on the issues and controversies behind the plays.

A few words are in order about the critical standards by which I evaluate the plays. Documentary theatre tends to put the process by which it is created into the fore by including references to that process within the performance itself. In this way it breaks down the normal expectation of fiction on stage. At the same time it tends to include references and techniques which authenticate the play's claim to factual veracity. In so far as these tendencies inherently reject the traditional discourse of dramatic narrative they seem ideally suited for structuralist analysis. The fact of collective creation is itself a critique of the traditional role of the dramatic author, and in most of these plays authorship must be seen as a group process. In that sense, these plays make traditional dramatic criticism, with its textual orientation, difficult. I have attempted to overcome this problem by discussing each play as a way of using theatre to transform actuality into a performance of findings that is both ongoing process and created text. Ultimately, these plays are atextual; they repudiate the idea of a fixed, unchanging text which exists as a blueprint, as it were, for a performed interpretation. Hence, when I refer to 'text' in this book, I mean the particular text generated by the actors in a particular performance.

Because this book is primarily a discussion of the development of a theatrical genre, its basis is empirical. It does not proceed from one governing theoretical position, at least not explicitly. Instead I have tried to approach each play with the critical perspective that seems best able to explain the performance in its historical context. In so doing I have borrowed analytical techniques from several critical theories, but in all cases I have tried as much as possible to avoid specialized jargon.

Finally it is necessary to stress that the plays discussed in this book are drawn from the English language theatre in Canada. There is no attempt to examine the very different conditions and resulting genres of the French language theatre. Although the two principal theatre cultures in Canada have much in common, they have many differences. Responding to different social pressures, guided by different ideological priorities, the francophone and anglophone theatres have evolved unique genres that require separate study. Only after defining the particular development of each culture will scholars be able to embark on the more comprehensive synthesis that examines these developments in relation to each other.

In the course of researching and writing this book I have been helped by many people. I wish to thank the office staffs of Catalyst Theatre, Globe Theatre, Northern Light Theatre, and Theatre Passe Muraille for their cheerful assistance in locating archival material. Shirley Martin of the University of Saskatchewan Library and Susan Puff of Toronto Workshop Productions deserve thanks for their help in finding photographs. As well, I am indebted to the staff of the Metropolitan Toronto Library Theatre Department for guiding me through their invaluable archive.

I wish to thank as well the artists who helped me reconstruct the performances I describe. David Barnet, Rex Deverell, Ken Kramer, George Luscombe, Jan Selman, Guy Sprung, Andras Tahn, and Paul Thompson all were generous with their time and insights.

The research for this book was helped immeasurably by Diane Bessai, whose pioneering inquiries into Canadian documentary theatre guided my path, and Chris Brookes, who provided inspiration and hospitality. To Mary McDougall Maude of University of Toronto Press I owe special thanks for her painstaking editorial assistance.

Finally I wish to thank the two people who saw this book grow from its inception. Michael Sidnell's critical advice and Susan McLennan's patient encouragement were of greater value than they perhaps realized at the time.

The Farm Show, Theatre Passe Muraille. Original audience in Ray Bird's barn

The Farm Show. Left to right: Ann Anglin, Miles Potter (top), Paul Thompson, Fina
MacDonell

On tour in Wales. *Left to right:* local Welsh farmer, his cow Mary Bell, Linda Griffiths, Mary Walsh, Ted Johns

Ten Lost Years, Toronto Workshop Productions. Cast of the 1975 production on the set. *Left to right:* Diane Douglass, Peter Millard, Ross Skene, Heather Ritchie, François-Régis Klanfer, Sandy Crawley, Judy Crocker, Rich Payne, Grant Roll, Rosemary Dunsmore

Publicity still showing men of the 1981 revival. *Left to right:* Norm Hacking, Kim Vincent, Ross Skene, Sten Hornborg, Grant Roll, Peter Millard, François-Régis Klanfer (Photo: Vid Ingelevics)

No. 1 Hard, Globe Theatre. Linda Huffman

Left to right: Debra Scott, Linda Huffman, David Miller, Kim McCaw

Paper Wheat, 25th Street Theatre. *Taking a bow left to right:* Bill Prokopchuk, Peter Meuse, Skai Leja, David Francis, Sharon Bakker

Meeting the audience

David Francis, Sharon Bakker, Lubomir Mykytiuk (Photo: Pat Close)

Buchans: A Mining Town, The Mummers Troupe. *Left to right:* Donna Butt, Bembo Davies, Allen Booth, Lee J. Campbell, Connie Kaldor

Left to right: Lee J. Campbell, Allen Booth, puppet, Howie Cooper, Connie Kaldor, Bembo Davies

Left to right: Allen Booth, Bembo Davies, Lee J. Campbell, Howie Cooper, Connie Kaldor

It's About Time, Catalyst Theatre. Ed Lyszkiewicz, Robert Winslow

Robert Winslow, Ed Lyszkiewicz

Stand Up for Your Rights, Catalyst Theatre. *Left to right:* Dennis Robinson, Shelley Irvine (Catalyst TV)

Left to right: Jane Heather, Susan Sneath, Frank Pellegrino

COLLECTIVE ENCOUNTERS

1

The Evolution of Documentary Theatre in Canada

There is an enduring cliché to the effect that Canadian culture has an inherent predilection to the documentary in film, literature, theatre, and visual art. Like many clichés, this one is founded on a reasonable observation. That the documentary has an important place in Canadian culture is readily apparent, but it does not follow that Canadian culture is more partial to the documentary than other cultures, or that Canadians are better – or even more prolific – than others at making documentaries. The idea of cultural bias towards one mode of expression is troublesome. It denies that cultures are processes of changing relationships, and that the artistic forms a culture develops reflect deeper changes.

The idea that a documentary impulse is inherent in Canadian culture was first formulated by Dorothy Livesay in her influential 1969 essay 'The Documentary Poem: A Canadian Genre.' Livesay maintained that a preference for the documentary is as old as Canadian literature, and she identified a tradition of narrative poetry 'based on topical data but held together by descriptive, lyrical and didactic elements.'[1] Although she suggests that this style, especially in the 'long storytelling poem' of such writers as Isabella Valancy Crawford and E.J. Pratt, is deeply representative of the Canadian character, Livesay's argument is pure hypothesis. Her definition of documentary is elastic enough to cover most narrative genres which 'create a dialectic between the objective facts and the subjective feelings of the poet.'[2] Although she argues the case for a distinctive Canadian narrative voice, Livesay fails to explain why this documentary impulse should be so imbedded in the Canadian cultural psyche.

A later generation of critics, accepting Livesay's proposal, have attempted to account for a Canadian partiality to documentary in terms of a post-colonial insecurity. Rick Salutin, the left-wing playwright whose plays such as *1837: The Farmers' Revolt* and *Les Canadiens* draw heavily upon documentary techniques, has argued that the documentary 'is the curse of Canadian culture.'[3] It is, he says, 'a style for people who have trouble taking their own experience seriously.' His explanation is important enough to quote at length:

The documentary style – in film, theatre, prose, whatever – says: count on this, we've got it down in pictures, quotes, documentation, in the speech rhythms of daily life and all kinds of tiny corroborative details. This (story, movie, play) feels like fact because it has the texture of the news in your daily paper. It is true to life and reliable in the way an on-the-spot report on 'The National' is. Boring, perhaps – but real. Our works of the imagination seem to require the perpetual reiteration – through the documentary style – that this is all about something real.

Salutin completes his argument with the suggestion that despite its commitment to historical fact, the documentary may distort reality by providing an illusion of actuality at the expense of true analysis.

Both Livesay and Salutin attribute the modern documentary trend in Canada to John Grierson's work at the National Film Board of Canada (NFB) in the 1940s and 1950s. This suggestion has even found favour among those who create documentary theatre. Paul Thompson, whose work at Theatre Passe Muraille gave Canadian documentary theatre its characteristic style, told an interviewer in 1973:

In The Farm Show and Under the Greywacke we went out into a community to bring back a kind of living community portrait or photograph, filled with things that we observed and that they would like to say about themselves. I suppose that's based on all sorts of traditions of documentary that we have in this country, like the work of the CBC and the NFB.[4]

The existence of such a tradition remains a matter of speculation, but what little evidence there is suggests that the case has been exaggerated. That the documentary form was remarkably popular in the 1970s, in theatre and film, is beyond doubt, but that popularity cannot be ascribed to inherent cultural bias or to Grierson's work in film thirty years earlier.

When Grierson established the National Film Board it quickly began to fulfil a propagandist function based on his own theories and necessitated by the Second World War. The NFB did indeed embody a documentary tradition, but it was not native to Canada; rather it followed Grierson's previous work with the British Government Post Office (GPO) Film Unit, and it was influenced by American newsreels like The March of Time and Why We Fight. If we are to ascribe to the NFB a major influence in Canadian culture since the Second World

War, it may be because the board created an institutional framework which provided facilities and funding for novice film-makers. Canada was by no means the only country to sponsor the production of documentary film (although the NFB was widely copied abroad), but in Canada those documentaries occupy an important place in the history of film. This may reflect something more material than a native cultural bias: in Canada the work of the NFB stands out in stark contrast to the underdevelopment of other cinematic genres until the post-war era. When Grierson piloted the NFB to world renown, the Canadian feature film industry was at a standstill, and film-makers who might otherwise have directed their energies to full-length features instead produced documentaries. Similarly, when theatres began producing documentary plays in the early 1970s, there was a dearth of Canadian plays fit for the stage, and would-be directors were forced to encourage new writers and make their own plays. The same principle holds true of the CBC; it attained legendary proficiency in the production of radio documentaries – but so did networks in other countries.

Nevertheless, if the revival of documentary after the war did not arise simply out of a native tradition, but out of a complex of material and cultural processes, it is true that it played a special role in the development of contemporary Canadian culture. This suggests that there must be some element in that culture that is best expressed in the documentary mode, at least at this particular stage of its development.

To come to terms with this problem it is necessary to separate the rise of the modern documentary theatre from its related genres and historical sources. Although the thematic tendencies of the Canadian documentary theatre can be attributed to the populist nationalism of the alternative theatre movement, its specific forms emerged in large part from the intersection of two distinct sources: a tradition of didactic historical drama in Canada, and the international tradition of documentary theatre that originated in Europe in the 1920s.

Canadian drama has from its beginnings been partial towards what might be called the authority of factual evidence. This can be seen in a long line of plays that seek to revise Canadian history, a list that begins in the early nineteenth century and continues to the present day. There is a direct line of descent from historical dramas like Sarah Anne Curzon's *Laura Secord* (1887) and Charles Mair's *Tecumseh* (1886) to the contemporary didactic plays of writers such as Sharon Pollock and Rick Salutin. Invariably, the self-appointed task of the Canadian historical dramatist has been to promote a specific ideology, and, in most cases, that ideology has been overtly nationalistic – even though the definitions and programs of Canadian nationalism have changed radically over the past century.

Just as Pollock and Salutin incorporate documentary evidence in their plays, so did their predecessors. Mair's *Tecumseh*, certainly the most celebrated Canadian play of its day, offers a case in point. Mair wrote the play ostensibly to celebrate the Indian chief Tecumseh's contribution to the British cause in the War of 1812, but the play celebrates as well the dubious tradition that Canadian nationhood was won on the field of battle by the Canadian volunteers. *Tecumseh* is a hymn of praise to a conservative, anti-republican, and pro-monarchist Canada. By adopting the form of Shakespearean blank verse tragedy, Mair effectively appropriated the British literary heritage to produce a new tradition that would abide by its roots while 'tasting of the wood.' The lyrical descriptive passages in the play, the many references to Canadian flora and fauna, Indian lore, geography, and most notably the extensive footnotes appended to the play all reveal Mair's desire to authenticate romantic action in terms of verifiable reality. Mair's faith in actuality extended to his dramaturgy, in which he tried to stay 'as close to history as exigency would permit.'[5] Ten years later, Mair's contemporary, James Bovell Mackenzie, wrote his own Indian play *Thayendanegea* (about Joseph Brant) in rebuttal, with less skill but even more exacting fidelity to historical fact. Arguably the most inept playwright in Canadian history, Mackenzie, in his appeal to 'Thespis' undistorting camera, was typical of the polemic dramatists of his day.[6]

This tradition of polemic drama is related to a minor tradition of civic and professional pageants, which themselves followed Louis Parker's historical pageants in Britain in the 1910s. Properly speaking, polemic drama and pageantry are antithetical: pageantry, with its emphasis on iconography, by definition precludes the reasoned argument that is implicit in the idea of polemic drama. In practice, however, the two forms have often overlapped, generally at the expense of true polemic. *Tecumseh*, for example, illustrates but does not prove its polemical thesis, and it incorporates elements of iconographic pageantry (songs, patriotic marches); portions of the play were performed at patriotic rallies in Mair's own days.

Although the tradition of pageantry has had little apparent influence in the development of Canadian drama, the first example of a Canadian play which relies heavily (although not exclusively) on actuality in performance may be Denzil Ridout's *United We Serve*, a 1927 pageant of the history of the United Church of Canada which incorporated original speeches by John Knox and John Wesley. Such pageants introduced dramatic techniques that would later recur in the documentary theatre: in *Paper Wheat*, one of the most successful Canadian plays of the 1970s, we find elements virtually identical to features in Minnie Harvey Williams's 1923 pageant, *The Romance of Canada*.

The polemical tradition in Canadian drama was entrenched by the turn of the century, but the first example of a play that deserves consideration in a discussion of documentary theatre emerged out of a different tradition. *Eight Men Speak* (1933) was an agitprop response to a political event – the jailing and attempted murder in prison of Communist Party leader Tim Buck. *Eight Men Speak* was not a documentary, in that it did not incorporate actual material directly. Indeed the four authors of the play (Oscar Ryan, E. Cecil-Smith, Frank Love, and Mildred Goldberg) took care to disguise, however thinly, provocative details that could lead to libel suits. The federal minister of justice, Hugh Guthrie, is known in the play as New Dufrie, and the governor of the Kingston Penitentiary is given an invented name.

Originally conceived as a mock trial of the prison guard who fired his rifle through Buck's cell window, *Eight Men Speak* is typical of the international tradition of revolutionary agitprop developed in the 1920s by workers' theatres in Britain and the United States, deriving from the revolutionary theatres of Germany and the Soviet Union. Agitprop is advocacy rather than analysis: it presents a polemic statement on an issue and depicts the ideological meaning of events rather than the events themselves. Like pageants, agitprop relies on an iconographic reduction of reality.

Eight Men Speak was written in six acts, which vary in style and which together embrace the full range of agitprop techniques. The first act is a simple political lampoon in which the bourgeois villains of the piece are parodied as hypocrites; the second takes the expressionistic fugue form common to radical drama of the 1930s (similar to that used by Irwin Shaw in *Bury the Dead*); the workers' court of the third act is a more solemn trial scene which uses rear projections and mime; the fourth act introduces the direct address techniques of the mass chant; and the final two acts return to the presentational form of the workers' court. In the mass chants and the trial scenes in particular, the use of direct address and exhortation, the editorial techniques of montage, and the use of monologues as an anti-illusionistic device anticipate the techniques of the documentary theatre of the 1970s. The theatrical vocabulary of *Eight Men Speak* was borrowed from international models, at a time when 'international' was a rallying cry for the left wing. There is little aside from the particulars of the subject that was uniquely Canadian in the play.

Although there is no direct line of descent from *Eight Men Speak* to the contemporary Canadian theatre, the play did initiate a tradition of agitprop that is still active. The first production of the Mummers Troupe in 1972 was a short agitprop performed in a shopping mall in support of a cinema projectionists' strike. In Ottawa, the Great Canadian Theatre Company has produced numerous agitprops for local labour and community organizations, and in the 1980s there has been a notable resurgence of agitprop among women's groups.

Eight Men Speak may be the first major agitprop in English Canada, but more pertinently, it was the first Canadian example of a play developed primarily by theatrical rather than literary techniques. As such it is an important predecessor to the plays discussed in the following chapters. It is the first example as well of a play in which factual material is utilized for specific political purposes, and consequently it is the first important example in English Canada of what has since become known as 'popular theatre,' in which the significance of the theatrical event requires a personal or ideological relationship between audience and subject matter.

The first playwright in Canada to use the techniques of documentary theatre was Irish-born John Coulter, who arrived in this country in 1936, three years after *Eight Men Speak*. Coulter had already established himself as a writer of historical dramas for radio in Britain, and he would continue to experiment with the genre for the rest of his life. In the late 1930s he worked briefly for CBS radio in New York, writing for its 'Living History' series. Presumably it was in New York that he became familiar with the work of the Federal Theatre Project's Living Newspaper Unit, which pioneered a form of documentary play about current social issues. In 1942, once again residing in Toronto, Coulter wrote *Mr Churchill of England* which in his words introduced '... a new stage technique which I think has not yet been seen in Canada nor in any but a few big towns in the U.S.A. It is the technique of the stage documentary, the so-called "living newspaper." '7

This is the first reference to documentary in Canadian theatre, but in fact *Mr Churchill of England* is not a documentary. The play, which has never been published, is a selection of highlights from Winston Churchill's career, and, with the exception of montage techniques derived from radio and the Living Newspapers, it is not in essence different from standard dramatic biographies. The warm reception accorded the play when it was produced at the Arts and Letters Club in Toronto in 1942, and later on CBC radio, may be attributed to its topicality. Of the many characters in the play, only Churchill, his wife, and Admiral Jackie Fisher speak lines taken from actuality; the rest is invented. In this Coulter followed the example of the Living Newspapers, which did not hesitate to invent characters when necessary. His debt to the Federal Theatre is obvious in such newsreel-style scenes as this:

Black Out
(During the black out: newspaper sellers Paper! Belgium mobilized! Paper! War threat nearer! Latest on the war! Paper! Paper! Belgium mobilized! War threat nearer!
– and so on till:)
  Light up on Admiralty and Mr Churchill as before.

CHURCHILL
This morning, the cabinet veto, on mobilisation of the Naval Reserves, was decreed.
Yet – Germany now having declared war on Russia ... To disregard the cabinet
veto, and order mobilisation on my own responsibility ...
Hazardous! Even illegal.
Occasions ... when great responsibility must not be evaded.
(Pause, Rising)
I order – immediate mobilisation of the Naval Reserves.
Telegram. (Telegram is heard transmitting.)
Black out.[8]

Such scenes are however the exception rather than the rule in the play. The
greater part of *Mr Churchill of England* dramatizes famous incidents in the life
of its hero. Written as it was during the war, the play is unashamedly patriotic;
it ends with Churchill delivering his famous 'We shall never surrender!' speech.

Coulter is best known for his trilogy of plays about a very different kind of
hero: *Riel* (1950), *The Crime of Louis Riel* (1966) and *The Trial of Louis Riel*
(1967). Taken together, these plays reveal clearly the difficult relationship
between historical drama and documentary.

Riel follows the tradition of the heroic martyr play. With its Elizabethan-
style staging and epic structure, it is far from documentary, but it does include
elements that have the appearance of documentary actuality, especially in the
climactic trial scene. Most of the dialogue in the trial is in fact Coulter's
invention, freely paraphrased from the original transcripts. *Riel* is typical of
modern didactic historical drama which explores the meaning of an historical
event by focusing on a 'world-historical' character who typifies his epoch. The
political world in which Louis Riel lives, and which he affects radically, is the
external complement of an inner conflict, as Riel passes from religious faith to
militant heresy and returns to faith while he awaits execution. When he hears
mystic voices, the audience hears them too; we are drawn into the subjective
world of a man whose actions shaped part of our history. In this way,
Coulter, like many historical dramatists, explains history through individual
psychology.

Following *Riel*, Coulter wrote two more plays on the subject. The first of
these, *The Crime of Louis Riel*, is a shorter acting version of *Riel*, but in the final
play, *The Trial of Louis Riel*, Coulter turned away from the inner dialectic of
character action and history to concentrate on the external events of Riel's trial.
He described the play as 'a factual documentary in which I omitted any
imaginative interpretation and crammed what had transpired in four or five
days into two or three hours.'[9]

The tribunal play based on actual court records is perhaps the most easily identifiable form of documentary theatre, and perhaps the most deceptive. No matter how faithful to the transcripts on which the play is based, imaginative reconstruction is at work in the selection and arrangement of material. The procedure of the courtroom makes it possible for the author's editorial cuts and emphases to pass without notice, and the implicit bias of the play is supported by the apparent authenticity of the court protoool.

This suggests that no matter how authentic a documentary play may appear to be, an audience has no sure means of separating fictional invention from actuality within the discourse of the text. Documentary theatre requires the audience to accept it as true, and for that reason must in some way back up its claim to veracity with some form of authentication. In the case of the tribunal play, the authentication is to be found within the form itself, which reminds the audience that the trial was an historical event. Perhaps the most famous example of this is Peter Weiss's *The Investigation* (1965), a documentary re-enactment of the Frankfurt trials of former Auschwitz camp guards. In that play, the success of which may have inspired Coulter to write his own trial play, Weiss edits the court transcripts to make an overt statement about the relation of fascism to capitalism.

In *The Trial of Louis Riel*, Coulter does not just edit the material and paraphrase when necessary, he departs from it with a freedom that is deceptive to those who accept the play as an authentic re-creation of the trial. Virtually every passage in the play departs from the original, sometimes for editorial convenience, as when Coulter eliminates a translator and has a French-speaking witness speak in Enqlish with a 'marked accent,' but more often for dramatic effect. This may be illustrated by comparing a typical passage from the play with its predecessors in *Riel* and the original transcripts.

Midway through the trial, Riel interrupted the proceedings to ask permission to question a witness, arguing that the defence counsels were unaware of certain significant facts. This led to a lengthy discussion of Riel's faith in his counsels, during which the following exchange took place:

PRISONER
If you will allow me, your Honor, this case comes to be extraordinary, and while the Crown, with the good talents they have at its service, are trying to show I am guilty – of course it is their duty, my counsellors are trying – my good friends and lawyers, who have been sent here by friends whom I respect – are trying to show that I am insane –

MR JUSTICE ROBINSON
Now you must stop.

PRISONER
I will stop and obey your court.[10]

In *Riel* Coulter re-creates the incident as more impassioned:

RIEL
(Rising again). Your Honour, this case comes to be extraordinary. The Crown are trying to show that I am guilty. It is their duty. My Counsel, my good friends and lawyers, whom I respect, are trying to show that I am insane. It is their line of defence. I reject it. I indignantly deny that I am insane. I am not insane! I declare ...
JUDGE
Now you must stop.
RIEL
The chance to ask important questions of this witness is slipping by. My good Counsel does not know what questions to ask because he does not know this man and because he is from Quebec and does not know our ways out here ...
JUDGE
I have said you must stop. Now stop at once.
RIEL
I will stop and obey your court.[11]

In *The Trial Of Louis Riel*, the passage deviates even further from the original:

RIEL
Your Honour, this case comes to be extraordinary. The Crown are trying to show that I am guilty. It is their duty. My Counsel, my good friends and lawyers whom I respect, are trying to show that I am insane. It is their line of defence. I reject it. I indignantly deny that I am insane.
DEFENCE
(Trying to break in) Your Honour ...
RIEL
(Not giving way) I am not insane! I declare that in rousing and leading my people against cynical disregard and neglect by Ottawa ...
JUDGE
Stop! Now you must stop!
RIEL
The chance to ask important questions of this witness is slipping by. My good Counsel does not know this man. Counsel is not from this part of the country and does not understand our ways, and so ...

JUDGE

I have said you must stop. Stop! Obey!

RIEL

I will obey the Court. But I repeat my life and honour are at stake. If this man ...

JUDGE

(Peremptory) Stop at once! (Riel sits down) [12]

Coulter's deviation from the original transcript changes the basic nature of the trial, and of Riel's character, to express more clearly the underlying reality of the event. This is the traditional task of the historical dramatist, who selects particular episodes because of the normally invisible motives and meanings they reveal. Coulter's Riel is more vehemently passionate and excitable than the real Riel was at his trial, and the proceedings of the trial seem more explosive, and perhaps less fair, than they were in fact.

Coulter's purpose is most apparent in his treatment of Riel's final speech to the jury. In the transcript of the trial, that speech fills fourteen pages, and a subsequent speech delivered before the passing of sentence fills another twenty-one. In these speeches Riel examined the major issues of the trial as he perceived them, and he discussed in detail the specifics of the charges he faced. Coulter's version abstracts from these speeches their rhetorical peaks and simplifies the legal and political issues. His Riel is a more obviously militant, less discursive, and arguably less intelligent man than the records reveal.

As a documentary, The Trial of Louis Riel sacrifices actuality for ideological interpretation and dramatic effect. Coulter was too much a dramatist to subordinate his creative impulse to the historical record. This is the first true documentary in Canadian theatre, but it is a problematic one, because in the end it does not live up to its claims to portray reality. This historical fact may be especially significant when we consider that the play has been produced annually since 1967 by the Regina Chamber of Commerce as a tourist attraction and ostensibly an accurate re-creation of history.

This problem of interpretation and authenticity is unresolved in The Trial of Louis Riel; in fact the very structure of the play effectively denies that such a problem exists. The credibility of the play depends ultimately on our faith in the authority of the playwright. In its theatrical context, there is no attempt to authenticate the text in the performance itself. The actors serve the text in a manner that might be termed arbitrary; although they give the appearance of historical authenticity, they are no more or less 'true' than any actor in any costume drama. They play roles defined strictly by the text to which they bear no personal relation, and they do not have the liberty or the means to interpret the reality they depict. The documentary tribunal play is in that sense a genre of historical drama which argues its case by means of the aesthetic illusion of reality.

Less than a decade after *The Trial of Louis Riel*, Coulter's attempts at documentary were eclipsed by a new movement that addressed these issues directly. In the documentaries of the 1970s, and especially the collective creations inspired by Theatre Passe Muraille, the responsibility for authenticating the material of the play was passed onto the actor, who in effect reported the findings of his own research. Coulter himself dismissed this new movement:

Are not the directors and actors attempting to banish the playwright, to improvise their productions, each contributing whatever random idea comes into his head in a sort of comment ... What we are seeing in such parades is a company of actors interpreting not a playwright, not a play conceived and shaped into unity and meaning by a playwright, but their own notions of what a play might be ... Extemporized plays are merely theatrical statements, a good experimental use of the stage.[13]

Jealous of his prerogative as a playwright, Coulter greatly underestimated the dramatic intelligence the new documentaries brought to bear. In fact, it was because there were too few playwrights like Coulter that companies such as Theatre Passe Muraille were able to redefine the idea of documentary theatre in Canada.

This new movement developed quickly across Canada, and just as quickly displaced the pioneering efforts of Coulter's generation of playwrights who laboured in isolation, often with no access to a professional stage, to develop an indigenous Canadian drama. In the decade following *The Trial Of Louis Riel* new theatre companies produced well over a hundred documentary plays and several times that number of more conventional plays.

The documentaries that came after Coulter bore little resemblance to his plays. They represented a different tradition, as the emerging alternative theatre, in its search for new forms capable of expressing new analyses of Canadian culture, created an indigenous documentary shaped both by native experiment and international influences.

The influence of foreign traditions of documentary on the Canadian theatre is difficult to determine, because there is no single coherent 'international' model of documentary theatre. Rather there have been interconnected experiments in the form, arising out of various cultures throughout this century. In most cases where a form of documentary theatre has developed as an ongoing tradition (as in Weimar Germany, the United States in the 1930s, and Canada in the 1970s) it appears to have developed as a necessary stage in a cultural crisis. The documentary theatre seems to thrive in periods when new cultural imperatives cannot be expressed within the framework of traditional dramatic forms. Concerned as it is with the presentation and verification of cultural material as evidence, the documentary form effectively reorders the fundamental relation of artist and society, and in so doing proposes new structures of dramatic language and metaphor upon which literary drama is based. At the core of the documentary impulse is an implicit critical statement that the conventional dramatic forms of the culture in question no longer express the truth of the society, usually because those conventional forms cannot accommodate rapid social change. The documentary approach provides a way for artists to realign the theatre to these changes.

I have suggested that the Canadian documentary is related in part to parallel traditions of historical drama and agitprop. In this the Canadian experience recapitulates the general principles of documentary theatre as it first evolved in Germany in the 1920s, mainly through the work of Erwin Piscator. It was in reference to Piscator's 'epic theatre' that Brecht first applied the word 'documentary' to the theatre in 1926 – in the same year that John Grierson coined the word in English to describe the films of Robert Flaherty.[14]

Like his successors in Canada a half-century later, Piscator evolved his documentary theatre out of several sources, the most important being historical drama, film, and agitprop. Of these, the relation to film is at once the most obvious and the most troublesome (as it would be in Canada). Piscator incorporated projected film into his plays, but more important is the fact that cinematic techniques had a major impact on dramaturgy in the early years of this century. From the motion picture, directors learned new ways of lighting, staging, and composition. Even so, many of the dramaturgical techniques that seem to derive from film, such as flashbacks and cross-fades, actually anticipate it, having their origin in the proto-expressionist drama of the late nineteenth century.

That the cinema influenced Piscator is apparent enough, but whether it had a more significant influence on him than it did on his entire generation of play-wrights and directors is uncertain. Whatever the Piscatorian documentary's relation to film, its origins in historical drama and agitprop are clear. Piscator was steeped in the romantic tradition of the literary 'world historical' play, which sought to dramatize the workings of history as a dialectical force. The idea of drama as a vehicle of philosophic speculation was an invention of the Enlightenment, and during the following century, after the examples of Lessing and Goethe, playwrights experimented with dramatic forms that moved away from an emphasis on the fate of individual characters. In the most notable plays of this genre, such as Ibsen's *Emperor and Galilean* (1873), the structure and inner logic of the play embodies the dialectic of philosophic reasoning. In his story of Julian the Apostate, Ibsen sought to include the unconscious 'World Will' of history as a dramatic force, almost a character, in its own right.

The development of this genre of panoramic historical drama shows a clear progression from character drama to a form of proto-documentary as playwrights began to include historical evidence to support their theses. The philosophical abstraction of the 'world historical' play was brought down to earth during the First World War, when Viennese editor and satirist Karl Kraus attacked the distortions of language that concealed German and Austrian war guilt in his massive *The Last Days of Mankind*. In this play, which Piscator wanted to stage, Kraus redirected the panoramic drama by compiling dozens of incidents of official hypocrisy and deceit within a discursive dramatic frame. In his preface to the play, Kraus wrote the first articulation of the documentary principle in the theatre:

The most improbable deeds reported here really happened. The most improbable conversations that are carried on here were spoken word for word. The most glaring inventions are quotations. Sentences whose insanity is indelibly imprinted on the ear grow into a refrain that stays with one forever. A document is a dramatis personae; reports come to life as personae; personae breathe their last as editorials; the feuilleton acquires a mouth that speaks itself in a monologue. [15]

In its form and internal discourse, however, *The Last Days of Mankind* is a variation of historical drama. Its claim to documentary veracity is not authenticated within the text. Kraus's concept of documentary is inherently dramatic, and his play is the first of a continuing tradition of 'docudramas': didactic historical plays that present re-creations of historical events, or which attempt to present a recognized historical reality in terms of narrative fiction. This tradition of documentary drama is exemplified in Canada by the plays of Rick Salutin and Sharon Pollock, both of whom have written plays about 'real' events. In the final analysis 'documentary drama' is troublesome; it often describes nothing more than the tendency in didactic drama to move away from the single protagonist of the Aristotelian drama.

It was Piscator who found the operative principles of documentary theatre in the structure of the performance rather than the dramatic text. Piscator himself did not make this distinction; as a revolutionary eclectic he used every means possible to bring his political world to the stage. Piscator's major contribution was his development of non-literary genres in such plays as the 1925 *Despite All!*, an historical pageant for the German Communist Party, which stands as the first play to consist entirely of documentary material (newspapers reports, testimonials, and projected slides figured prominently). In Piscator's documentaries the material on stage was authenticated by the absence of plot and by the deliberate repudiation of dramatic illusion. Out of Piscator's work emerged the fundamental principle which distinguishes documentary theatre from the documentary genre in other arts. In the cinema, for example, the documentary is a mass medium, a powerful tool of persuasion designed to reach as wide an audience as possible. Piscator's theatre, like that of his successors, spoke to a particular community defined by a common experience. In his case that community was made up of left-wing revolutionaries and the unemployed of Berlin.

The two principles that characterize Piscator's work in the form provide the common ground for all subsequent developments of documentary: it is a genre of performance that presents actuality on the stage and in the process authenticates that actuality, and it speaks to a specifically defined audience for whom it has special significance. Typically that actuality is authenticated by the internal conventions of the performance, such as Piscator's use of projected slides and titles, or the Federal Theatre Project's use of a loudspeaker 'Voice of the Living Newspaper.' These techniques are essentially rhetorical, and they evolve in accord with changing images of verisimilitude. It may be, for instance, that the widespread reliance on presentational monologue in Canadian documentary theatre may be related in part to our general acceptance of the authority of the television news 'talking head.'

The Canadian documentary can be traced back to Piscator's pioneering efforts through the development of the form in Great Britain, where Unity Theatre, which began as a merger of several left-wing amateur troupes, and the more celebrated Theatre Workshop, both influenced in equal measure by Piscator and the Federal Theatre Project, created a series of living newspapers in the 1940s and 1950s. Of these troupes, Theatre Workshop would have the most direct influence on the later Canadian theatre because of its connection with George Luscombe, who acted for Joan Littlewood and used her company as a model for his Toronto Workshop Productions in 1959.

Joan Littlewood and Ewan MacColl formed Theatre Workshop in 1945 to carry on the work of their pre-war troupe, Theatre Union. It was with Theatre Union that they had created their first living newspaper, *Last Edition*, in 1940. The new Theatre Workshop quickly established itself as a major voice of politically engaged theatre in post-war Britain, with adaptations of classics, new left-wing plays and living newspapers such as MacColl's *Uranium 235*. For the first few years the company survived by continuous tours working out of Manchester and Glasgow until in 1953 Littlewood took over the Theatre Royal, Stratford East, London. Twenty years after the war she revived the documentary style with the famous *Oh What A Lovely War,* a music-hall pierrot show which juxtaposed songs and satiric sketches of the First World War with the grim statistics of trench warfare. *Oh What A Lovely War* was a refinement of the living newspaper idea and it popularized a satiric technique that would prove a major influence in Canada as well as Britain.

As developed by Piscator and his successors, documentary theatre was essentially propagandist in function. It presented the facts of a situation within an editorial context, so that the form of the performance, the songs, projections, sketches, and scenes delivered information and evaluated it at the same time. By representing historical characters, the actors in such documentaries create the illusion of historical reality when necessary to illustrate the material they present. In that sense, the actors embody the editorial perspective of the documentary, and although we in the audience recognize that the scene before our eyes is a rehearsed re-enactment of reality, we can accept it as authentic providing we agree with its editorial stance. The actor in the Piscatorian documentary bears a symbolic relation to the material he performs.

The Canadian documentary tends to document experience rather than facts. and the actor generally has a first-hand relation to the material of the play. In this it is a development of an approach formulated by the British director Peter Cheeseman who, although influenced by Littlewood, evolved his form of documentary for reasons that resemble the Canadian experience. Cheeseman wished to create a truly provincial theatre at the Victoria Theatre in Stoke-on-Trent, but he found himself without a resident writer when Alan Ayckbourn left for London in 1964. Cheeseman turned to the documentary as a method of creating plays about the local community without a writer.

Of the various forms of documentary theatre, Cheeseman's has the closest resemblence to film. Cheeseman stressed what he saw as an obligation to adhere totally to the documentary material. In his introduction to *The Knotty,* one of the first of his Stoke-on-Trent documentaries, he wrote that 'words or actions deriving from the events to be described or participants in those events are the only permitted material for the scenes of the documentary. If there is no primary source material available on a particular topic, no scene can be made about it.'[16]

Cheeseman's belief that theatre can document the experience of a community has had considerable impact on Canadian theatre, and his emphasis on first-hand field research has become a standard feature of Canadian documentaries. In Cheeseman's work, the focus of the documentary shifted from political to sociological and cultural analysis, and with that shift came increased reliance on factual accuracy. In his performances, the actors authenticated the material by assuming the role of the informant, in the sociological sense, and by incorporating references to the process of research into the play.

In literary documentary drama the actor's imitation of an actual person is justified and made possible by the narrative action of the text, by the re-enactment of the event (especially in tribunal play), or by the topicality of the production. Cheeseman's work came closer to an actor-created text, to which the actor brings his own experience with the subject. Cheeseman did not use collective creation to the extent that his successors in Canada would, but he introduced the complexity of the actor who bears a personal relation to the material he performs. In fact, the actor's presence can affect the material he documents. This is most evident in *Fight for Shelton Bar*, a documentary about a community struggle to prevent the closure of a steel mill. The struggle was still underway when the play was made in 1972, and the actors found themselves performing incidents on stage in which they themselves had participated in real life. In effect, the actors were documenting their own intervention in the community.

Although Cheeseman was the first to explore the principles that would later emerge to define the Canadian documentary, he was only one of three main links between the European documentary tradition and the Canadian theatre. The first of these links was George Luscombe's connection with Joan Littlewood. Luscombe acted with Theatre Workshop for five years in the 1950s and when he returned to Canada in 1959 to found the company that would become Toronto Workshop Productions (TWP) he sought to continue Littlewood's ideas of popular theatre. Luscombe was the first director in Canada to explore collective creation and documentary staging techniques, and, although his work had little influence on the alternative theatre movement that followed him, he developed his own documentary tradition that found its greatest expression in the 1974 production of *Ten Lost Years*.

The second connection was Paul Thompson, who, like Luscombe, apprenticed in Europe and returned to Canada to adapt the ideas and techniques he learned there. Thompson worked with Roger Planchon in France, whose ideas of populist theatre later led Thompson to experiment with collective creation. On his return to Canada in the late 1960s Thompson became familiar with the 'jeune théâtre' movement in Quebec, where collective creation and documentary techniques developed earlier than they did in English Canada.

The third link, Cheeseman's work at Stoke-on-Trent, influenced the emerging Canadian alternative theatre through two separate connections. In 1972, Cheeseman visted Toronto as a guest of Theatre Ontario, an umbrella organization of professional and amateur theatres. The program of his activities included this note:

His company at Stoke have developed the art of documentary theatre indigenous to, and springing from, the very roots of the history and lore of the region. Perhaps from a similar philosophy and dedication will the elusive Canadian theatre identity emerge. [17]

The anonymous author of that note prophesized none too soon, for even as Cheeseman screened films of his plays, Paul Thompson was taking his actors to a farm near Clinton, Ontario, to create just such a documentary. Thompson did attend one of Cheeseman's lectures, but by that time he had already developed his own quite different attitudes to documentary. [18]

In that same year, Theatre Ontario helped to fulfil its own prophecy when it provided a grant for a young director named Ray Whalen to work under Cheeseman as an assistant director. In 1974 Whalen and Sylvia Tucker founded Open Circle Theatre in Toronto to produce documentaries modelled on Cheeseman's work, although in the end Open Circle's documentaries more closely resembled Thompson's than Cheeseman's. The second Cheeseman connection is to be found in Regina, where Ken and Sue Kramer established the Globe Theatre in 1968. The Kramers had worked with Brian Way's Theatre in Education program in Britain, and, while this provided the initial thrust for the Globe, they had also become acquainted with Cheeseman's documentaries, and harboured a desire to create similar plays in Saskatchewan.

The indigenous documentary tradition that emerged in Canada in the 1970s naturally assimilated foreign influences but for the most part it must be seen as a unique development. The documentary theatre was perhaps the most distinctive expression of the alternative theatre movement, but it is important to note that the documentary was in fact a secondary stage of that movement, and that few of the theatres that became known for their documentaries actually started with it in mind.

Martin Kinch, one of the founders of the Toronto Free Theatre and hence one of the pioneers of alternative theatre in Toronto, has suggested that the initial impulse of the alternative theatre came out of the 1960s 'counter culture' rather than an analysis of Canadian culture:

The first thing to realize about the Canadian Theatre Movement is that it began with little or no nationalist aspirations; beyond the aspirations of its founders to create situations in their own country, in which they could begin their careers ... It was not however the dream of a truly Canadian Theatre or the desire for a specifically Canadian experience ... The real influences were Fritz Perls, and Timothy Leary, Peter Brook and Jerzy Grotowski, Tom O'Horgan, Cafe La Mama, Julian Beck, Judith Malina and the whole ensemble of the Living Theatre; in short a host of European and American artists, most of them primarily dedicated to the ethic and aesthetic of 'doing your own thing.' [19]

Kinch's comments point to one of the two most important factors that defined the shape of alternative theatre in Canada. Although the alternative theatre may be said to have begun with Luscombe's founding of TWP in 1959, it remained a series of isolated experiments until the arrival of the generation that emerged in the late 1960s with an interest in the arts and an awareness of foreign cultures. Many, if not most, of the directors who founded theatres in the late 1960s were trained in American graduate schools or European theatres. Their desire to establish theatres in Canada was encouraged by large-scale funding from the Canada Council and provincial arts councils, and more importantly, from such federal make-work schemes as Opportunities for Youth and Local Initiatives Program. Even as the Canada Council was investing massive amounts of money into the building of a professional 'regional theatre' network across the country, a younger generation was taking advantage of other federal programs to challenge that system. The 'Canadian Theatre Movement, if we date it from the founding of TWP, is no younger than the established theatre to which it was the 'alternative,'and which it has since to a large extent absorbed.

Despite Kinch's reminder of the influence of the American experimental theatre on its early development, there can be no doubt that the alternative theatre was in part the manifestation of a new era of Canadian nationalism. Whatever their initial impulses, the alternative theatres found themselves in the forefront of a popular nationalist movement. In the theatre the issues of post-colonial cultural independence were particularly visible and, deliberately or not, theatres forced into a nationalist posture by the lack of good Canadian plays and the apparent preference for British plays and directors in the regional theatres found themselves typed as radical. The alternative theatres provided a market for aspiring playwrights, who felt themselves locked out of the larger theatres; this situation in turn contributed to the nationalist debate that was emerging in all sectors of Canadian society.

This nationalist revival, coupled with the economics of the alternative theatre, made it possible for playwrights to realize the long-standing dream of an indigenous Canadian dramatic literature. The desire for an indigenous drama has been a common thread in dramatic criticism in Canada throughout this century, although until the post-war era that drama was normally conceived through British-educated taste. A number of critics realized, however, that an indigenous drama requires as a precondition an independent theatre. In 1913 critic B.K. Sandwell called for a 'theatrical declaration of independence' from the United States.[20] This would be best achieved, he wrote, 'by a localized system' of theatres across the country, producing Canadian plays. Twenty years later, Archibald Key visualized 'Canada's National Theatre in the form of a little red schoolhouse, a Ford Sedan with trailer, a few drapes, props and an elementary lighting set.'[21] These were the first intimations of the two wings of the Canadian theatre that would develop after the Second World War, and although both of them, the regional theatre system and the alternative theatre, were influenced by foreign examples, they were at the same time fulfilments of a nationalist vision.

Perhaps the most important manifestation of the desire to define an indigenous culture, in the theatre at least, was the recognition of regionalism as a determining factor in Canadian culture. The question of regionalism is of paramount importance to an understanding of the Canadian documentary.

As social motivating force and thematic subject alike, regionalism in Canadian theatre is related to an ideology of political populism. Although regionalism has become critical orthodoxy in Canada, there have been few attempts to define its exact meaning when applied to culture. In her essay 'The Regionalism of Canadian Drama,' Diane Bessai makes the important point that regional drama 'draws its strength from the audience interest it thereby generates.'[22] Bessai ascribes the emphasis on regional identity in Canadian theatre to the determining influences of geography and colonial settlement in Canadian history. In her analysis, regionalism is a manifestation of a post-colonial sentiment. In this she takes exception to Northrop Frye's distinction between regionalism, which he defines as 'a decentralizing movement,' and what he dismisses as 'mere localism.' Bessai argues that 'localism in its contemporary theatrical forms is a demonstrably important phase in the establishment of a mature, decentralized culture.'[23]

Bessai's analysis of localism as a post-colonial impulse does much to explain why regionalism in Canadian theatre tends to express itself in grass-roots populism. That populism is perhaps the most important reason for the Canadian documentary's affinity with collective creation. In order to make that connection, however, it is necessary to examine the problem of regionalism a little more closely.

All of the plays discussed in this book can be defined as localist, but not all are explicitly regional, in the sense that not all are 'about' the particular features – cultural, social, or geographic – of a particular region. As used by Frye and Bessai, localism has a geographic value: localist documentaries like *The Farm Show* explore the dimensions of a culture as defined in the terms of a specific community. But if we expand the sense of the term, all of the plays discussed here are localist in that they document issues relevant to a particular community of shared experience – whether it be the community of prison inmates in *It's About Time*, of prairie grain growers in *No. 1 Hard*, or the more diverse community of Canadians who share the historical experience documented in *Ten Lost Years*. In each case the audience brings a special interest to its understanding of the performance.

Localism, it appears, is an integral part of documentary theatre. In Canada it has also been a cultural strategy which has tried to define the processes by which community experience may be translated into art. It is when localism is placed in a political context that regionalism emerges as a major consideration. In Canada, the uneven historical development of the several regions has engendered an idea of separate regional cultures distinguished by geography, history, demography, and language. If localism can be defined as the expression of issues relevant to a particular community, then regionalism may be the expression of issues relevant to a community defined in the more complex terms of geography, language, and political history.

The differences between the two 'isms' in practice are apparent in the plays examined in this book. In *The Farm Show*, which stands as the prototype of the localist community documentary, community is defined entirely in terms of personal experience. The play documents a social net of families who live and work in proximity to each other, but it does not explore the history that brought them together. In comparison, *Paper Wheat*, the most consciously 'regional' of these plays, defines a regional culture of shared political and historical experience. A concern for regional culture and identity is characteristic of documentaries (as well as other dramatic forms) from the western and Atlantic provinces, which have traditionally perceived themselves as colonies subordinate to centralized economic and political power in Ontario. In Ontario, the regional impulse has typically manifested itself in pan-Canadian nationalism or in essentially apolitical explorations of local culture.

Localism and regionalism are closely related attempts to define the contours of an indigenous Canadian culture. Regionalism provides a context in which the description of localist matter or historical experience conveys deeper cultural meaning.

The inherent populism of the search for cultural identity in community experience found an ideal expression in collective creation. On one level, the vogue of collective creation, in which the actors contribute directly to the compilation or writing of the performance text, was part of the international movement to challenge the traditional hierarchies of theatrical production. In Canada that radicalism, like the initial radical impulses of the alternative theatre in general, facilitated the search for indigenous theatrical forms and images. In the absence of a national dramatic literature, Canadian actors had traditionally trained in the classics of the British and American dramas. Collective creation made it possible for actors to find indigenous models of performance, and to explore personal (often romanticized) responses to the sources of Canadian culture. In the localist documentaries the Canadian actor found the patterns of characterization and speech that a British actor might find in his national repertoire. At the same time the process of documentary research and collective creation drew actors to the most easily accessible themes and character types. In this way, the documentary theatre enabled actors and directors to locate and test the raw material out of which playwrights could begin to fashion a national drama.

2

Documentary and Collective Creation:
The Farm Show

The dominant form of Canadian documentary had its birth in an unused barn near Clinton, Ontario, in August, 1972, when Theatre Passe Muraille premiered *The Farm Show* to an audience of local residents and farmers. *The Farm Show* is important both as a play and a cultural phenomenon. It stands as one of the finest works of the Canadian theatre, and it became the model for a form of community documentary theatre based on the actors' personal responses to the source material. *The Farm Show* inspired numerous imitations across Canada, most of which applied techniques of collective creation developed by Passe Muraille's artistic director, Paul Thompson. Few of those successors equalled the original in dramatic intelligence, as indeed did few of Passe Muraille's later experiments in the form. The reasons for *The Farm Show's* brilliance are several, but in the end they must be ascribed to the pioneering inventiveness of Paul Thompson, who conceived and directed the play.

As a director, playwright (although never with pen and paper), and *animateur*, Thompson has been one of the most influential figures in modern Canadian theatre. He gave Passe Muraille – and through it, alternative theatres across Canada – a vision of regional culture and a methodology for transforming localism (Thompson's preferred word was 'particularism') into art, and as a director he, more than any other person, was responsible for the development of a new acting style in Canada. The Passe Muraille house style was characterized by a combination of dialect realism, improvisation, and presentational story-telling.

Thompson's emphasis on the actor's creative encounter with reality and his delight in pure theatricality were shaped in large part by the two years he spent as a *stagiaire* – an apprentice director – with Roger Planchon in France in the late 1960s. Perhaps even more significant to the development of Passe Muraille's documentaries was Thompson's belief that theatre can locate and define the motifs and images which identify a culture. For Thompson, these motifs and images point to the formative myths of a society. The concept of myth recurs throughout Thompson's work; it lies at the heart of *The Farm Show*, and it explains why in subsequent shows Thompson moved beyond documentary actuality to a new form of actor-created dramatic literature. As Thompson once told Urjo Kareda, then drama critic for the *Toronto Star*: 'Myth is no longer a fashionable word. But a myth, in the Canadian context, is a thing so obvious that eventually you cannot deny that it exists; even the guy at the garage will nod his head.'[1]

In 1974, Thompson told an interviewer that all of his productions 'function on the level of myth'; six years later he expanded his meaning to the same interviewer by relating the concept of myth to the function of the actor:

In *The Farm Show* and *Under the Greywacke*, for example, we didn't just talk with the people we ended up portraying, we listened to their speech patterns trying to understand them through a kind of verbal interplay. The actor's ear for detail was a very strong point. They were not just recording cameras. In the midst of talking and listening they were already imbuing the experience with a mythic dimension. They were already conscious of how the person they were talking to represented more than himself; like he may be one person, but he was a type.[2]

At the core of Thompson's approach is a fascination with 'the magic that comes out of the discovery of the actor coming to terms with something.'[3] It is from this that his interest in what he has called 'extended language' derives. In the early days at Passe Muraille, Thompson led his actors into the exploration of a specific event or community. In his later work he became increasingly interested in working with writers. Although he had introduced a playwright to the creative collective as early as 1973, when Rick Salutin helped create *1837: The Farmers' Revolt*, Thompson grew more interested in collaborating with novelists. This interest coincided with a growing fascination with the culture of western Canada. As Thompson began exploring the history and culture of the prairies, he turned to prairie novelists for an understanding of a region with which he was essentially unfamiliar. This in turn led to collaborations with such novelists as Rudy Weibe (with whom he created *Far As the Eye Can See*) and Robert Kroetsch (whose *The Stud Horse Man* he adapted). From these experiences he gained an appreciation for the novelist's descriptive powers and sense of language which influenced his subsequent work.

Under Thompson's leadership, Passe Muraille moved from the attempt to define the sources of local culture to an active exploration of culture in the deeper sense. Thompson's search for a theatre that spoke to 'the guy in the garage' led him away from documentary even as he gave the Canadian documentary its typical form. Even in the beginning, Thompson was suspicious of documentary actuality. His disagreement with Cheeseman's rigid adherence to actuality has already been noted, and in 1974 he told an interviewer that

people keep telling us that some of what we're doing is close to documentary theatre techniques. I think it's folk theatre because in many cases we're not interested in fact. If an emotional, exciting lie makes better theatre and gets the point of the scene across better, then I'm more interested in the lie than the fact.[4]

Six years later he maintained:

Documentary is a dead end as far as theatre is concerned. And the reason is that you can end up 'handcuffed by history,' which means that you keep digging into the facts and, in the end, find those facts limit your ability to portray a full experience for the audience.[5]

Despite these disavowals, more than one critic has divided Thompson's work at Passe Muraille into two categories: 'sociological' plays like *The Farm Show* and *I Love You, Baby Blue,* and 'historical' plays like *1837* and *Them Donellys.* When examined in terms of a conscious attempt to define the myths that shape Canadian culture, this distinction is facile. As this chapter will show, *The Farm Show* is by no means sociological in tone or substance. Similarly, the historical plays differ from the contemporary plays only in the period covered. Theatrically and ideologically, these two categories are the same. Thompson has proposed the term 'folk theatre,' which may be more useful, although technically inaccurate. (Used correctly the term refers to 'non-formal' theatrical traditions passed on through generations.) Folklorists and anthropologists might dispute this use of 'folk theatre,' but it at least acknowledges that all of these plays require a special relationship between actor and audience, that they are essentially non-literary, and that they exist only in performance.

The significant factor defining Thompson's work at Passe Muraille is collective creation, and it is in that context that *The Farm Show* is best analysed, for the process by which the play was made is in part the substance of the play itself. In all of Thompson's collective creations the actors transform their communal experiences in researching the material into an integral part of the performance text: the specifics of the material and the make-up of the collective account for the different forms and styles of the various plays.

In his decade at Passe Muraille, Thompson directed or supervised over thirty collective creations, as well as dozens of other plays. Most of the collectives drew upon a small corps of actors skilled in improvisation and committed to Thompson's brand of populism. Like many of his contemporaries, Thompson was passionately nationalistic. This sense of struggle against the forms of colonial culture led him to demand that actors create 'texture' in performance. In the year after *The Farm Show*, he said:

I keep talking to the actors about texture because one of the things missing in Canadian theatre is an identifiable base for the characters. Instead there's a kind of general base and you see too much of what I call movie-acting where, for example, if you want to do a small-town character, everyone's trying to be Paul Newman in *Hud* instead of going out to a small town and sitting in the corner drug store, finding out how people really are, catching their rhythms and building off that.[6]

Ted Johns, who worked closely with Thompson as an actor and playwright, described his method:

For example, when auditioning actors one time, Thompson asked each actor to do five Canadian accents. Well, that floored 'em. So Thompson would say, 'You're taking all your models from the movies or TV. I ask for a tough guy and I get Marlon Brando. I ask for sincerity and I get Robert Redford.'[7]

Thompson's style of collective creation varied with each play, depending on the contributions of the actors, the subject matter, and his own experimentation, but it had certain constants. The most important was the actors' combination of a realistic 'identifiable base' with a non-realistic presentational technique that freed them from naturalistic portraiture. The fusion of these two approaches resulted in a form of gestural story-telling.

Perhaps the most concise example of Thompson's theatricality can be found in a brief passage from *The West Show* (1975). At the beginning of the first section of the second scene of the play, an actress tells the audience:

The west is full of enormous individual and enormous collective efforts. That was a true story about a man. The next story is about a woman. That's not me so I'll show you what she looks like.[8]

In this passage we find the basic elements of Thompson's theatrical vision: a direct relationship between actor and material, an informal presentational style, an appeal to a collective sense of community, an emphasis on truth (whether actual or 'mythic') which is formulated in terms of stories, and an implied reference to the process by which the play was made. This is manifested in the gesture of 'showing' the image or fact to the audience.

The actress in this scene describes her character in concrete visual terms:

I'm four feet high and four feet wide. I have black eyes with circles around them like a racoon. And I have big ears that hang down like my grandfather's.

The passage bears comparison with a similar piece from the rehearsal process of *1837*, as described in Rick Salutin's diary of the play:

1st day of rehearsal.
Before splitting up, we asked each of the actors to present an 1837 object. The best was Clare [Coulter]. She set herself before us and said:
I'm William Lyon Mackenzie's house. My feet are spread wide and my feet are firmly planted. My hands are on my hips and I look straight ahead. I have *lots* of windows and any question you ask me I'm not afraid to answer.[9]

This technique of showing and naming is both the basis of the dramatic text of plays like *The Farm Show* and the means by which the actors discover and invent the text.

Thompson is rare among Canadian directors in his reliance on the actors to discover not just the form and the structure of the play but its content and scope as well. Thompson would normally begin rehearsal of a play without any preconception of the final product. In 1974 he told an interviewer

I quite like the chaos. In a lot of the work we're doing there's a lot of chaos, it looks chaotic … up until about opening night. And sometimes even after that, but the presence of an audience, the pressure of an audience puts a discipline on it.[10]

In the words of Miles Potter, one of Thompson's regular actors:

It took me two plays of working with Paul Thompson to realize he isn't bluffing when he says he doesn't know what to do. For days we sit and sit and sit, thinking that sooner or later Paul will produce something. Then, maybe on the fourth day, we start rolling.[11]

A glimpse into Thompson's working method can be found in an article in the *Clinton News Record* by a reporter who sat in on an early rehearsal 'jam' of what would become *The Farm Show*. Thompson had asked each of the actors to create a physical description of an image through movement:

Fina, arms over her head, suddenly becomes a slanted roof with pigeons under the eves. Janet's body described the grey walls of a barn with orange tiger lilies growing next to it. Evidently not satisfied, she commented, 'It's hard to concentrate hard enough into a non-literal movement.'

Paul Thompson answered her, trying to help her feel comfortable with the exercise. 'It is the physical taking over and extending the metaphor,' he said.[12]

A more graphic illustration of this same principle is Linda Griffith's description of the process of creating *Les Maudits Anglais* (1978):

We'd been working on one crucial scene in which I played an Anglo journalist trying to explain the English Canadian position to a separatist, I'd tried everything – intellectual, political, and economic arguments and nothing was working dramatically. Suddenly Thompson, who'd been sitting quietly at the back of the theatre all this time, said, 'I think you're on the verge of something but you're not going there.' That's all he said. And I just cracked right down the middle and came out with this tremendous emotion, one I didn't even know I felt, and I stood there with my arms outstretched and my head back, crying out this image of a highway stretching right across the country. And that was the scene.[13]

Such moments became the hallmarks of Thompson's productions. Because he was more interested in the process than the final product, more interested ultimately in theatre than drama, Thompson's collective creations were usually awkward in structure – a problem that became more apparent when he moved towards an integration of documentary and mimetic plot in plays like *Torontonians* (1981). Thompson seldom recaptured the brilliance of *The Farm Show* in his later work, in part because of the unique conditions that made that play possible, and in part because of his commitment to 'expand the collective form.' Shortly before he left Passe Muraille, Thompson told an interviewer:

The straightforward nature of something like *The Farm Show* works for an audience but it isn't enough for actors who want to grow with their material; their needs become larger. And my needs as a putter-together of structures also become more complex. I think it has to do with needing to surprise the audience but also needing to surprise yourself. I mean, sure, in the middle of a show you can bring in a marching band or a dancing elephant and that's a surprise, but after a while you start figuring that maybe the surprise should come out of the work you are doing in the first place.[14]

In his earlier work, Thompson never hesitated to bring on the dancing elephant. As he told an interviewer in 1974, 'If an actor could yodel, for example, then I'd really like to put his yodel into a play.'[15]

In his earlier shows, beginning with *The Farm Show* in 1972 and including *Under the Greywacke* (1973), *Oil* (1974), and *I Love You, Baby Blue* (1975), Thompson allowed the dramatic structure to emerge out of the rehearsal process, with no attempt to shape it into an obvious pattern of meaning. In his preface to the published edition of *The Farm Show* he wrote: 'There is no "story" or "plot" as such. The form of the play is more like a Canadian Sunday School or Christmas Concert where one person does a recitation, another sings, a third acts out a skit, etc.'[16] In the opening speech of the play, an actor advises the audience that 'the show kind of bounces along one way or another and then it stops.'[17] As we shall see, the disclaimer is somewhat ingenuous, for the *The Farm Show*, even more than the plays that came after it, reveals a genuinely dramatic coherence. Even so, Thompson's early plays at Passe Muraille are characterized by an episodic structure that allows for star turns by the actors, in which apparently extraneous elements might be added – the dancing elephant – at no expense to the overall structure of the play.

Thompson's willingness to display the actors' virtuosity resulted in some of the most memorable highlights of his productions, but it could also detract from the play itself. Virtually every one of the Passe Muraille collective creations contains scenes in which the theatrical metaphor expresses nothing more than its own cleverness. It is however axiomatic for Thompson that a good performance is its own justification if it 'connects' with the audience. The most extreme example of this is perhaps the 'Human Levitation' number in *I Love You, Baby Blue*:

ACTRESS
(To audience) Ladies and Gentleman, right here on this very stage (She covers a hole in the back drop with her hat) the most amazing phenomenon will take place. Yes! Before your very eyes, presenting the colossal, the magnificent, the stupendous ... Human Levitation! (Removes her hat and we see a penis hanging out of the hole.) Watch it rise, watch it rise. Higher and higher, no strings attached. (She demonstrates the fact.) Ladies and Gentleman, we must all think harder ... harder ... Ladies! Gentleman! (By now the penis has either risen or not risen. If it did she said ... 'The Human Levitation!' and hung her hat on it; if it didn't, she said, 'The Human Levitation has a headache!' and she'd cover it again with her top hat ...)[18]

Typically in a Passe Muraille collective creation the audience responds to the theatrical moment rather than the development of a governing idea; the meaning of the play is a result rather than the cause of the arrangement of material. The exceptions to this rule are those plays that take their structure from an event, as in *1837*, with its chronological arrangement of didactic scenes. This emphasis on episode rather than fable encouraged the development of an acting style that is at once informal in appearance and highly mannered in fact.

It should be noted too that Passe Muraille's characteristic style was formed in part by the theatrical spaces in which the plays were performed. *The Farm Show* was performed in auction barns before it arrived in a real theatre; *Under the Greywacke* was performed in a church; *1837* in an old school house; and *Adventures of an Immigrant* in a Toronto streetcar. These two conditions called for actors who were at their best when playing in close proximity to their audience but who could appear most natural when performing larger-than-life theatrical 'turns' in a direct presentational style.

This seeming informality could express considerable dramatic subtlety, as it does in *The West Show* and to a lesser extent in *The Farm Show*, but when combined with overt attempts at plot making it paradoxically works best with grandiose language and gesture. This is the case with *Far As the Eye Can See*, written with Rudy Weibe. The different contributions of novelist and actors are easily discerned in the text, which juxtaposes a documentary-style drama about a citizen's protest against a strip-mining plan in rural Alberta with a rhetorical conceit utilizing the spirits of three 'Regal Dead.' These three historical characters (Princess Louise, Crowfoot, and William Aberhart) function as a chorus to the action; their scenes are the most effective in performance but the most awkward on the printed page. Conversely, the conventional realism of the romantic sub-plot and the documentary style of the main plot both seem banal and artificial in contrast. *Far As the Eye Can See* works best when it is most consciously formal. This is in keeping with the Passe Muraille tradition: the grandiose verbal gesture of the 'Regal Dead' scenes is directly related to the physical theatricality of *The Farm Show*. In both cases the actor employs an anti-naturalistic rhetoric. The informal physicality of *The Farm Show* and the elevated language and conceit of *Far As the Eye Can See* derive from the same source.

At its best, Thompson's technique created plays of extraordinary power, generated by performers critic Urjo Kareda once described as 'awesome in the depth and fullness of their commitment.'[19] We might ask why it is that the same techniques, applied to different subjects, employing a basically similar group of actors, should result in plays of vastly differing quality. Why, for example, is *The Farm Show* a work of notable complexity when *I Love You, Baby Blue*, despite its great popular appeal, falls apart under close scrutiny? That the level of dramatic intelligence varied in Thompson's work may be ascribed in part to the problems of what Thompson has called 'consumer values': if a particular technique works well, there is always the temptation to repeat it. As Mary Jane Miller has suggested, 'the trauma of haying becomes the trauma of mining ore becomes ...? Six actors with portable props in a play adapted to any playing space must impose severe and repetitive limitations on themselves.'[20]

Thompson's deliberate decision to avoid repetition meant that in a sense his plays were all experimental. At the same time, he moved towards ever more complex subjects requiring a higher degree of risk from the actors. The problems of researching and commenting on the sexual mores of Toronto were more complex than those of getting to know the people of Clinton, just as the demands upon an actor in creating a narrative plot in a play like *Torontonians* were more complex than those of piecing together an episodic 'Sunday concert.' It is perhaps unfair therefore to extoll the brilliance of *The Farm Show* to the detriment of later, more ambitious projects. As the prototype of the collectively created documentary, *The Farm Show* set a standard that successive shows could not equal without imitating. The example of *The Farm Show* colours all of Passe Muraille's later work. It is axiomatic that a first venture will point the way to later experiments which must implicitly refer back to it, but this does not explain why *The Farm Show* stands out among Thompson's work. Its significance may be explained by its place in Passe Muraille's history, but its excellence cannot. To account for that we must look at the circumstances of its creation.

BACKGROUND TO THE FARM SHOW

When Thompson joined Theatre Passe Muraille in 1969, it was an avant-garde 'counter-culture' collective working out of Rochdale College, an alternative housing co-operative in Toronto. Under the initial direction of Jim Garrard, who wanted to make theatre 'as popular as bowling,'[21] Passe Muraille made its debut with contemporary American plays, like Rochelle Owen's *Futz* (for which the theatre was closed by police) and Paul Foster's *Tom Paine*. When Thompson assumed the job of artistic director in 1971 (following Martin Kinch, who had succeeded Garrard), he continued the theatre's open-door policy, inviting other groups and directors to make use of Passe Muraille's meager facilities. In 1974, Thompson told Robert Wallace:

You know, our logo has four arrows running off in four different directions: I think, in a sense, it's really good, to have people who aren't working in the same style ... Like, I'm the only one here who's really into Canadian textures and nationalism in the sense of putting Canadian voices and people on stage.[22]

Thompson's first venture into Canadian 'textures' was the 1971 *Notes from Quebec*, an adaptation of Jean-Claude Germaine's *Diguidi, Diguidi, Ha! Ha! Ha!* Fluently bilingual and familiar with French theatre after his period with Roger Planchon, Thompson was naturally attracted to the remarkable theatrical renaissance in Quebec in the late 1960s. Upon his return from France he had spent a winter in Montreal, and was one of the few anglophone Canadian directors to attempt to bridge the gap between the two cultures. (His most notable attempt came some years later, with the 1978 production of *Les Maudits Anglais* in which a cast of anglophone actors improvised a play in English which they then performed in French to Montreal francophone audiences.)

Thompson's first attempt at a collectively created documentary was very much a transitional work. *Doukhobors*, produced in 1971, anticipated the theatricality of *The Farm Show* but relied heavily on more traditional documentary techniques, including projected titles and photographs. Like *The Farm Show*, *Doukhobors* is episodic in structure and presentational in style. In it Thompson introduced his techniques of juxtaposing monologues with physical transformations. In the later plays, this technique became the rhetorical basis of the text, but in *Doukhobors* it is a feature introduced to illustrate an essentially literary text.

In his introduction to the published edition of the play, Thompson wrote:

We created an impressionistic approach to the Doukhobors. It was what we knew about them. We chose the title *Doukhobors* instead of *The Doukhobors* because we didn't feel that we knew enough to say 'This is what the Doukhobors are about.' It became: 'Doukhobors – what we knew about them as people living in Ontario.' Some of our scenes are intentionally built on these prejudices. The point is – What do we know about Doukhobors? Basically the headline stuff.[23]

Perhaps the most telling difference between *Doukhobors* and Thompson's later work is that this admission of subjectivity is not made explicit in the actual text. In its performance style, *Doukhobors* derives from the environmental theatre of the late 1960s, with an anti-illusionist technique stressing ensemble performances. The program notes to the play suggested a parallel between the Doukhobors and the ideology of the 1960s 'counter culture'

The Doukhobors were pioneers in more ways than one.
They unanimously took a stand opposing all wars.
They lived together communally.
They questioned the validity of our education system.
They discovered effective means of protesting government interference in their lives.

In his review of the play for the *Toronto Star*, however, Urjo Kareda noted that this parallel 'mercifully ... stops short of cheapening both the present and the past by wilfully lashing them together.'[24]

To convey a sense of authenticity, the actors alternated between an accented English for the monologues and a stage 'Russian' for the improvisational scenes. Reviewing the play, Herbert Whittaker noted that the actors were 'more expressive when using a convincing Russian speech than when interpreting themselves in broken English.'[25] In fact, the 'Russian' was an invented gibberish, although, according to Thompson, it actually communicated concrete facts and jokes.

The actuality of *Doukhobors* is authenticated by the text rather then the performance. Thompson had not yet developed his basic method of incorporating the process of research into the performance. The relation of actors to subject in *Doukhobors* is indirect; the play was based on published secondary sources rather than primary research by the cast. The first two weeks of the six-week process saw a continual turnover of actors. Janet Amos, who would become one of the mainstays of Passe Muraille as an actor and director, told Kareda: 'I dropped out after I'd been coming to rehearsals for a week and every day there would be a different cast except for Paul and myself.'

The reasons for this turnover are not difficult to guess: the actors were unpaid, and the collective process of play making, always uncertain, had not yet been validated by a triumphant success. In addition, Thompson noted in his introduction that one actress quit the cast because she 'couldn't come to grips with the whole nudity question. She thought it was silly.'

The nudity of *Doukhobors* was its most notorious aspect, at a time when the fact of nude bodies on stage excited controversy. Four years later, in *I Love You, Baby Blue*, the commitment to nudity and explicit sexuality on stage was a necessary condition of the play. As one of the actresses in *Baby Blue* said: 'The show was very raw, and titillating and sexy, and that's something that's hard to admit. Lots of people came for tits and ass. It was truly the best show in town for that.'[26] *Baby Blue* certainly appealed to the baser instincts of the audience – the play was the most successful in the history of Passe Muraille – but its explicitness was necessary to a play about sex. The nudity of *Doukhobors*, in contrast, was essentially iconographic, with an implied reference to the libertarian attitude of the day. In that sense, the brave climax of *Doukhobors* became the starting point of *Baby Blue*.

The principal difference between *Doukhobors* and the plays that came after it has to do with the composition of the collective and its relation to the material it performs. It is in this regard that *The Farm Show* was a major breakthrough. In *Doukhobors* the cast had no personal relation to the subject; the play was conceived essentially as an intellectual exercise.

It is apparent that certain subjects, more readily than others, can unite a group of actors into a genuine collective capable of expressing a synthesis of individual attitudes and discoveries. In collective creation, the group mind must reconcile its differences to create a community statement. This can happen in one of two ways: either the cast is united by ideological consensus in the analysis of the subject (as in *1837*), or the circumstances of making the play become a shared experience which then becomes part of the substance of the play itself. This is the case with *The Farm Show*.

When Thompson took his actors to Clinton in the summer of 1972 he was participating in a theatrical movement happening throughout Europe and North America. In the late 1960s, for example, Scandinavian students were creating comparable community plays, as were a number of Québécois theatres.[27] Thompson himself told an interviewer that 'the going out to communities is from things we'd read about happening in China.'[28] In 1974 he explained the genesis of the play in less romantic terms: 'Somebody said one day, making fun of your leftist outlook, by the way, "next time you'll be making a show like they have in Russia, about some guy in love with his tractor" and I thought, "that's an idea."'[29]

That remark was made in 1972 when Thompson was teaching a course at Brock University. He 'kicked the idea around' with Ted Johns, then a fellow instructor, who returned a few days later with a concrete proposal. He had a relative with an empty farmhouse which Thompson might be able to use. Owned by Ray Bird of Clinton, the farm was located close to Listowel, the town where Thompson had grown up. This personal connection was the single most important factor in the success of *The Farm Show*; it gave the actors the credibility to make contacts and overcome suspicious in a tightly knit community.

There was a second and perhaps even more felicitous factor in the play's success. Offering only thirty-five dollars a week and free accommodation in the farmhouse, Thompson gathered a cast of remarkably inventive and intelligent actors: his wife Anne Anglin, Fina MacDonell, Janet Amos, Miles Potter, and David Fox. A sixth actor, Alan Jones, quit the show after its first performance. Having grown up on a farm, he argued against Thompson's requirement that the actors meet the local farmers by assisting them in work that was usually miserably hard. When Jones left, Thompson took his place for the subsequent tour; in the revival the next year he was replaced by Ted Johns.

THE FARM SHOW: ANALYSIS

Throughout *The Farm Show* we are reminded of the process by which it was made, and we are always aware that the actors themselves are characters in the play. *The Farm Show* is not simply about an Ontario farming community. Rather, it is a play about the experiences the actors passed through in the course of researching the material. The performance documents the actors' growing consciousness as they make sense of the lives of the farmers. In that sense, the actors are a community looking at a community.[30]

The aesthetics of a documentary devised for the very people it purports to document must in the end defy empirical analysis; the specifics of character are transformed in performance into a broader typology of character – Thompson's 'myth' – and the actors stand midway between audience and subject, speaking for both in the play. This process can be outlined by examining two related scenes that incorporate the making of the play into the text.

The first of these scenes (act 1, scene 2) is a short comic encounter between Miles Potter and a farmer named Jack Merril. As Merril, played by David Fox, moves bales of hay, Miles introduces himself as an actor from Toronto and offers to help. The scene is a satiric admission of naïvety, which contrasts Merril's matter-of-factness with Miles's awkwardness:

MILES
... Boy it must be great being a farmer ...
JACK
Oh?
MILES
I mean you get up in the morning and get your hands down into that good honest dirt. What time do you get up in the morning Mr. Merril?
JACK
Oh, six, sometimes earlier.
MILES
Six! Eh. (a little surprised pause) Boy, this sure is a great old barn, Mr. Merril. (whistles) Hand-hewn beams! I'll bet it's one of those antique barns.
JACK
It's pretty old, I guess.
MILES
Sure would like to get some of these boards ... take them back to Toronto and make a coffee table out of them.[31]

This is the first mimetic scene in the play, following the presentational introduction and the ensemble 'Auction song.' As such it fulfils several distinct functions. As a comic skit it reminds the audience that everything in the play is learned through first-hand experience, and it demonstrates the process of that experience. Secondly the comic tone of the scene establishes the dominant light-hearted mood of the play. Miles may be a caricature of the actors' original naïvety, but that is merely a genial exaggeration of the actual state of affairs, and any suggestion of patronizing self-parody is offset by David Fox's sincere representation of Jack Merril. This is the first of many such impersonations in the show, and the contrast between the two characters in the scene is a tangible reminder of the distance the actors travelled in the course of making the play. Miles may satirize the initial awkwardness of the actors, but Fox's performance graphically demonstrates the final result of that awkwardness. In that sense the scene is the play in miniature.

When performed to the original audience in Clinton, the scene has an even more basic purpose. It effectively deflects whatever suspicions the audience may have of the actors by showing that they can laugh at themselves. The scene assures the audience that the play will be both humorous and sympathetic. When removed from the original audience the function of the scene is simplified: it becomes a straightforward introduction to the research process. If rural audiences could be expected to see the scene from Jack Merril's point of view, urban audiences could be expected to empathize with Miles, the city boy trying to make contact with an unfamiliar culture.

In the second example (act 1, scene 5), Miles returns to the subject of baling hay. In one of the most celebrated scenes of the play, Miles delivers a long monologue that describes the miserable day he and another actor spent helping Mervyn Lobb store hay in his barn. As he tells the story in the past tense, he performs it in the theatrical present, miming the work and mimicking the sound of the machinery. The monologue builds into a graphic and extremely funny and demanding situation. At the conclusion of the story, Miles collapses in exhaustion – made even more real by the strenuous physicality of the scene – and says to the audience:

> Now I ask you ... why? Why would any human being *choose*, for the better part of his life, *twice* a year, to put himself through this total and utter hell? I didn't understand then and I don't understand it now.
>
> (43)

In Michael Ondaatje's documentary film *The Clinton Special*, about the 1973 revival of the play, Potter explains the genesis of the scene. He had come home to the farmhouse from the baling tired and angry at Thompson for putting him through the ordeal. In rehearsal the next day he described the work to vent his rage and found that in the telling the story acquired unintended humour. According to Thompson, the transformation from agony to humour in the scene was a way for the audience to laugh at their collective demons: 'The scene gets him, but he gets them – pointing to the audience in effect and saying, "are you nuts?" And they have to agree, they are.'[32]

Throughout *The Farm Show* the actors transfer their experience of the process to the audience, through direct reportage, as in this monologue, or by implication. The latter technique is most obvious in the character monologues, which create a sense of mirror imagery by retaining the verbal interpolations and deixis of the original speaker. We see this first in act 1, scene 3, 'Round the Bend,' a collage of brief monologues that introduces the community as a network of neighbours and relations:

BETTY FEGAN

Oh hi! (other actors freeze) Come on in! No we're not busy. We saw the light on over there. We knew you were there but we didn't go over. You know, we didn't know what to expect. You must be Janet. Look who's here, Ross! (26)

This technique is used in every monologue in the play. The actors perform the characters just as they themselves met them. This is one of the more obvious authentication techniques in the play, and it highlights the dual nature of the performance. The original audience see themselves reflected through the actors, and the later audiences see the original audience as the actors met them. In the first case, the technique plays upon a level of recognition absent in the second. That *The Farm Show* works in both contexts may have been a happy accident but it is a major factor in the play's success.

It is easy to forget that the shape of *The Farm Show* was arrived at through accident and experiment rather than design. Despite the avowal that the show 'bounces along'; it has a definable structure. Any arrangement of scenes will manifest some kind of structure, no matter how haphazard, but in this case, the encounter of communities, the incorporation of the process into the text, and the dual nature of the play combine to form a suprisingly coherent dramatic statement. According to Thompson, the play had no shape at all until the first performance; by the mid point of the process certain scenes (including Miles's hay-baling scene and the 'John Deere' recitation that closes the play) were obvious 'keepers.'

The process of creating the play was one of discovering what it could be about. Collecting the monologues was the least complex task, although, as Janet Amos admits in *The Clinton Special*, the actors gravitated to the more outgoing and familiar members of the community and shied away from meeting others until pushed. The presence of tape recorders may have been an inhibiting factor, responsible in part for the self-consciousness of the informants. Significantly, the most intimate portrayal in the play is that of Jean Lobb, performed by Janet Amos at the beginning of the second act. In *The Clinton Special*, Jean Lobb recalls that she had no idea she was being taped when she spoke to Amos, who had told her the tape recorder wasn't working. Instead of resenting the taping of her speech as a breach of trust, Jean Lobb gave her permission for it to be used – further indication of the acceptance the community accorded the actors.

The monologues are only one part of the substance of the play. The contiguous part, the improvisations and theatricality of the play, was a more complex challenge in rehearsal. The specific theatrical techniques of the play can be explained in terms of the exercises Thompson gave the actors. These exercises gave the actors the basic tools to transform their perceptions and experiences into theatrical gesture, and at the same time they were the building blocks of the play itself. The five principal exercises, in Thompson's words, were 'portraits' of local characters; 'landscapes,' in which the actors were asked to create visual images; 'mythologising'; 'show and tell'; and 'transformations,' turning objects into something else. In each of these exercises the actors were asked to give their discoveries in concrete imagery and gesture.

In the course of a typical rehearsal the actors would work through many such exercises, and the most promising would be noted as potential scenes. Instead of proceeding analytically, Thompson encouraged the actors to discover the possibilities of the play in their daily attempts to come to grips with the material in rehearsal. This accounts for the narrow focus of *The Farm Show*; only those experiences that could be transformed into effective theatre made their way into the play. The relation of this process to the performance text of the play may be clarified by taking each of these exercises in turn and examining a scene that developed from it.

From the 'portraits' exercise came the character studies that are the heart of *The Farm Show*. Thompson saw this as an essential part of the myth-making in the play: 'Even though we particularized a character like Jean Lobb right down to the way she laughed, we somehow made a connection with something larger.'[33] We can see how this process works in practice in Michael Ondaatje's film, which juxtaposes David Fox's representation of Les Jervis with footage of Jervis himself as he describes his home-made wildlife park. Jervis comments that Fox 'mimicked me pretty good.' In the rehearsal exercise, the actors were asked to represent their characters so that the Clinton audiences could identify them. This appears to have been successful. Reviewing the original performance in the *Goderich Signal*, Liza Williams wrote:

And everyone who knew Les Jervis recognized the character sketch done by David Fox. As a matter of fact, those in the audience who were from the area recognized most of their neighbours in the scenes. Howls of laughter and groans of embarrassment burst continually from the straw bleachers.[34]

Yet when we compare Fox to Les Jervis in *The Clinton Special* it is clear that the actor does not strive for an exact imitation of the original. The words and the inflections are those of Les Jervis, but the voice and presence are those of David Fox. The actors signal the characteristics of the original without surrendering their own individuality. In that sense, 'mimicry' is an accurate description. This principle carries over to an audience that does not know and cannot recognize Les Jervis. As the six actors portray a whole community, they create a theatrical synthesis of it. This underlies the general movement of the play: even as it defines the community, the play gives that definition a concrete unity in the presence of the actors. All of the characters represented by David Fox, for example, acquire his characteristics. Although these characters may be differentiated by gesture and inflection, they share a commonality in the actor.

In the context of the original audience, the actors perform on stage much as they presented themselves in real life to the community. In chapter 5 we see a variation of this in the case of the Mummers Troupe's *Buchans: A Mining Town*; in that play the actors extend their natural personalities into more general character types in the play, adding in effect a level of pretense between performer and audience. In *The Farm Show* the actors consistently return to an informal performance style. This distinction tends to disappear when the play is removed from that original context. When played to an unfamiliar audience, especially in the city where the audience in all likelihood has little sense of community, at least not in the geographic sense, the informality of the performance becomes a theatrical device; it aquires a sense of artifice.

Only once in the play is portraiture developed in a radically different manner than that of the Les Jervis scene. At the beginning of act 1, scene 8, Janet Amos tells the audience:

Last summer we asked one of the farmers if he knew anyone in the area who was considered eccentric. Someone who was a bit strange and outside of the community. He said that the only man he could think of was a man named Charlie Wilson. (57)

The actors create a portrait of the deceased Charlie Wilson through a montage of impressions and memories. Charlie Wilson had been a local recluse, a self-educated handyman who suffered terribly from a facial tic. The scene is constructed around David Fox as Charlie, writing a letter to a friend in town. The letter, which describes Charlie's readings and his observations of nature, is authentic. The props in the scene are Charlie's own possessions, but they acquire a greater value. As Thompson has said, in his work 'objects become metaphors.'[35] (He has also remarked: 'My plays come out of Charlie Wilson's tools.'[36])

Effective as it is, the 'Charlie Wilson' scene points to one of the limitations of Thompson's methodology. By framing the story of Charlie Wilson in terms of the people who knew and remembered him with fondness, the actors accept the community's image of itself. Although the scene originated with the desire to find someone 'outside' the community, the scene suggests that in fact the community is all-inclusive. Despite his reclusiveness, Charlie Wilson was very much a part of the social matrix. By the fact that the scene is created by the memories of people who knew and dealt with him, Charlie Wilson is defined as a man among friends, not an outsider but 'one of us,' and the real hardships of his life suggested in the scene are softened. It is easy to forget when watching *The Farm Show* that the actors spoke to only a few members of the community as a whole, and that they could only express certain aspects of it. The 'Charlie Wilson' scene is the most traditionally documentary in the play; in its structure and substance it assumes an appearance of objectivity, principally because the actors could not meet Wilson. In most of *The Farm Show,* the informality and subjectivity of the performance deflects the question of honesty and interpretation. In the 'Charlie Wilson' scene, because it is more apparently objective, that question cannot be avoided.

A community documentary can only succeed if the actors accept the community's values and image of itself. It must avoid controversy, even when dealing with controversial subjects, if it is to win the approval of the community it documents. An unflattering portrayal of Charlie Wilson, for instance, would have been unacceptable to the original audience of *The Farm Show*. The scene is not just about Charlie Wilson's impact on the community as a whole; it is about his relation to those members of the community who cared for him.

This principle of partiality can also be seen in two of the scenes that extend Thompson's 'show and tell' exercises. In the first of these, act 1, scene 7, the actors recreate their impressions of the Orange Day parade they witnessed in Goderich. The scene is a collage of public addresses and monologues, framed by the actors' mime of a marching band. The event is recreated as a joyful festival, with particular emphasis on the ornaments and ceremony of the parade:

LODGE MEMBER
Thank you, Mr McKinley. Thank you very much. (shakes his hand vigorously) We want you to remember that Mr McKinley is the Member of Parliament for this region, and we're very *proud* to have ... (cut off by True Blue, exits backstage with McKinley)

TRUE BLUE
Banner!
Loyal Orange Lodge Number Seven Oh One.
Faith of our fathers!
They suffered death rather than submit to popism.
We have here the Boys of Derry and some monks kneeling, with a crucifix before them.
GRAND MARSHALL
(Actor miming a man riding a frisky and unruly horse)
King William of Orange! On a white horse.
Grand Marshall, Loyal Orange Lodge, Goderich.
(Parade continues with fewer people at a slower pace)
SPEAKER
Well, now, I'd like to tell you one of those Newfy jokes ...   (52–3)

The actors are not interested in the ideology or historical significance of Orangism in Huron County, as they might be in a sociological documentary. Even the religious aspects of the ceremony are presented as a kind of authentic folk theatre. In the Orange Day parade the actors show the community at play. It is the form and not the substance of the occasion that attracts their attention.

In the second of these scenes, act 2, scene 7, two actors recreate a township council meeting. The stage directions to the scene describe the theatrical game on which it is based:

Each councilman has a characteristic voice and manner. Before speaking a line attributed to one of the men the actor must quickly move into his place and assume his character ... In the course of the scene each of the actors plays each of the five men once or several times.   (91)

This is a typical example of Thompson's use of the gesture of showing. The mundane routine of the council meeting is transformed into exciting theatre by what Thompson has called 'the kick of virtuosity.' Like the 'Orange Day parade,' this scene lacks inner substance. Our engagement is with the telling of the story rather than the story itself. The scene does comment implicitly on the nature of democracy in the community – the councillors are local farmers, and the meeting is conducted with casual informality but this is not expanded into an overt observation.

Rarely in *The Farm Show* do the actors venture into territory where the preference for form over analysis creates difficulty. Although the play has been criticized for its avoidance of political and economic complexities (including the threat to personal farms by corporate 'agribusiness'), it protects itself against such criticism for the most part by looking at the culture, not the business, of farming.[37] Only in certain scenes, such as 'Orange Day Parade' and 'Township Council' do the larger issues intrude, and then only because the scenes invite questions the play is not prepared to answer.

The remaining three rehearsal exercises were designed to help the actors express perceptions as concrete images. In the first of these, Thompson asked the actors to transform landscapes into theatrical gesture. There are three notable examples of this in the play, in each case as a brief preface to a larger scene: at the beginning of act 1, scene 4, again in act 1, scene 6, and finally, before act 2, scene 6. Thompson has joked that these theatrical poems come from 'our understanding of Japanese theatre.' The piece preceding Fox's Les Jervis monologue is typical:

FIRST GIRL
(enters stage left and mimes while speaking)
A tall wire fence – bent
Thick fence posts,
Enclose a smooth, flat pond.
A water-wheel,
Turning.
Above it,

A sign written in black.
Time.
(sits centre stage with hands like two ducks heads)
Ducks!
Swimming on the pond ...   (44)

This vignette begins as a rhythmic interpolation between two monologues. It punctuates Miles's hay-baling scene which precedes it, and it sets the scene for the Les Jervis monologue. More importantly, its restraint and formality create a poetic expectation in contrast to the direct realism of the Les Jervis speech. On a structural level, the vignette performs a more complex function: it brings about a momentary unity of performance rhythm, dramatic substance, and theatrical gesture. As Fox begins his Les Jervis monologue, the actors become the animals in the sanctuary they have described in the poem. The vignette starts as a structural punctuation device and moves through verbal imagery to physical theatricality. The animal mimicry in the Les Jervis scene is established in the poem when Fina MacDonell illustrates her words by turning her hands into ducks. Typically, in Canadian collective creations, the montage techniques used to create transitions from one scene to another have little or no organic relation to the scenes so connected. The subjectivity of *The Farm Show* enables the actors to establish an essentially poetic unity.

In another exercise, Thompson asked the actors to transform various objects into something else. In the opening scene of the play, an actor shows the audience the props scattered about the stage:

> We also brought back a few things from Clinton.
> This is part of a bean dryer.
> These are straw bales, not to be confused with the hay bales you'll hear about later.
> An old cream can. Some crates. An actual Clinton shopping cart. (19)

These objects, like Charlie Wilson's tools, take on metaphorical significance in the play. They are rarely used as themselves. Any thing can become any other thing in performance. In act 1, scene 3, 'Round the Bend,' there is a brief monologue in which a man displays his collection of curiosities:

> Here's an interesting item. (carelessly picks up an old mailbox or whatever) Nobody knows exactly what this is – not even the experts. (30)

This dialectic of mutability and exact actuality is a principal feature of *The Farm Show*. The actor invests the object with significance by usage. This principle of transformation is generally applied to give documentary fact theatrical life, allowing us to witness the creative process of the actor transforming fact into meaning. It can also serve as the starting point, and in the end the *raison d'être* of a scene. The 'Winter scene' (act 1, scene 4) is a complex theatrical game made possible by such transformations. The scene is established by a poetic vignette similar to the one that precedes the Les Jervis scene. Following the vignette, two actors, as husband and wife, re-enact a typical day in the life of their family. The actors take on a number of voices in a collage centred on the stage props. At the end of the day the couple go to a barn dance: they huddle out of sight under the bean dryer, which they shake and bounce to simulate the activity of the dance. The bean dryer, the crate, and the shopping cart 'car' are the 'rules' which make the scene possible. On the most basic level, this principle of transformation applies to the representation of characters as well as animals and things. The actors transform themselves into other people while retaining their own individuality, just as they transform themselves into objects which can elevate a simple monologue to virtuosity. In act 1, scene 9, for example, Miles Potter delivers a monologue about the dangers of driving a tractor. Three other actors form the tractor, which Miles drives around the stage, demonstrating his point with a gestural transformation.

The final rehearsal exercise deals with a less tangible kind of transformation, that of turning a perception into 'myth.' There are two major examples of this, one of which provides the structural unity of the second act. The first example is the recitation that ends the play, a twenty-three-verse heroic ballad about John Deere, who gave his name to a popular make of tractor. As the universal tool of the farmer, the tractor figures prominently in the play as a symbol of work and death. In act 2, three successive scenes focus on tractors and related farm machinery: act 2, scene 2, is a monologue by a woman who recalls injuries caused by tractors; scene 3 describes two separate incidents of similar injuries, and scene 4 is a comic 'gargantuan war of the tractors' in which two actors, representing two popular makes, engage in a tractor-tug.

The 'John Deere' recitation describes how the legendary hero, derided by his friends for his faith in the newfangled machine, saves some children from drowning and dies in a final attempt to save a kitten:

With a kitty on board, all scared and wet,
But no sign of John – we ain't seen one yet.
Some say he pulled himself ashore below
And he's savin' kittens still – but I don't know.

But one thing come of that fateful day
And I'm proud that I can stand here and say,
'Whenever men gather be it far or near,
And there's a tractor of that make, men named
her – John Deere.'   (107)

As the finale of the play, this recitation may seem an odd choice. Its only thematic relation to the play is the fact that John Deere is said to have lived in the precise area *The Farm Show* documents. By transforming the story into a folk legend and setting it in a popular form, the actors give the community is own history back to them in the form of a heroic myth. The recitation in that sense embodies the idea of the play.

The second, more complex, attempt at defining a myth is embodied in the recurring song about the Lobb family in act 2:

Mobs of Lobbs, Lobb-in-laws, ready-on-the-job Lobbs
All along the Maitland and the 16th line.
If you go out driving there, any time,
Looking out your window you too will see

That ever-spreading, farming, Lobb Dynasty,
dynasty. (74)

The 'myth' of the Lobb dynasty is one of the main structural features of *The Farm Show*. Most of act 2 centres on various members of the family, and the act is given unity by the recurrence of the Lobb song, which charts the family's several generations. In act 1, the Lobbs are present but not pre-eminent, but in the second act they come to the fore to represent the community as a whole. As a structural device, this focus on one family seems to have emerged as an obvious choice in rehearsal. It was through the Lobbs that the actors entered the community, because of the family connection with Ted Johns, and as they met the large number of Lobbs in the district they discovered a community in miniature.

The decision to string together a number of monologues centring on Lobbs with the Lobb song may have been a dramaturgical expediency, but it had a qualifying effect on the thematic structure of the play. *The Farm Show* is not structured to express particular themes, but, rather, themes emerge out of the theatrical arrangement of material. The first act charts the territory of the play, marking the boundaries of the community. The logic of the act is associative: the scenes form a general collage while they simultaneously describe the process by which the play was made. The act follows a basic movement from the general to the specific, from the montage of impressions in 'Round the Bend,' (which gives us seventeen different characters – all neighbours – to the public celebrations of Orange Day and the detailed portraits of Les Jervis and Charlie Wilson. The act ends with a segment about women. In act 1, scene 10, Janet Amos, sitting in a washing machine, outlines a typical day in the hectic life of a farm wife, until the constant interruptions by her family build to such an intensity that she turns into a chicken. The scene turns into a square dance to a ballad about a farmer's wife who sells her husband at an auction. Within the frame of the ballad, two brief monologues and a vignette comment on sex and marriage.

In this first act, the play defines the community by the patterns of its daily life and work. In the second act, the play looks more closely at the life cycles of the commmunity. Here the narrative function of the Lobb song is crucial. The act begins with Janet Amos's Jean Lobb monologue in which she describes in detail the various weddings in her family. Following the monologues comes the first verse of the Lobb song. Its function is to name Jean Lobb's family:

When Mervyn sang tenor in the old church choir,
There came an eager lady who would him inspire,

To sing in parts the best there can be,
Soon he learned to sing to her, marry me,
marry me.

Then it started growing, that old Lobb tree,
Don and Bruce, Murray and Hugh, Gord and Jeannie.
They all grew straight and tall and strong,
And all settled down around Clinton town,
Clinton town.   (74)

The play then moves into the three monologues of the accident sequence:
marriage and birth are followed by injury and death. The second verse of the
Lobb song follows the 'tractor-tug' that rounds off the accident sequence. In this
verse, the song describes the second generation of Lobbs:

Bruce saw Diane waiting on tables and
When she brought him coffee, spilled it over
his knee.
Oh, how he burned for her until one day
He bought a wedding ring for her and stole
her away, stole her away.

Then it started growing that old Lobb tree
Michael, Christopher, Jack a bundle of three
They're learning their bible and they know
God's way
Will lead them to another family some day.   (81)

This is the introduction to the 'Jesus Bus' scene, in which Diane Lobb
describes the trip she took with her husband and another couple to Halifax to
bring back a double-decker bus for her evangelical church. Their journey is
marred by repeated breakdowns, which become the theatrical basis of the scene;
one actor plays a wounded 'bus' nursed along by two other actors. In
counterpoint to the monologue, an evangelical 'witness' testifies to the 'four
steps to salvation.' This is one of two references to religion in the play (the other
being the 'Orange Day Parade' scene), and it serves a double purpose. As a
sympathetic portrayal of Bible-belt fundamentalism it acknowledges the
important role religion plays in the community, and it demonstrates the
diversity of the Lobb family. This is continued in the next scene, again
introduced by a verse of the Lobb song, in which we meet Diane's sister-in-law

Alison. She describes her volunteer work at the local Sunday School, even though, as she says, 'I'm not religious – You might even say I border on the agnostic.'

There is no attempt in these scenes to reconcile or explain the differences within the family. The scenes function on two levels: the 'Jesus Bus' scene, for example, is about a woman's religious faith, but it is also about the Lobb family, which can accommodate diverging views. The 'myth' of the Lobb family develops as the contrasting scenes juxtapose differing attitudes.

Alison Lobb's monologue is a commentary on the various community events in which she has taken part, including the Ladies Guild, the Township Council, and various celebrations. In the Jean Lobb monologue, the family was introduced as a closed group; in this scene it is described in the larger social context. This monologue leads rather arbitrarily into the 'Township Council' scene described earlier.

Following the council scene, the play moves into its final segment, with act 2, scene 7, 'Picture Frame,' which precedes the final verse of the Lobb song. The picture frame is a theatrical metaphor of changing attitudes towards farming. Five actors stand in a row while a large wooden frame is lowered in front of them. As two of the actors, representing a husband and wife, describe the history of their farm their children in turn step out of the frame and tell the audience why they chose to leave it. The scene ends when an auctioneer 'sells off' the picture. This is as close as *The Farm Show* comes to historical analysis; the scene is a sentimental suggestion that all that has gone before represents a vanishing way of life.

Originally, this scene was followed by a concluding speech by Don Lobb about the mechanics of farming, but for the 1973 revival it was replaced by the Bruce Pallet speech found in the printed edition of the play. According to Thompson, this speech grew out of a letter the company received after a sequence of the play was broadcast on CBC radio.[38] The letter suggested that Passe Muraille drop in on Bruce Pallet's Sunday School class in Orangeville. Thompson met Pallet and set up a further meeting with David Fox, who brought back to the company the monologue that takes the play to the final 'John Deere' recitation. Pallet's speech addresses the issues of the 'Picture Frame' scene in more explicit detail. He describes the rate at which farm land is lost to other development in Ontario, and he details the economic plight of the farmer with passion. His final angry words stand as the company's concluding admonition:

> Y'know, I just want my kids to make a *living* at it. I got *grandchildren* I want to make a living at it.
> So what else can I *do*? Y'know, how else do you *build a nation*? (102)

The juxtaposition of the narrative structure of the Lobb sequences and the thematic structure of life cycles on the farm gives the second act its apparent complexity. As Thompson admits, the overall structure of *The Farm Show* is not complex: it can be perceived in terms of general patterns governing the arrangement of material. These patterns are not in themselves complicated, and the arrangement is frequently arbitrary. There is however little profit in judging *The Farm Show* by the standards of textual dramatic criticism. The play was after all conceived, researched, devised, and rehearsed in six weeks, a span of time that a more traditional theatre might allot to the rehearsal of a literary drama.

When judged as a theatrical statement in performance, however, *The Farm Show* is a complex work of art that succeeds because the actors were able to document the community from within. As a documentary about farming in Ontario, *The Farm Show* may not stand up to analysis but, as a frankly subjective report of a personal encounter with farmers, it remains one of the most innovative works of the Canadian theatre. *The Farm Show* introduced a tradition of populism that would come to define the Canadian documentary, and its influence reaches into all the plays discussed in this book. It is perhaps too soon to ascertain the actual extent of Paul Thompson's contribution to Canadian theatre. He was not the only director to conceive of a community documentary, nor was he the first to explore the possibilities of collective creation. Thompson was, however, the first to bring these two developments together, and, although the movement towards a collectively created populist documentary form was perhaps an inevitable historical development, Thompson gave that development its initial expression. In his own words, *The Farm Show* was 'a blueprint of how to do something in a place where nothing had been done.'[39]

3

Documentary and Popular History:
Ten Lost Years

The Farm Show initiated the dominant form of Canadian documentary theatre, but the play that may be said to have established the documentary as a popular genre in the minds of critics and audiences derived from another tradition entirely. In February, 1974, less than two years after *The Farm Show*, Toronto Workshop Productions opened its adaptation of *Ten Lost Years*, a popular and well-received anthology of oral memories about the Great Depression compiled by Barry Broadfoot. Adapted to the stage by Jack Winter, Cedric Smith, and George Luscombe, *Ten Lost Years* went on to become one of the most successful productions in the history of Canadian theatre. Judged in terms of critical acclaim and box office popularity, it set a standard that few Canadian plays, let alone documentaries, could match.

Despite its unparalleled success, *Ten Lost Years* remains an anomaly. If it is the most successful Canadian documentary, it is also the least representative. In theme, performance style, and dramaturgical technique, it differs significantly from the other plays in this book. At first glance, *Ten Lost Years* appears to have much in common with *The Farm Show*: both forego invented text in favour of a montage of oral source material; both define a collective experience from a populist perspective; both use the techniques of ensemble performance to present documentary actuality; and in both the actors juxtapose documentary realism with anti-illusionist theatricality.

Beneath these similarities, the two plays rest on very different perceptions of the relation of documentary and culture. *The Farm Show* initiated a tradition which responded to the perceived need to define local or regional culture with an implicit rejection of 'international' artistic standards and models. In its theme and style, *The Farm Show* was a conscious exploration of localism as a defence against 'cultural imperialism.'[1]

In contrast, *Ten Lost Years* represents the successful transplant in Canada of a theatrical technique developed in Britain in the 1930s, and it followed upon fifteen years of systematic exploration of that technique at Toronto Workshop Productions. George Luscombe had founded TWP in 1959 a few years after a five-year stint with Joan Littlewood's Theatre Workshop at the Theatre Royal, in Stratford East, London, and in his opinion, his theatre was the only true continuation of Littlewood's 'group theatre' vision. As he told Herbert Whittaker in 1979, 'of the original nucleus, I was the only one who built a theatre. The young people who run her Stratford East theatre now have a new policy.'[2]

If TWP represents the extension of a theatrical tradition that can be traced to the Workers Theatre movement of the 1930s and ultimately to Piscator, it is also true that it was the first of the alternative theatres in Canada. Luscombe himself has been referred to as 'the granddaddy' of the movement.[3] TWP thus occupies a prominent but problematic place in Canadian theatre: it is the only theatre which may be said to link the alternative theatre of the 1970s with its antecedents in the 1930s. The problem is that the link, although real, is indirect. TWP continues a tradition that developed in the 1930s, but it has no direct link with the Canadian theatres of that decade.

Ten Lost Years was at once a culmination of Luscombe's continuation of Littlewood's vision, and an important transition for his theatre. Its success gave TWP a new lease on life, as well as renewed esteem in the eyes of its critics. More importantly, the process of adapting Broadfoot's book led Luscombe to further refinements of the techniques he had inherited from Littlewood. These refinements made it possible for him to realize long-held ambitions of adapting historical material to the stage in such subsequent documentaries as *The Mac-Paps* (1979, about Canadian volunteers in the Spanish Civil War) and *The Wobbly* (1983, about the International Workers of the World).

Despite its success, *Ten Lost Years* has had virtually no discernible influence on the work of other theatres in Canada. *The Farm Show*, Paul Thompson's 'blueprint' for collectively created community documentary, inspired numerous imitations; *Ten Lost Years*, despite its greater popularity, inspired none. In this, *Ten Lost Years* is typical of Luscombe's work. TWP prepared the way for the alternative theatre in Canada but had little effect on its actual development. It has produced only one minor playwright in Jack Winter and, with the exception of the 1983 publication of *Ten Lost Years*, has not made its plays available to the public. Although Luscombe frequently collaborated with playwrights, he had no apparent interest in playwriting as such, and consequently no real interest in the struggle to establish a national dramatic literature that was an important feature of the alternative theatre.

TWP remained peripheral to the alternative theatre movement not simply because of differences in theatrical emphasis, but because of deeper differences in political and cultural analysis. In 1978, Robert Fulford, editor of *Saturday Night*, observed of Luscombe that 'somehow, compared to the Young Turks of experimental theatre, he represented what the Old Left was to the New Left: an honourable but faintly boring leftover from the bad old days before the breakthrough.'[4] The political simile is more appropriate than Fulford may have intended. Luscombe's politics were indeed those of the 'Old Left,' with its emphasis on trade unionism and international socialism. For all of its superficial similarities to *The Farm Show*, *Ten Lost Years* is the product of an older tradition of political documentary that defines issues in terms of class struggle. In that sense it is as closely related to a play like *Eight Men Speak* as it is to its contemporaries.

To understand why Luscombe's approach to political theatre has had no significant effect on other Canadian theatres, it is necessary to examine his commitment to the theory and practice of 'group theatre' as the term was used by Joan Littlewood. Luscombe's commitment to Littlewood's techniques of combining ensemble performance, text, direction, and design in one inseparable whole had its source in his early interest in the idea of a popular political theatre. As a young man in Toronto in the 1940s, Luscombe acted in plays and wrote sketches for the socialist Co-operative Commonwealth Federation, and formed a song and dance troupe which performed for variety shows, rallies, and on one occasion from the back of truck to striking factory workers. In 1948 he joined the short-lived People's Repertory Theatre in Toronto, formed by students from the Royal Conservatory of Music under the direction of E. Sterndale Bennett. Despite its name the troupe had no interest in political theatre, performing instead British rep standards such as J.B. Priestley's *Dangerous Corner*. It was, however, one of the first attempts to tour professional non-commercial theatre to small towns in Ontario, a practice Luscombe would revive briefly in his early years at TWP.[5]

In 1950 Luscombe moved to Britain to gain experience on the stage. He took what roles he could, including a season as young male lead in a touring 'fit-up' company in Wales until 1952, when Littlewood accepted him into her newly expanded Theatre Workshop. He joined Theatre Workshop just as it was settling into its first permanent home at the Theatre Royal, Stratford East. The five years he spent there set the course of his future work.

In the words of its manifesto, Theatre Workshop's aim was 'to create a flexible theatre-art, as swift moving and plastic as the cinema, by applying the recent technical advances in light and sound, and introducing music and the "dance theatre" style of productions.'[6] The most important step in realizing that goal was the creation of an acting ensemble that could develop group skills through successive productions. When Luscombe joined it, Theatre Workshop was on the verge of its most fruitful period, during which Littlewood led the ensemble through a variety of modern and classical texts. Luscombe acted in productions of *Lysistrata*, *The Good Soldier Schweik*, *Volpone*, and *Arden of Faversham*, among others. Later in his own theatre he would continue Littlewood's eclectic program and pay tribute to her with productions of Ewan MacColl's *Travellers* and Brendan Behan's *The Hostage*, both of which originated at Theatre Workshop, as well as a new adaptation of *Schweik*.

His time at Stratford East introduced Luscombe to the specific techniques of 'group theatre' and to Littlewood's arduous discipline, both of which he would emulate. From Littlewood he learned the value of improvisation as a method of training actors, and he absorbed the staging techniques that won her recognition as the most innovative British director of the day.

The Theatre Workshop company took regular classes in voice, and, perhaps more importantly, in the movement and dance techniques of Rudolf Laban. From 1948 on, the company had the advantage of a resident teacher in Jean Newlove, one of Laban's original British students. The application of Laban's methodical analysis of human movement gave the company a method of unifying dramatic text with stage movement that freed them from the realist conventions that dominated the British stage. In his research Laban had analysed basic movement 'efforts' in terms of time, space, and energy. In the classes the Theatre Workshop ensemble explored the ways in which an understanding of these efforts could define the physical and psychological shape of a character. Laban himself wrote to Littlewood: 'For the first time in this country I have met a group who is tackling the fundamental problems of movement as affecting the individual actor and the group as a whole in such a way as to affect the rhythms of contemporary life.'[7] For Luscombe, Laban's exercises provided a system though which he could continue to refine Littlewood's theories of staging, and throughout his career at TWP he held classes in Laban technique for his actors.

It is in the nature of 'group theatre' that the qualities that make it unique are the most ephemeral, but the debt that Luscombe owes to Littlewood can be illustrated by comparing descriptions of their respective staging techniques. David Scase, an actor in *Johnny Noble*, Ewan MacColl's 'ballad opera' about a merchant seaman during the Second World War, describes Littlewood's mastery of theatrical illusion and effect:

Five men and a gun, fighting off an attack on their convoy. Joan asked me to show what each man in the gun crew did. By repeating the movement over and over again, the orders and the shouts, Joan actually created a ballet, a dance sequence out of it; but by incorporating realistic sound, bombers coming in, guns and shots, the scene had all the drama of a gun crew fighting off an aeroplane.[8]

Littlewood's signature technique of portraying realistic action through mime and sound effects became the identifying feature of Luscombe's staging also; it is one of the basic principles in the performance of *Ten Lost Years*. In 1965, Nathan Cohen gave a concise description of this technique used to great effect in Jack Winter's Jonsonian comedy, *The Mechanic*:

Later on the mechanic lectures his naive assistant on the actual and pretended repairs of a car and how to gull the customer. His sermon is illustrated by players pantomiming the stirrings and workings of the various parts of the car. Sometimes depending on which part of the car he is talking about, just one player simulates an action of the engine, sometimes they're all gyrating and swirling in expertly worked-out unison. Meanwhile, each uses a deliberately incongruous instrument – a sewing machine top, for example – to produce the matching noise. When the whole engine is working, you have a symphony of moving parts and accurately appropriate sounds.[9]

Luscombe learned from Littlewood how to apply these techniques of group performance to non-dramatic material. At the same time he learned techniques of dramatic analysis derived from the great Russian actor and theorist Konstantin Stanislavski that could assist actors in developing character action in improvisation. In 1963, when Toronto Workshop Productions made the transition from semi-professional to fully professional status, Luscombe's playwright-in-residence Jack Winter, described the company as 'a genuine group theatre, founded on the principles of dynamic growth within an intimate and harmonious body.' The influence of Stanislavski is clear in his summation of Luscombe's working method: 'Once the units in the action and the objectives in the roles have been recognized the performers are free to act and interact in any way and all ways that are true for them and true for the play.'[10]

Laban technique gave Littlewood's, and later Luscombe's, actors a stylized movement vocabulary which extended natural impulses; Stanislavski's acting exercises gave them the tools to improvise around a subject without losing the dramatic thrust of a play. Although Luscombe's work has been referred to as collective creation, it is necessary to distinguish it from the method of collective creation popularised in Canada by Paul Thompson. For Thompson, improvisation is the starting point that leads to the discovery of dramatic text. For Luscombe, it is a method of expanding textual action defined in advance by the playwright and directors: 'I work in terms of unit objectives. I'm not interested in watching an actor look for an idea. You have to begin with an idea and look for its theatrical shape.'[11]

Together these two elements, Laban-inspired movement and closely super-vised improvisation, gave Luscombe the basis of his style, one that has confused several generations of critics. A third element may be found in Luscombe's demand that the actor 'achieve voice.'[12] Luscombe stresses the importance of the voice as a musical instrument, training his actors to be sensitive to rhythm and tempo while at the same time retaining colloquial speech patterns. Typically, Luscombe trains his actors to 'butt' their cues, so that lines are delivered without the actors' normal pauses between them. Coupled with stylized movement, the result is a performance in which physical and vocal gestures seem slightly larger than life. Like Littlewood, Luscombe perceives text in terms of its physicality. In his own words, 'nobody else in Canada *uses* the stage – they use it like radio.'[13] He has compared his use of the stage to opera:

Opera gives you the opportunity to lift out of life onto a very high frame that which is not realistic but rather, representational. That's what I want to do. Remember what Shakespeare said, '… as *if* into a mirror,' *not* into a mirror; and Stanislavski expressed it as *rendering* into artistic terms. That word rendering is very important. Theatre is the *element* of life transposed onto the stage.[14]

It was in part because of Luscombe's faithful adherence to the principles of 'group theatre' he learned from Littlewood that he developed a reputation as a 'tyrant' in Canadian theatre. When he founded TWP he was unique among Canadian directors in his determination to train his actors in a particular and rigorous style, and to instil in them the sense of purpose he brought back to Canada in 1957. That discipline even extended to the behaviour he expected from his actors in rehearsal: 'No one eats, drinks, reads newspapers or plays pinochle in my theatre.'[15] His adherence to one particlar style has also earned him a reputation as a director capable of brilliance, but whose productions, in the words of one critic, 'have a sameness about them.'[16]

Luscombe's return to Canada coincided with what he called 'the awful gap' of the 1950s: 'I came back to Toronto to find a lot of feverish pretence, and nothing really changed.'[17] Supporting himself as an actor, with CBC television and the Crest Theatre, he began drawing plans to revive Littlewood's vision in Toronto. One story frequently repeated at the time describes how Luscombe stood up at a meeting of theatre professionals, called to discuss the need for more professional theatre, to announce: 'If it's worth doing, I'm ready to give it ten years.'[18] In the end he would give it more than twenty-five.

Luscombe founded his Theatre Workshop in 1959, and shortly thereafter merged with the administrative remains of Basya Hunter's Actors Theatre to form Toronto Workshop Productions. In the summer of 1960 he took a program of Chekhov one-act plays and Pirandello's *The Evil Eye* on tour to resort areas of

Ontario; like the People's Repertory Theatre of the previous decade, the tour was 'designed to bring theatre to those who can't or don't bring themselves to theatre.'[19]

TWP's first attempt at a Littlewood-style production was the 1960 *Hey Rube!*, an improvised play written mainly by Jack Winter, Luscombe, and Anthony Ferry. Over the next two decades, *Hey Rube!* would be revived approximately every seven years in versions tailored to new casts. Its plot is little more than an extended sketch: it describes the ordeals of a tattered one-ring circus as it prepares to battle creditors and hostile townsfolk. Much of the performance consisted of circus acts mimed in the Littlewood manner, with orchestrated lighting effcts, music and sound cues, and group improvisation. The production found favour with critic Nathan Cohen, who called it 'an exhilarating experience.'[20]

In 1963, Luscombe made the difficult leap to fully professional status, a transition made possible by the Canada Council's desire to encourage new professional theatres. He auditioned ninety actors, of whom he chose twenty for a two-month training period without salary. In the end, he selected seven to form the nucleus of what he hoped would be an ongoing ensemble. Over the next decade, Luscombe continued his refinements of Littlewood's 'group theatre' in a series of classical plays, adapted novels, and new works. By 1970, when Luscombe was about to embark on what would prove to be his most popular and innovative period, critics commonly decried his adherence to a style they perceived as limited and dated. Although Luscombe continued to assert that his approach was still largely unexplored, that it was a way of using the resources of the theatre to their fullest and not simply a stylistic imprint, Nathan Cohen disagreed:

Of the dedicaton of George Luscombe ... of his integrity and capacity for leadership and aesthetic resourcefulness, no qualm or doubt is possible. But his inflexible devotion to the concept of company equality preached by his mentor Joan Littlewood of the now defunct Theatre Workshop of Stratford East, London, keeps pushing him towards the same immobilizing mists which eventually swallowed her.[21]

This would become a recurring theme in reviews of Luscombe's productions. As the alternative theatre of the 1970s concentrated more on the development of new playwrights, Luscombe's group approach seemed dated. Despite a series of critical successes and an increasing international reputation (two productions were invited to the Venice Biennale in 1969 and *Chicago '70* played for eight weeks in New York in 1970), critics found it difficult to assess Luscombe's achievement. In 1974, the same year as *Ten Lost Years*, Don Rubin barely mentioned TWP in his overview of Canadian theatre since 1945. Attributing the development of alternative theatre to Theatre Passe Muraille and Factory Theatre Lab, Rubin dismissed TWP with the note that it had

offered up through the years a number of original productions at a time when original productions were not considered chic. For this TWP deserves positive mention here. Yet, it must also be added, that most of TWP's original work did consist of adaptations of foreign literature, particularly American works and American concerns, and, as such, its contribution, while interesting, has not really been that significant.[22]

It is true that Luscombe did not develop new playwrights with the same zeal as the theatres that came after him, but it is also true that in the 1960s TWP produced nine original Canadian plays and four adaptations by Canadian writers of foreign works. Heir to the internationalist tradition of the left, Luscombe was not particularly interested in the new tide of nationalism that defined the contours of the emerging alternative theatre. At a time when Canadian theatres were divided by their stand on Canadian plays (and when critics like Rubin sought to define Canadian theatre in thematic terms), Luscombe turned his attention to wider political controversies of the day, in the belief that they had pertinence to Canadians. In the five years before *Ten Lost Years*, he produced plays on such topical issues as revolution in Latin America (Mario Fratti's *Che Guevara*, 1968); revolution in China (Rick Salutin's *Fanshen*, 1972); radical politics in the United States (*Chicago '70*, 1970); and racism in the ghettos (*Mr. Bones*, 1969).

If TWP was criticized for not paying sufficient attention to Canadian subjects, it was also criticized for paying too much. In 1970, Nathan Cohen revised his earlier caution that Luscombe was becoming immobilized by his group approach:

Uncharacteristically, Luscombe's theatre has failed most thoroughly in the things that may be said to have inspired it most profoundly. From a repertory company with a group of plays that were in constant revision, it has moved to the most conservative kind of stock company operation. Its poorest shows, esthetically and in terms of audience attendance, are those which pretended to have a Canadian impulse.[23]

Like Theatre Workshop when it moved to Stratford East, TWP's move to a permanent home on Alexander Street in 1967 signalled a change in its initial ambition to create a popular theatre that would reach out to working-class audiences. In its earlier years TWP made some effort to realize this goal literally, including three summers under a tent at Stratford, Ontario. Once established in its new home, the theatre had to admit the necessity of subscription drives and planned seasons; it had to reconcile its ideals with the economic need to draw a supportive and inevitably middle-class audience.

Luscombe showed an early interest in the performance of topical material, but he did not explore the possibilities of documentary actuality until TWP was well established with audiences and critics. In 1967 he opened his new theatre on Alexander Street with Jan Carew's *Gentlemen Be Seated*, a play about the assassination of Abraham Lincoln and the emancipation of the slaves. Performed as a minstrel show, the play drew parallels with the racial tensions that burst into riot throughout the United States in the mid-1960s. Two years later Luscombe revised the play as *Mr. Bones*, and revised it again in 1972. In his revisions, he focused more overtly on the contemporary situation, using Lincoln as the 'Interlocutor' of the minstral show. *Mr. Bones* included authentic speeches and factual material, but combined them in an invented context; in its approach to documentary it followed Littlewood's living newspapers of the late 1940s.

Luscombe's first attempt to create a play entirely out of documentary actuality was in Herbert Whittaker's judgment TWP's 'first hit in ten years (and 37 shows).'[24] *Chicago '70* played for ten weeks in Toronto, from March to May 1970, followed by an eight-week run at the Off-Broadway Martinique Theatre in New York. Its success was due to its topicality: *Chicago '70* brought to the stage the controversial proceedings of the 'Chicago Seven' conspiracy trial that followed the 1968 Democratic National Convention. The trial was still in session when the play opened, and, as a *cause célèbre* of the day, it virtually guaranteed a hit. Reviewing the show in *Canadian Forum*, Paul Levine commented:

Although the judge and prosecuting attorney did not agree, the Chicago Conspiracy trial had all the elements of great theatre: a generational conflict as old as Greek theatre, a dispute over the meaning of justice as basic as breathing (*conspire*, as Abby Hoffman is fond of pointing out, means literally 'breathing together'), and the greatest cast of a comic actors since the old Marx Brothers movies.[25]

Luscombe was attracted to the trial because of its importance as a political confrontation and because of the defendants' celebrated attempt to exploit the media coverage to turn the proceedings into a kind of electronic theatre. It was this relation of revolutionary politics and overt theatricality that Luscombe attempted to express in his adaptation.

In so far as it recreates on stage the proceedings of an actual trial, *Chicago '70* may be numbered in the genre of court-room documentaries that enjoyed wide popularity in Europe and North America in the 1960s and early 1970s, but it departs radically from such typical examples as *The Trial of Louis Riel* or Peter Weiss's *The Investigation*. *Chicago '70* is a partisan challenge to the the very idea of objectivity and for this reason it makes no attempt to create a sense of authenticity. As Luscombe told Whittaker, 'we were not looking for an Agatha Christie trial or documentary realism. We wanted to say what the trial means to us. The judge isn't Judge Hoffman – who may even be a nice man – it is him as part of the system.'[26]

Chicago '70 was not an attempt to report a trial that was already well documented in the mass media, but to portray it as a political morality play by framing selected highlights with improvised commentary. Luscombe arranged to have daily transcripts sent to him by a friend who sat in on the trial in Chicago, and complemented them with eyewitness reports of the riots and trial from the underground press: 'The twenty actors in the company compiled the text themselves. We laid it all out on the front two rows of the theatre. Then as the transcriptions came in, still wet, we read them out and seized on this other material and read it in where it fitted.'[27]

Luscombe's ensemble approach was well suited to express the theatricality of the original trial. To find a theatrical metaphor for the defendants' strategy of turning the trial into a parody of itself, Luscombe embellished the transcripts with songs, monologues, gags, fashion parades, class-room drills, and agitprop scenes from American history. A 'court reporter' wrote notes on the blackboard that surrounded the set, and from a clear plastic booth beneath the judge's bench, a 'disc jockey' acted as occasional narrator. In one notable scene, Luscombe used the trial from *Alice in Wonderland* as a satiric metaphor of the proceedings. The result was, in the words of *The Nation*'s reviewer in New York, 'a choreography of judicial nuttiness whose malignancy is acknowledged but whose farce is played to the hilt.'[28]

The satiric approach to the play found great favour with audiences and reviewers, although some critics suggested that it obscured the important issues of the trial. According to Levine, 'Luscombe and his group have provided a metaphor for what the defendants have already transformed into a metaphor: the trial as pure Yippie theatre ... In short, we are permitted to treat the Chicago trial as *nothing* but theatre.'[29]

The improvisational satire that framed the documentary material may have restricted the possibilities of true political analysis in *Chicago '70*, but at the same time it brought theatrical technique and subject together in a mutually enhancing unity not always seen in Luscombe's productions. That unity is to be found in his earliest work: in *Hey Rube!* the ensemble performance embodies an aspect of circus life essential to the play which the text itself cannot express. In much of Luscombe's subsequent work, however, the relation of performance and subject is less direct.

In *Chicago '70*, the improvisational humour embodies both the defendants' strategy in court and the public perception of the trial itself. This complex view is made possible by a paradoxical attitude towards documentary actuality. The transcripts are included in the play as the factual evidence upon which the company builds its analysis. In that sense, *Chicago '70* adheres to the established pattern of court-room documentaries. At the same time it presents that evidence in terms of caricature and lampoon in order to satirize the American judicial system. Consequently, in *Chicago '70* documentary evidence is at once the means and the target of political criticism.

In terms of Luscombe's development in the use of documentary actuality, *Chicago '70* is of particular interest because of its relation to *Ten Lost Years*. Despite their differences in style and attitude towards documentary evidence, in both plays group performance functions as an integral part of the narrative structure of the text. To some extent, this is true of any 'group theatre' production, but in *Chicago '70* and *Ten Lost Years* the essentially metaphorical relation of performance and text embodies a deeper level of meaning that contributes to the thematic unity of the play. In *Chicago '70* that meaning is found in the parallel between ensemble performance and the theatricality of the original trial. In *Ten Lost Years* it is found in the narrative tension of historical event and modern memory, and in the gradual unfolding of an implicit historical argument.

TEN LOST YEARS: ANALYSIS

Luscombe's interest in factual material on stage evolved from his commitment to a political theatre that would speak for, and whenever possible to, working-class audiences. In that light, documentary actuality has no inherent value; it is useful as one of a number of textual strategies in the creation of polemical theatre. In this regard Luscombe, like Littlewood before him, followed in the tradition established by Piscator.

Considered in this context, *Ten Lost Years* was a departure for Luscombe. Not only was it compiled entirely out of documentary evidence, but the authenticity of the material is an important theme of the play. In his previous work, Luscombe had used documentary evidence to enhance the presentation of a theatrical argument. In *Ten Lost Years*, the argument is never stated, only implied in the arrangement of evidence.

Like *Chicago '70*, *Ten Lost Years*, is an adaptation of an already existing text, in this case Barry Broadfoot's collection of oral history of the same name. As book, play, and later CBC television film, *Ten Lost Years* has been described as 'one of the most important cultural "happenings" to have taken place in Canada in years.'[30] Broadfoot's book was an immediate national best seller when it was published in the fall of 1973; in its first year it went through three printings and sold more than thirty thousand copies. Equipped with a tape recorder, Broadfoot had travelled across the country, talking to hundreds of people about their experiences in the Great Depression. Their recollections are arranged in thematic sections, with chapters on such subjects as relief camps, hobos, entertainment, domestic life, and political events. The result is an anecdotal overview of a 'forgotten' decade.

Broadfoot was inspired by American writer Studs Terkel who had compiled a similar oral history of the Depression in the United States under the title *Hard Times*. Unlike Terkel, Broadfoot did not name his sources, with the result that anonymous memories 'speak for themselves.' Broadfoot has admitted that the memories are enhanced by editorial selection:

I used a tape recorder whenever I could but I also made notes or remembered the stories and words as closely as I could and wrote them down when the interview was over. I had to do some editing because people just do not talk simply or economically. Listen to anyone tell a story and you will understand; they ramble. So I did compress the story when necessary, although I always tried to keep the individual flavour of the storyteller's style.[31]

The anecdotes in the book are consequently more articulate than one would expect from speech. The richness of the language contributed to the popularity of *Ten Lost Years* as book and performance. As one reviewer wrote, 'The peoples' marvellous imaginations, their powers of description, their easy use of the English language, and what is more interesting, their spirit of survival and ability to view things with honest detachment, made the book hard to put down.'[32]

The stage version of *Ten Lost Years* opened at TWP in February 1974, just three months after the publication of the book. Cedric Smith, an actor and member of the musical group Perth County Conspiracy, brought the book to Luscombe and offered to write the music for a stage adaptation. Luscombe secured the rights to the book, despite a competing bid from the Citadel Theatre in Edmonton, and adjusted his season in the hope that the play would prove a success.[33] It was an unprecedented hit for TWP, running for seventeen weeks in Toronto before setting out on an eleven-week national tour. As was the case with *Chicago '70*, *Ten Lost Years* owed much of its initial success to its topicality and, according to Broadfoot, to a wave of nostalgia for the 1930s.[34]

When rehearsals began, Luscombe had no fixed plan in mind for the show. He trusted the material to suggest narrative possibilities. The ten actors in the cast were encouraged to find material that suited them.[35] Their research took them to other sources as well; the play includes occasional material from two other primary sources on the Canadian Depression, James Gray's memoir, *The Winter Years* and Michiel Horn's collection of documents, *The Dirty Thirties*.[36]

Luscombe has described the process of adapting the material:

> We just spread the book and we all read it. Then the actors would come to me and say, 'We've got to do this story George' or 'This is a great story George.' We looked at them all and we tried them all. Some times they would work on stage and sometimes they would not. We talked about them, and we changed them and we kept doing this until we a collection of stories that seemed to fit together.
>
> Then we would try to make a dramatic sequence out of them ... If we didn't have a finish we would just leave them out and go on ... Then we'd get another collection and soon they would start to come together, to shape up.[37]

After the actors had worked the basic sequences, Luscombe brought Jack Winter into the process to assist in arranging the material.

The final text of the play reflects this process. As in *Chicago '70* the ensemble performance gives the text its narrative context. The performance juxtaposes the retrospection of the stories (all delivered in the past tense) with a presentational montage of mime, dialogue, and music which draws the action into a theatrical present. This principle is enforced in Luscombe's production design. The action takes place on a bare stage surrounded by platforms which serve as 'homes' for the four women in the cast. The men in contrast, and in keeping with the play's emphasis on unemployed drifters, are 'homeless.' Anecdotes follow by association and mood rather than causal narrative action, and recurring references to memory and the act of remembering remind the audience that the telling of the stories is as important as the stories themselves. The resulting interplay of past and present gives the play its narrative shape; Winter's contribution as dramaturge helps to clarify the thematic development which compensates for the absence of explicit historical analysis.

As book or play, *Ten Lost Years* makes no attempt to analyse its subject systematically. History is presented in emotional terms. Luscombe has said that he wanted to avoid nostalgia: 'I wasn't going back to celebrate the worst years of my life.'[38] But the absence of explicit analysis and the natural tendency of the actors to select material for its emotional and dramatic power give the play what one reviewer called a 'sepia-toned' nostalgic romanticism.[39] According to Brian Arnott, writing under the pseudonym Brian Boru:

The political premises of *Ten Lost Years* were, however, belied by the charm of the TWP production. Those who bore the brunt of the Depression were depicted as grass roots people with a down home resiliency and a baggy pants look which made them at once both admirable and sympathetic.[40]

Ten Lost Years is an anthology of heroism and hardship, but it is also popular history as people chose to recall it. The anecdotes in the play, which number over a hundred, were selected as the most promising stories from hundreds of hours of selective oral memories. The overall effect of the play is thus one of intensified experience. It portrays the Depression as a time of greater extremes than our own, a time in which moral issues were less ambiguous and shared adversity gave birth to a social unity since lost. The long process of distillation from actuality to the stage imbued the material with a romanticism that was perhaps inevitable. The play makes no attempt to validate the stories; they are presented as true because they are the *vox populi*. In that sense, *Ten Lost Years* is also a play about language and the way people express memory. Much of its appeal stems from the colloquial idioms and accents in which anecdotes are couched. The combination of romantic nostalgia, simple morality, melodrama, and familiar dialects enhances the actuality to a level of poetic intensity.

The adaptation of the book to the stage required that Broadfoot's decision to present the anecdotes as anonymous voices be modified. Rather than trying to create a realistic character for each monologue, Luscombe had each actor develop a distinct character type without specific identity. As listed in the published text, the four women consist of 'Quiet Woman,' 'Farm Wife,' 'Young Girl,' and 'Strong Woman.' The six men are identified as 'Farmer,' 'Salesman,' 'Young Man,' 'Hobo,' 'Quiet Man,' and 'Balladeer.'[41] This last was the character played by Cedric Smith who, in addition to acting, composed and performed most of the music.

These character types impose a sense of commonality on the diverse material they perform, and taken together they provide an analogy of the social structure expressed in the stories. There is no attempt to conceal character inconsistencies from one story to the next; although defined as types, the actors remain identifiable as storytellers who stand outside the specific reality of the anecdotes. The Salesman, for example, performs material appropriate to his type, signified by a suit and tie. When telling a story he creates a momentary sense of realistic character, giving it a particular inflection or rhythm. The ensemble performance which gives the play its shape thus consists of an interplay of presentational theatricality and emotional realism.

The performance structure of *Ten Lost Years* is more complex than its text. The anecdotes are arranged in a polyphonic collage which combines monologues, representational dialogue, overlapping music, and mime to link the various sequences. In the construction of these sequences, the contributions of Luscombe as director, Winter as dramaturge, and Smith as composer are inseparable. It is virtually impossible to recreate the performance from the published text, which omits description of the mime and divides the action into thirty-four titled scenes corresponding roughly but not entirely to the unit sequences in performance.

In the process of adapting the book to the stage, Luscombe applied three main techniques which together form the basic structural principles of the text in performance. The monologues of the book tend to be discursive: Luscombe and Winter edited them so that a typical story of seven hundred words might survive in two hundred words on stage. In the book the stories follow in a linear progression; in performance they overlap, so that two or more stories might develop concurrently. A typical example contrasts two opposing points of view about the On to Ottawa Trek.

FARMER OR BALLADEER
I can't remember why we left the relief camp and went on to Vancouver, but it had something to do with chicken-shit regulations.
YOUNG MAN
I've never considered the Regina Riots and the box car march anything more than a skirmish.
FARMER OR BALLADEER
We met Art Evans. He was a real hard nut, but he could organize. And he was doing something, and that was more than anybody else was doing.
YOUNG MAN
The communists thought they had everything going for them and really they had nothing.
FARMER OR BALLADEER
He said: the only way to get anything done was to go down to Ottawa and see R.B. Bennett.
YOUNG MAN
Most of the reds were Ukrainians and Jews. (106)

In a common variation of this technique, a monologue might be interrupted by short sentences extracted from other stories to provide endorsement or ironic contrast.

The second major adaptation technique transforms the stories even more radically. In those cases where the original story was too complex or colourful to reduce to a short monologue, the actors improvised dialogue within the frame of a presentational monologue. This technique gives the play much of its theatrical variety and, like the intercut monologues, occurs in several variations. In a typical example the actor who begins the monologue becomes the narrator of the scene:

BALLADEER
There was a sort of informal group, a bunch of us, management at a lower level than plant superintendant, and we used to met and drink a bit and play poker, and it was a good bunch to belong to and I enjoyed it.
SALESMAN
Well, Bert, I'm going to trim some more fat this week.
BALLADEER
That might have been a foundry or a sawmill.
YOUNG MAN
How many?
SALESMAN
Ten sawyers and half a dozen sizers.
YOUNG MAN
Okay Harry. Let me know if there's a ruckus and, if not, I'll wait a week and match you.
BALLADEER
I saw maybe 15 or 20 or my good friends dealing in men's lives and doing it just like they were raising each other at stud poker. (90)

Together these techniques of contrapuntal collage and reconstructed dialogue transform the original material by placing the single point of view of the anecdote in a social and thematic relation with the unfolding argument of the play as a whole. In that sense the specific reality of each monologue is transformed into a general experience shared by the ensemble.

This principle is even more obvious in the third important technique of adaptation. Throughout the play Cedric Smith's songs counterpoint the action with moral commentary and ironic lyricism. It is in the songs that the political perspective of the play is most overt. Several of the songs are adapted directly from the book. In Chapter 5, for example, there is an evocative description of a train passing an isolated farm:

I loved the long whistle of a train, at night, moving down the valley six miles south of our farm, the long call to other places. Always at night, as I lay in my little bed in the attic. You know why I loved that sound? Because that train, a passenger train, I knew that train was going on to Vancouver, or to Winnipeg and then on to Toronto. Escape. Get away. Leave the farm.[42]

The natural rhythm of the speech is retained when it is turned into a song:

I love the long whistle of a train at night,
Moving down the valley, a call to other places where
things might be right.
As I lay in my bed, I loved the sound of that train,
Telling me escape, get away through the mountains.
A passenger train, going to Vancouver
Or to Winnipeg, then on to Toronto.   (80)

These techniques combine with the presentational performance and its emphasis on physicality and quick transitions to give *Ten Lost Years* its theatrical structure. Together they compensate for the absence of a governing narrative structure in the text. This transformation from an anthology of independent stories to a montage of memories and theatrical images makes possible the revelation, in part deliberate and in part inadvertent, of a political morality that is significantly more unified that that which is found in the book.

To understand the qualitative effect of Luscombe's montage technique on the unfolding themes of the play, it is useful to look briefly at another theatrical adaptation of Broadfoot's book, performed under the same title by Edmonton's Northern Light Theatre in 1977. Compiled and directed by Scott Swan, the Northern Light *Ten Lost Years* is little more than a staged reading in two parts. The first act consists of memories framed by modern hindsight, as in the book; the second act contains the stories in a theatrical recreation of a hobo jungle.[43] Like Luscombe, Swan wanted to 'eliminate any sentimentality which might still surround the era.[44] Swan's version focuses more specifically on the prairie experience of the Depression. It begins with memories of the dust storms, proceeds through sories of calamity and survival, and concentrates in the final segment on the experiences of homeless men. Political events are mentioned in passing and stories are punctuated by songs from the 1930s.

Unlike Luscombe, Swan let the monologues speak for themselves with little theatrical adaptation. His only concession to the fact of performance, other than the songs and the hobo jungle, was the arrangement of tableaux to create mood. In his version the monologues are more faithful to the original. They follow in thematic sequence, but because they are not contained in a meaningful performance structure they do not express a level of argument or a perspective by which the play as a whole might be understood.

The Northern Light *Ten Lost Years* is documentary theatre at its simplest; because it does not attempt to place the material in a critical context, it expresses little more than the nostalgia it purports to deny. Like Broadfoot's book, the play is limited to the insights and analyses of the people it quotes. In the end, it functions as a localist documentary which offers verbal images of the Depression. It defines the matter, not the meaning, of the historical experience. Luscombe, in contrast, attempts to synthesize the diverse and self-reflective insights of the original material into a governing point of view by imposing a political morality which influences the internal relation of the material.

Ten Lost Years differs from most Canadian documentaries in that its subject does not provide an obvious thematic focus. Unlike *The Farm Show*, which documents a cohesive community, or *Paper Wheat*, which examines a narrowly defined historical event, *Ten Lost Years* attempts to survey an entire decade in the history of a nation. The material is too broad to suggest a single dominant theme. Luscombe and Winter selected the material to develop two parallel themes of natural disaster and class exploitation, and their development expresses an essentially moral critique of capitalism. The play implies that the Depression was caused by an economic system that had neither the interest nor the ability to save the land from natural calamity, but it does not support that implication with specific evidence. Rather, the speeches in the play function as testimony in a moral judgment of history.

The thematic development of *Ten Lost Years* can be analysed in terms of eleven major units. Their order is determined by theatrical considerations but their internal relation generates the implicit argument of the play. The first of these units, consisting of scenes 1 to 4 in the text, introduces the Depression in terms of its memorable images, and at the same time establishes the convention of the ensemble performance. At the beginning of the action the actors enter miming a horse and buggy. The Balladeer begins the play by explaining the scene:

> You ask me what a Bennett Buggy was? Well, in the 20s farmers bought automobiles – Chevs, Fords, Hupmobiles – kinds they don't make anymore. Then came the crash and the drought and nobody had money for gasoline, let alone repairs, and they'd already thrown away all those fine old buggies every farm used to have. So what was left? A horse, pullin' a car that wouldn't run. (55)

The retrospective nature of this first speech establishes the role of memory in the play and it suggests a relation of actor and audience as storyteller and listener. The realism of the monologue is offset immediately by an ensemble song:

> Get out the Bennett Buggy,
> Let's go for a ride in the lovely countryside

Two horsepower, five miles an hour,
When Dubbin and Dolly go back to work again.

The mimed buggy unites monologue and song, so that the first moments of the play introduce three main elements of performance – text, music, and theatricality – as related expressions of a common idea.

At the end of the buggy scene the actors introduce a collage of short impressions and memories with fragments of typical Depression-era songs. The memories in this scene are as yet unrelated: the Quiet Man for example remembers Bible Bill Aberhart, while the Farm Wife recalls clouds of grasshoppers darkening the sky. The collage establishes the actors as character types, and announces the authenticity of the material:

FARMER
Something else you oughta know is that the songs and stories you're about to hear are the real stories of the real people all across Canada who survived the Depression. And they're all true. (57)

The memories in this preface are all framed by a representative story in which the Salesman describes how he talked a farmer's wife into signing for a new piece of machinery in her husband's absence. The salesman in the story is a good-natured predator who knows that the farmer cannot afford the machinery but will honour the sale. The story is played as a monologue with occasional dialogue through which the other, unrelated memories in the scene are interspersed.

This first sequence indicates the major themes of natural disaster and social exploitation, and it defines the basic adaptation strategies. With the introduction of the character types, the sequence creates an impression of multiple perspectives which in the end enables the play to present its conclusions as the authentic voice of typical Canadians.

The second sequence (scenes 5 and 6 in the text) describes the human cost of the Depression. Scene 5 is a series of short statements framed by the Farmer, who describes the effect of the drought on his land. Alternating with his speech, the other characters describe other contributing factors to the Depression: large families with no means of support, and an oppresive economic policy that favoured the banks. The relation of natural and social causes is summarized in the final statements of the scene:

SALESMAN
We were all of us – from R.B. Bennett down to the lowest of the low, some

Bo-hunk smelling of garlic – in one gigantic insane asylum.

FARMER

The land just blew away. (60)

The second part of the sequence consists of seven longer monologues. It begins with the Quiet Woman, who recalls how the Depression forced her family to revert to the 'old ways' of living without power or machinery. The Strong Woman then describes how her husband worked for starvation wages in a coal mine. Interrupting her story, the Farm Wife tells of a similar incident, and the Quiet Man recalls his experience as a thirteen-year-old miner. Their stories alternate, and the sequence concludes with the Strong Woman's memory of her husband's death.

The general impressions of the Depression continue in a somewhat lighter vein in the third sequence (scenes 7 and 8). In contrast to the sombre monologues of the previous scenes, this sequence makes full use of Luscombe's theatricality. It begins with the Hobo's humorous description of his ingenious method of hitch-hiking by posing as a 'motorist in distress.' The Farmer comments that it was considered criminal to be alone and poor and homeless, and the Salesman describes how he would chase drifters out of his barn every morning. These contrasting views of unemployed transients conclude with an emotional plea in the form of a lyrical song:

Please take another look, what history has done,
People in a restless place, and what about our sons.
Good kind people, gentle lovers of the earth,
The truth has long been sold, and greed has taken away our mirth. (62)

This is the cue for a mimed scene of considerable virtuosity, which follows from the Salesman's final image of 'Freight trains, covered with men, going absolutely nowhere.' As the song ends, the Quiet Woman describes the sight of trains covered with men looking for work, passing in both directions by her farm. During her speech, a special light illuminates a rectangular area in the centre of the stage. The women create trains sounds with incongruous instruments (rubbing coins on a washboard to simulate the sound of wheels on tracks, for example), and the music provides the driving rhythm of a train in motion. The lighted rectangle wavers, and the men run and leap aboard the 'moving' boxcar. According to Luscombe, the actors spent three days in rehearsal practicing this mime, so that lights, sound, and movement would create a sense of verisimilitude.[45]

This boxcar scene is the first and shortest of two such scenes in the play. It is introduced at this point only to place the fact of 'riding the rails' in larger context. On the boxcar the Farmer describes the pleasure of travelling on a sunny day, and as he speaks he sees his brother passing on top of a train moving in the other direction. After a brief shouted dialogue the brother leaps from one train to the other. The mime ends abruptly as he lands; the men fall flat on their faces to pass into a tunnel, and the boxcar disappears in darkness.

The sequence ends with a continuation of the song, followed by the Farmer's recollection of riding into Montreal, 'a fortress commanded by a couple of hundred Englishmen and Scotsmen to keep two million Frenchmen in line.' The Quiet Woman, speaking with a French accent, then describes the sweatshop garment factory in which her mother laboured under oppressive conditions. The plight of a single mother struggling to support her family is an ironic contrast to the comparatively carefree though desperate drifting of the men.

To this point, the play has introduced the Depression in terms of its worst effects. The next sequence (scenes 9 to 11) changes direction abruptly. In scene 9, the Strong Woman recalls the school assembly in which she hears Edward VIII deliver his abdication speech. The other actors mime the assembly, and the Salesman imitates the king, speaking into a microphone which is signified by a banjo held upside down. His speech is fragmented by appropriate sounds of static interference. The Strong Women's final comment, 'Looking back on it, I think what a great movie those days would have made,' provides the associative link to the next scene. The schoolchildren rearrange themselves to represent children in a movie theatre. They hurl abuse and objects at a mimed romantic film, which in the following scene gives way to an imitation of Shirley Temple performing 'The Good Ship Lollipop.' The Quiet Woman recalls the Shirley Temple dolls that she sold as a clerk in the Eaton's store in Toronto. Her reminiscence grows increasingly more bitter:

> I'd stand there and watch the faces of those little girls. Little faces, they needed
> food. You could see a lot who needed a pint of milk a thousand times more than
> they needed a Shirley Temple doll. (65)

The sequence introduces Shirley Temple as a figure of humorous nostalgia, and transforms her into an image of social hypocrisy. In the woman's memory, Shirley Temple is associated with the working conditions at Eaton's. The fifth sequence of the play examines the matter of work more closely. Scene 12 is an excerpt from a Royal Commission hearing on working conditions, taken from Horn's *The Dirty Thirties*, in which a woman identified as Miss Nolan testifies to the inequities of piece-work at Eaton's sewing shop.[46] In one of the most overt editorial juxtapositions in the play, her description is followed by a statement, also from the Horn anthology, in which John David Eaton recalls the Depression as 'a good time for everybody.' The scene ends with a ditty about the widespread use of Eaton's catalogues as toilet paper.

In scene 13, which follows a verse of a song about welfare relief, the Quiet Woman and the Quiet Man describe their jobs in municipal relief offices, and the Strong Woman relates an incident in which her neighbour broke down and cried when his young daughter lost the first wages he had earned in five years. These stories consist of overlapping memories, framing short dialogue scenes.

The sixth sequence completes a pattern of alternating themes. Just as the freight train sequence, with its focus on displacement, leads to the nostalgic sentimentality of the abdication and movie scenes, the bitterness of the relief sequence is followed by a light-hearted series of scenes about the place of radio in domestic life. In scene 14 the actors create the theatrical reality of a general store, in which they meet and discuss radio reception and favourite programs. In scene 15 they listen to a typical radio show, consisting of an anecdote of about an Indian awaiting execution recast as a radio dialogue, a speech by R.B. Bennett, and a 'real life true Canadian drama.' The drama is in fact a story from Broadfoot's book, about a family who survived the Alberta winter by building an igloo. In the next scene the actors listen to a Joe Louis fight while engaged in such typical activities as typing, picking beans, and scrubbing the floor.

The theme of escapism suggested by the radio is reinforced ironically in the final scene of the sequence. Scene 17 is a monologue by the Strong Woman, who tells of the day she found the body of a neighbour who had hanged himself in despair. The contrast of fantasy and suicide as forms of escape is typical of Luscombe's attempt to reduce the role of nostalgia in the play.

The idea of escape provides the bridge to the final sequence of the first half of the play. Consisting of scenes 18 to 21, the sequence begins with the'Other Places' song described earlier, sung by the women. Under the music the Young Girl recalls her romantic dream of escaping from the farm to the seashore. The remainder of the sequence exposes the naïvety of her dream by detailing the experiences of the hobos who crossed the country seeking work. Scene 19 begins with the angry statement by the Quiet Man: 'If they wanted you to pick fruit in a hurry you were an economic saviour, the rest of the time you were shit.'(80)

At this point the lights and sound effects re-create the train image. The Quiet Man explains the technique of hopping a boxcar; the men chase the train and leap into the open car; the doors 'close' and the sound effects are muted. In the car the men trade stories. The theatrical reality of the car gives way to a dialogue scene in which the Young Man tells of his experiences running rum across the American border. The actors mime a madcap automobile chase to the sounds of piano and kazoo, and at the conclusion of the story the chase sounds cross-fade into the trains sounds and the boxcar is re-established.

The effect of this superimposition of one theatrical reality on another is the opposite to that of the recreated hobo jungle in the Northern Light *Ten Lost Years*. In that production the verisimilitude of the hobo jungle attempts to authenticate the stories by placing them in a realistic dramatic context as the hobos swap stories around a fire. In this case the actors create the necessary reality as a form of anti-illusionist story-telling. The boxcar gives the rum-running story a narrative context, but there is no attempt to draw a causal connection between them.

Following the car chase scene, and maintaining the technique of superimposed realities, the hobo tells of his experience in 'boondoggling' on a make-work project. Again the memory gives way to a dialogue scene. Based on a passage taken from James Gray's *The Winter Years*, the scene describes the angry encounter of an indignant citizen with men picking dandelions to earn their welfare relief.[47] The scene ends with the re-establishment of the boxcar.

The remainder of the sequence completes the pattern of displacement and escape that gives the first half of the play much of its thematic unity. The two boxcar scenes have defined the freight trains as a last-resort means of escape; the play now examines the hobo jungle as a place of final refuge. Scene 20 is a series of monologues and dialogue units which describe aspects of jungle life. It concludes with three contrasting points of view which summarize the superficial romance of life on the road. The Farmer declares that a criminal record for vagrancy is a badge of honour; the Quiet Man boasts of the golden tongue that has enabled him to make his way through life as a bum; and the Balladeer describes how in the jungle 'each man had his own nickname and his own set of stories.'

The final scene of the sequence exposes the hobo jungle as a place of waste and violence. It begins with the Hobo, who recalls the time he saw one man murder another over a trivial argument. As he narrates the story, the men act it in mime, and the women accompany it with the mournful 'Hobo's Lullaby,' one of the few authentic period songs in the show. The men pick up the body of the dead hobo and place it on a mimed railway track. The sounds of an approaching train intensify under the music and as it passes (indicated by lights and sound), the body on the track convulses as if hit.

The senseless violence of the jungle is contrasted to the deliberate violence of the railway police by the Young Girl, who remembers the day she discovered that her kind neighbour was a brutal railway cop. Following another verse of the lullaby, the Salesman describes a gruesome instance of revenge in the story of a railway policeman found crucified to the side of a boxcar. The actors perform the mime, probing the dark yard with flashlights, opening a boxcar door, and staring in horror at the audience. The entire cast then joins in for the final verse of the song. With its combination of intensified experience, lyrical structure, and atmospheric mime, the scene is a perfect example of Luscombe's masterful staging.

By this mid-point in *Ten Lost Years*, the major themes have been declared in a simple moral scheme which couples the natural calamities of the Depression with the man-made calamities of poverty and unemployment. The memories that comprise the text are those of the victims of that compound disaster, few of whom reflect on the economic or social causes of the Depression. The performance itself gives narrative coherence to the memories, but in the end the analysis it develops is moralistic rather than intellectual. The play takes the moral view of the survivors in aggregate, suggesting a consensus that is in fact a result of editorial selection.

The second half of the play develops the moral scheme which identifies the victims of the Depression as its authentic spokesmen. Even more than in the first half, the sequences in the second half follow a logical pattern: the first sequence deals with class exploitation; the second with economic solutions; and the third with political solutions. The fourth and last sequence attempts to resolve the play's historical analysis chronologically with the suggestion that the outbreak of war ended the Depression with massive military recruitment.

The first of these sequences is the longest in the play. Consisting of scenes 22 to 28, it begins with a song and monologue about farmers leaving their land when natural disaster results in foreclosed mortagages. Scene 23 relates several stories of men and women who profited from the Depression; the dramatic frame is a poker game played by managers who collude to reduce wages and manpower. This condemnation of profiteering is followed by a lengthy monologue by the Strong Woman, who tells how she had to submit to the sexual demands of her employer to keep her job in a restaurant. Scene 24 comprises three monologues criticizing the middle class. In the first, the Young Girl condemns bankers as 'cruel men dedicated to a cruel system'; in the second the Quiet Woman recalls the fashionable socialist values of her university friends; in the third the Hobo tells of a Saskatchewan farmer who, not knowing what else to do with it, used the dried cod sent by church groups in Ontario as shingles for his outhouse. An ironic song in praise of endurance connects the three stories.

The following scene (scene 26 in the text) stresses the psychological damage caused by poverty. It begins with a dialogue scene narrated by the Farm Wife, about a gentle couple driven to despair when their budget precludes tea and tobacco. The Young Girl then remembers her mother's obsession with knitting mittens, and the Hobo tells of a man who stole a funeral wreath from a door to put on his own. The Young Man concludes the series with his recollection of the time he started a fire in a mail box in an irrational fit of frustration.

The final two scenes of the sequence show more harmful consequences of poverty. In scene 27 the Young Girl narrates a scene about the relief officer who gave her mother welfare chits in exchange for sexual favours. In scene 28 the Hobo describes forced auction sales, and the Young Man recalls the time he and his friends tarred and feathered a landlord. The Salesman then places the scene in ironic context with his comment:

> No, we never thought of the poor people. The reliefers. We'd see them on these
> make-work jobs, cleaning up back lanes, digging dandelions, hauling coal. I
> never thought to pity them or help them. Far as I know, nobody did ...   (99)

The next three scenes outline three possible solutions to the problem of mass unemployment. The first is economic. Scene 29 describes life in the government relief camps in a series of short monologues narrated in the present tense by the Quiet Man. His description of the camps is one of hopelessness and despair. Scene 30 consists of a monologue by the Strong Woman describing the sight of her sister's abandoned farm, followed by a lively song about dust storms and grasshopper plagues.

The final scene in the sequence depicts one family's attempt to flee the ravages of the Depression by moving to northern Alberta to homestead. The scene is one of the theatrical highlights of the performance: the family struggles through muskeg, bad roads, and clouds of mosquitoes until its horses drop dead of exhaustion in the middle of the bush. In the final monologues of the scene, the Farmer, speaking as a Métis, condemns the government for its institutionalized racism, and the Strong Woman curses R.B. Bennett for his statement that nobody died of starvation in Canada.

The sequence concludes with a reprise of the 'Bennett Buggy' song that begins the play. Initially a humorous evocation of a popular image of hard times, it appears here as an ironic condemnation of the prime minister who was incapable, the play suggests, of finding a solution to the Depression.

The reference to Bennett serves as a bridge to the next sequence, which recalls two important political events. The first is the On to Ottawa Trek and the subsequent Regina Riot, described by the Farmer (or Balladeer) and the Young Man from opposing points of view. There is no attempt to explain the historical background of the trek, although the original performance included a scene in which the trek leaders present their case to an unsympathetic Bennett. The account of the trek is the first mention of political radicalism in the play, and it ends with the assertion that Bennett turned the trek into a 'snow job' by discrediting the marchers as communists and allowing the police to provoke the riot.

In the second half of the scene the Farmer and the Hobo recall their experiences in the Spanish Civil War as members of the Mackenzie-Papineau Battalion of the International Brigade. This is the only reference to international events in the play, and it suggests that the fight against fascism in Spain was a natural extension of the fight against oppression at home. The scene ends on an ironic note, with the Hobo's angry recollecton of the Canadian government's refusal to enlist 'Mac-Pap' veterans in the army in 1939, despite the fact that they were the only men in the country trained in modern combat conditions.

The focus on political action at this late point in the play completes its thematic development with the implication that the oppression detailed in the previous sequences engendered a response in the form of grass-roots radicalism. Although consistent with Luscombe's ideological commitment, this suggestion points to what might be called a crisis in the play's narrative structure. The ensemble performance creates a narrative context in which modern prosperity recalls bygone adversity; in that sense Ten Lost Years implies a reconstructed present. The thematic structure of the play identifies political action as the necessary response to oppression and the precondition of reconstruction, but the two examples it presents were both failed causes for the radical left. The unfolding argument of the play requires that at some point the fact of modern memory be resolved with the themes expressed. In the end, Ten Lost Years lacks this resolution, in part because of the short process of adaptation which emphasized theatrical rather than dramaturgical solutions, and in part because of conflicting premises in the discourse of the play.

That conflict surfaces in the final sequence, in which the play switches to a chronological structure and attributes the end of the Depression to the outbreak of war in 1939. The sequence begins in the middle of scene 32 with a series of short statements about the imminent end of the Depression. The Salesman recommends that soccer leagues be started to divert idle men from talk of revolution; the Strong Woman reviles the memory of Prime Minister Mackenzie King; and the Quiet Man recalls a speaker who argued that the country could buy its way into prosperity if every family spent an additional fifty cents a day.

At the end of his speech, the Quiet Man takes on the character of a recruiting sergeant, and, as the Farm Wife describes the line of men waiting to enlist at the local armoury, the men march downstage in formation. In the following scene they reminisce about 'lining up to die,' and the sequence concludes with a lively recruiting song that connects the outbreak of war with the play's emphasis on class exploitation:

Come on boys and join the army,
Three square meals a day,
No need to worry, nothing to pay,
And sometime tomorrow we're sending you away.
For the war has finally come,
Bringing work for everyone,
Who will fight the hun – honey in the hive,
A job for everyone – who's still alive.   (109)

Even with the outbreak of war promising a return to prosperity, the typical
Canadian as defined by the play is still a victim, subject to the manipulation of
unspecified powers. The only exceptions are the radicals who marched on the
trek and carried their fight against oppression to Spain. In the previous scene the
Hobo has identified the Spanish Civil War as a prelude to a larger war against
fascism. Rather than developing that suggestion, this scene offers the more
cynical conclusion that the Second World War was merely another form of
exploitation. Reviewing the play in 1974, Brian Arnott perceived this problem
when he wrote:

The advent of war was offered, preposterously enough, to serve the day both
dramatically and historically. It seemed incredible that TWP (which this time last year had
been performing *Schweik*) could justify such an ending as being consistent with its *pro
populum [sic]* position, or could countenance its perversity.[48]

The cynicism of the recruitment scene is tempered in a brief coda to the play.
The Quiet Woman tells of her son Raoul, who graduated from school in 1932
and spent five years sitting on the verandah swing 'like a vegetable.' On the day
war broke out he enlisted, only to die at Dieppe. The final line of the play is an
epitaph for his generation:

He was a wonderful soldier, a very good soldier. You see, somebody wanted
him.
There was something for him to do.   (109)

Ten Lost Years thus ends on a note of sentimental irony which attempts to draw
together parallel themes of exploitation and heroic endurance. Raoul typifies
the Depression survivor as both hero and victim. The more complex question of
the relation of ensemble performance, retrospective text, and thematic
synthesis is left unresolved.

As Arnott suggests, the ending of *Ten Lost Years* owes more to theatrical
expediency than to historical analysis. To some extent, however, the ending is a

necessary concession to the very premise of the play as a documentary. Broadfoot's book, as indicated by its title, purports to survey the Depression as a decade of historical experience. With its more narrow focus, the play avoids considerations of chronology and historical survey by examining particular aspects of life within the context of the Depression as an isolated, or historically undifferentiated, event. The ensemble performance, with its emphasis on the act of remembering, compensates for the absence of historical overview. The thematic shape of the play, however, demands a reconciliation with its historical outline. By defining the outbreak of war as a solution to the Depression, the structure of the play is made in the end to conform with its historical premise.

Luscombe has said that his ensemble techniques elevate actuality to a higher plane of fiction. In *Ten Lost Years*, although performance and text enhance one another, they do not permit a final unifying narrative synthesis. This condition is largely a consequence of Luscombe's adaptation strategy, but it points to what may be the limits of his 'group theatre' approach.

As developed by Littlewood, 'group theatre' embodies a belief that together, actors, designers, playwright, composer, and director can explore a subject as a dialectical complex of inseparable expressions of a governing idea. In *Ten Lost Years* that idea emerges out of the documentary actuality without explicit textual commentary. The complexity of the group approach suggests an intellectual unity that is in the final analysis absent from the play.

Unlike the other plays in this study, *Ten Lost Years* does not allow for an admission of subjectivity or partiality in its performance structure. *The Farm Show* and the plays that follow it rest on their audience's recognition that the actors speak from personal experience or observation, and that the performance expresses their conclusions. In contrast, the actors in *Ten Lost Years* speak from within what is essentially a literary text, a narrative structure to which they bear an arbitrary relation. Their performance does not authenticate the actuality on which it is based.

It is perhaps because *Ten Lost Years* does not provide for this personal expression that it has had no discernible effect on other theatres in Canada, despite its popularity with critics and audiences. In part this lack of influence may be ascribed to the complexities of Luscombe's theatrical techniques, which had taken him twenty years to hone, and which were not easily imitated. This fact, however, is merely the most visible aspect of a more complex problem regarding the nature of political theatre in Canada. As is the case with most of Luscombe's work, *Ten Lost Years* may be described as political in so far as it deals with political issues and is predicated on an expressed political morality. But in a deeper sense (with which Luscombe would disagree), it is less political than the *The Farm Show*, which paradoxically ignores political issues in its portrait of its community. The alternative theatre movement, particularly in its collectively created documentaries, embodied a radical attempt to redefine Canadian theatre by exploring new forms for new audiences. It manifested a belief that theatre can be part of the process of cultural change. *The Farm Show* emerged out of a dialectic of myth making and iconoclasm. To define the images of indigenous culture it had to incorporate into its form a repudiation of received artistic models. That repudiation included a rejection of the traditional hierarchical relations of theatrical production, in which the actor is subordinate to the creative vision of the playwright and director.

If the alternative theatre chose not to emulate Luscombe's theatrical techniques, it was also in part because they were founded on fixed assumptions regarding the methods and hierarchies of production. Luscombe's concept of a 'group theatre,' developed over twenty years, subordinated the actor to the demands of the text. For Luscombe, the techniques of a 'group theatre,' provide the means of creating a dramatic text out of non-dramatic material. In effect, the innovations of his group approach were adaptations of established methods of theatrical production. The alternative theatre, in contrast, developed as a challenge to received theatrical and dramatic forms, and as a challenge to the very idea of dramatic text. This is the case with the collectively created documentary, which rejects a concept of text in favour of a performance of findings.

Luscombe's adherence to a theatrical approach which does not embody the process of radical redefinition of theatrical form typical of the Canadian documentary may be ascribed to a concept of political theatre which is retrospective rather than active. For Luscombe, politics is an intellectual framework that defines the meaning of an historical event. In the context of Canadian political theatre, Luscombe is a reflective commentator, an ideologue rather than an activist. In contrast to such groups as the Mummers Troupe and Catalyst Theatre, both of which have used theatre to intervene directly in the political life of a community, TWP under Luscombe was dedicated to a didactic concept of theatricalized politics.

It is because of this didacticism that *Ten Lost Years* cannot escape the nostalgic sentimentalism that Luscombe wished to avoid. To counteract that nostalgia, the play relies on a form of alienation. Typically, a series of overtly sentimental memories culminates in a graphic description of exploitation or death. Such irony, however, reinforces the sentimental appeal of the play. Luscombe's didactic ideology combines with the intensified emphasis on survival inherent in the memories to suggest a sense of collective pride in heroic endurance. Without a critical analysis, in both text and performance structure, capable of relating the miseries of the past to the present reality of the audience, the play isolates history from political context. Luscombe's ideological purpose is evident in the moral judgments that the play passes on the past, but it makes no reference to the present reality implied by the use of retrospective memories. Political theatre, by its very definition, assumes that an examination of its subject can in some way affect the lives of its audience. In *Ten Lost Years*, Luscombe introduces political criteria in his arrangement of the material, but his theatrical techniques do not permit an exploration of the political meaning of the Depression for a modern audience. It is ironic that those techniques had their origin in a movement which, like the Canadian alternative theatre, challenged fixed conventions of theatrical and dramatic form in order to participate actively in a process of political change.

4

Documentary and Regionalism: *No. 1 Hard* and *Paper Wheat*

In a period of just under a year, rural audiences in Saskatchewan had the rare opportunity to see two related shows that extended the relationship of documentary and regionalism first suggested in *The Farm Show*. In March, 1977, Saskatoon's 25th Street Theatre began the first of three tours of *Paper Wheat*, and eleven months later Regina's Globe Theatre presented its production of *No. 1 Hard*. The two plays had much in common. Both examined the history of Saskatchewan's grain industry; they were both collective creations; both attempted to promote an idea of culture that is at once regional and populist; and both forged connections with populist organizations: *Paper Wheat* with the Saskatchewan Co-op movement; and *No. 1 Hard* with the militant National Farmers Union. Beyond these similarities, the plays differed radically in form, style, and thematic ideology. These differences surpassed those one might normally expect when theatres in rival cities tackle the same subject for the same audience. They refer back to the deeper differences in the two main sources of Canadian documentary theatre.

Paper Wheat is the most famous descendant of *The Farm Show*, and the most successful result of Paul Thompson's policy of encouraging collective theatre across Canada. When Thompson arrived in Saskatoon in 1975 to create *The West Show*, he undertook to direct a collective revue for the fledgling 25th Street Theatre in return for rehearsal facilities. Andras Tahn, the theatre's founding director, was inspired by the experience of working with Thompson to venture a collective project of his own for the following year. The result was *Paper Wheat*, which went on from a shaky start to rival *Ten Lost Years* as one of the most popular successes in the history of Canadian theatre. After touring Saskatchewan twice (in two versions), *Paper Wheat* played to audiences across Canada, and reached even more as a CBC-TV special and a National Film Board 'Challenge for Change' documentary film.

The Globe, Saskatchewan's largest 'regional theatre' had planned to produce a grain industry show even before Tahn set to work on *Paper Wheat*, but as the *No. 1 Hard* project took longer to mature, it can in a sense be seen as a corrective to *Paper Wheat*. Directed by Ken Kramer, whose artistic policies at the Globe had long reflected his left-wing perspective, *No. 1 Hard* was a documentary in the manner of Peter Cheeseman. It adhered rigorously to the rule of primacy of authentic evidence. Although *No. 1 Hard* received an enthusiastic response in its home province, it did not go on – nor was it intended – to win the national acclaim accorded to *Paper Wheat*.

Behind the success of *Paper Wheat* and the relative obscurity of *No. 1 Hard* lies a paradox. Judged in terms of content and the presentation of material, *No. 1 Hard* is a more successful documentary than *Paper Wheat*. It builds its polemic on the basis of carefully researched evidence and editorial argument. *Paper Wheat*, in contrast, foregoes factual evidence and documentation in favour of sentimental 'myth,' in Paul Thompson's sense of the word. Yet it is *Paper Wheat* that has been received across Canada as the authentic voice of Saskatchewan, although the version that toured the country was directed, performed, and extensively revised by a cast who for the most part were strangers to that province. Although universally described as a documentary and applauded as a triumph of the form, *Paper Wheat* in fact contains very little in the way of documentary material. Rather it combines first-hand research with invented scenes in a revue structure.

Considered in terms of content, *Paper Wheat* may be more of an historical revue than a documentary, but it is nevertheless one of the most successful examples of the documentary style in Canada, and for that reason alone it merits close examination. *Paper Wheat* embellishes dramatic invention with the authenticating techniques of documentary performance, whereas *No. 1 Hard* relies on textual rather than theatrical authentication. Because it is the more complex and problematic of the two plays, this chapter will focus primarily on *Paper Wheat*, following a preliminary discussion of *No. 1 Hard*. By analysing their respective methods of creation, performance techniques and historical perspectives, this discussion will investigate the relation of regional culture to performance style.

The regionalism that these plays express is related to but significantly different from that of *The Farm Show*. In *Paper Wheat* and *No. 1 Hard*, the community is defined by broader geographic and historical boundaries: it embraces seventy years of Saskatchewan's agricultural history. In *Paper Wheat* that community is given a mythic proportion that unites the original sod-busters and their present-day descendants; in *No. 1 Hard* the community is defined in terms of economic class. Both plays appeal to a prairie and specifically

Saskatchewan sentiment and celebrate the tradition of co-operative socialism that has played so important a role in the history of Saskatchewan's artistic and political culture. In that sense, the community defined by these two plays has a political dimension not found in *The Farm Show,* in which the community is simply the aggregate of related individuals. The particularism of *The Farm Show* makes no appeal to political sentiment; the fact that the play documents a community in southwestern Ontario is of significance only in so far as the specific reveals the universal. In *Paper Wheat* and *No. 1 Hard,* the community is perceived more generally, and the individual is only present as the voice of a larger group. The regionalism of these two plays is no less particular than that of the *The Farm Show,* but because it is shaped by historical experience and delineated by the ruler-straight borders of Saskatchewan, it achieves wider relevance only when cast in terms of myth – as it is in *Paper Wheat* but not in *No. 1 Hard.*

NO. 1 HARD

No. 1 Hard (the title refers to a grade of wheat) was the first of three 'investigative documentaries' produced by Globe Theatre under the direction of Ken Kramer between 1978 and 1981. It is the only one of the three to be collectively created; the other two, *Medicare!* (1980, about the controversial struggle for socialized medicine in Saskatchewan) and *Black Powder* (1981, about the Estevan riot of 1931), were written by the Globe's playwright-in-residence, Rex Deverell. *No. 1 Hard* is also the only one that has not been published; it survives in a corrupt typescript and an audio recording of its songs.

From its beginnings as the Globe Theatre for Youth in 1966, the Globe has demonstrated an interest in socially engaged drama. In Deverell's words, the theatre entertained 'a notion that there is nothing wrong with the world that politics can't cure.'[1] Emerging as the largest theatre in the province in the 1970s, the Globe developed a mixed program of classics, new plays, and school tours familiar to regional theatres across the country, but – perhaps because of Saskatchewan's populist traditions – Kramer was able to introduce a strong political note in his programming. More importantly, he committed the theatre to the development and service of audiences outside Regina. Kramer's interest in the development of new plays was balanced by the need to produce a mixed season and the desire to speak to rural audiences. In his 1979–80 annual report, he made the point:

The hard fact of life is that a great number of the more visible playwrights in Canada are not produceable at The Globe because of their world-view (or lack of it), their geographical mind-sets, their subject matter or their language. Most of the work of French, Freeman, Bolt, Tremblay, Walker and Ritter, for example, either bear [*sic*] no relevance to our audience or would offend them greatly. On the other hand, some of our best work (*No. 1 Hard, Medicare!*) would not travel well outside of the Prairies without revision for export. We find this situation distressing only as it applies to quotas – we think particularization for specific audiences can only enhance that audience's self-image and reveal ourselves to ourselves.[2]

The Globe is not the only large theatre (especially in western Canada) to reject some of the more popular Canadian playwrights as irrelevant or unsuitable, but it is one of the few to balance that rejection with a concerted effort to develop its own version of relevant theatre. The Globe's commitment to socially engaged drama appears to be supported by its audience; for example, in its initial run, *Medicare!* played to 104 per cent capacity houses.[3]

The Globe's first venture into documentary came in its fourth season, 1969–70, with a collectively compiled staged reading about the Great Depression. Entitled *Songs and Stories of the Dirty Thirties*, the reading was devised hastily to fill an unplanned open slot in the season. The popularity of the performance led Kramer to commission Carol Bolt, then an aspiring writer in Regina, to write a longer documentary revue on the subject. Under the title of *Next Year Country* Bolt's play was included in the 1971 season, and it brought her wider recognition when Paul Thompson reworked it and presented it in Toronto as *Buffalo Jump*. In the course of that transition the play changed from documentary to satiric political revue.

Next Year Country was an emotional retelling of a crucial period in Saskatchewan's history, but there the resemblance to the documentary trilogy that would follow a decade later ends. In that trilogy, Kramer shows his debt to Cheeseman, whose work he had seen while working with Brian Way's Theatre in Education troupe in Great Britain. All three plays of the trilogy were conceived as investigations, in the manner of the Living Newspapers of the 1930s, and all three adhere, more or less rigorously, to Cheeseman's principle that the documentary must restrict itself to primary source material. In *Medicare!* and *Black Powder*, Deverell counterpoints documentary actuality with clearly indicated invented scenes depicting typical characters. This movement, from strict adherence to authentic evidence in *No. 1 Hard* to the inclusion of invented material in the subsequent plays, may be explained by the different processes by which the plays were made. According to Deverell, who served as 'editor-in-chief'of *No. 1 Hard*, 'it is difficult to arrive at a style of language in a collective situation.'[4] In *Medicare!* and *Black Powder*, Deverell as sole author had the freedom to explore the relation of literary style and documentary reality. For Deverell documentary is ultimately a literary concept:

Documentary theatre in a strict sense would be a rhetorical theatre, because the only access to the event is through the rhetoric of it. *No. 1 Hard* was the collective exploitation of rhetoric. In *Medicare!* rhetoric itself is revelatory, rather than the acting.[5]

Deverell has identified the relative lack of archival sources as the primary problem in adapting Cheeseman's methodology to Canada. The Globe documentaries rely mainly on secondary sources – newspapers, Royal Commission reports, published accounts – because, in Deverell's words, 'archivally, Saskatchewan has not yet got rich material.' The dialogue scenes in *Medicare!* and *Black Powder* replace the quoted diaries and letters of Cheeseman's plays. Like Cheeseman, Kramer and Deverell make extensive use of songs for editorial comment.

The conscious debt to Cheeseman has a political dimension as well. Kramer and Deverell have rejected what they see as the formalism and romantic populism of Theatre Passe Muraille. According to Kramer, 'Paul Thompson is interested in process. Cheeseman is interested in content.'[6] In Kramer's analysis, *The West Show*, for example, was a superficial and 'empty' treatment of its subject. In the end, Kramer's concept of documentary, like Deverell's, is explicitly textual.

The purpose of *No. 1 Hard* was, in Kramer's words, 'to take a whole industry and explain it to the masses.'[7] According to Kramer, the play was conceived to explain why the price of wheat had only doubled in price over fifty years, compared to much greater increases in other commodities. As well, Kramer was intrigued by the coincidence of the Biafra famine with the federal government's crop reduction plan, LIFT (Lower Inventories for Tomorrow). Deverell has described the process of researching the material:

Our first task was to understand the issue, the story, and, it soon became obvious, the rhetoric of the grain trade ... As the company divided itself into research groups we agreed we would seek only written material touching an issue or story. We set up boxes with files devoted to the specifics. If a file remained empty we would spend extra time figuring what kind of documents might exist to fill it, and then dispatch members of the troupe to find those documents.[8]

According to Kramer, the company included several points of view, 'from leftist to apolitical,' but it was 'an organic collective' of people who knew each other and worked well together. Working with the documentary material led to political cohesion. Deverell has made the same point: 'The actors began to feel that they had a responsibility to use the play to make a statement and that the play could enter the debate then raging in the industry.'[9]

They were not the only ones who saw that possibility. When *No. 1 Hard* was first mounted in a limited run of six performances in February 1978, Kramer invited a number of local labour and agricultural leaders to see it. It was at this point that the National Farmers Union agreed to sponsor the play on tour the following season. In the fall of 1978 a revised version with a cast of six actors embarked on a five-week tour to twenty-seven communities in Saskatchewan, fifteen of which had seen *Paper Wheat* the previous year.

According to Deverell, the two weeks allotted for the preparation of *No. 1 Hard* allowed 'enough time to collectivize around it, but not enough time to produce it.'[10] The original performances were in effect staged readings, with the actors reading the documents from hand-held cue cards. In the subsequent documentaries, Deverell and Kramer adapted Cheeseman's theatrical technique, by which the actors re-create the original event as closely as possible, without metaphor. *No. 1 Hard* relies on the theatricality of agitprop; the performance is an 'inventive commentary' on the text, but the relation between that invention and the matter under discussion is frequently arbitrary. The typescript of the play provides few indications of the performance style, but it is clear that the actors must illustrate the text with indicative gestures.

A typical example of this technique may be found in a scene in which Cargill, the American-based multinational grain company, applies to the Canadian government for permission to expand under the terms of the Foreign Investment Review Act.

CANADA
Well, as long as they don't get too big. I think Cargill can only be good for us in the interim.

MS CARGILL
Cargill has only 6% of the business.

CANADA
So long as they don't get too big.

MS CARGILL
I am a free enterprise. You never know how good you are until you're backed in a corner.

HERBERT HUMPHREY
Food is power. And in a very real sense, it is our extra measure of power. It may be the one thing we have in greater abundance and in the ability to produce than anyone else ... Herbert Humphrey.

MS CARGILL

If a person has power, Cargill finds a way to influence that person.

ANNOUNCER

In 1973, the multinational giants controlled in all fields, together with their banking allies, a $268 billion pool of capital ... [11]

In performance, Cargill was portrayed as a Playboy bunny who seduces the actor representing the Canadian government. Performing in the round with a minimum of props, the actors relied on exaggerated gestures and personal props (especially hats) to identify their function in a scene. In contrast to *The Farm Show*, *No. 1 Hard* makes little use of the actor's theatrical imagination to create images that at once embody and comment on the reality behind the play. As in *Ten Lost Years*, the actors in *No. 1 Hard* have no personal relation to the material they perform. *No. 1 Hard* is unique among the plays in this study in that it presents data rather than experience. Following the European tradition of investigative documentary, it implies a critique of the mass media in its attempt to correct conventional analyses of the wheat industry. Consequently, the actors function neither as story-tellers, as they do in *The Farm Show*, nor as activists, as in *Buchans: A Mining Town*, but as reporters. The absence of personal commentary directs attention to the facts they announce, rather than the manner of presentation.

The performance style of *No. 1 Hard* is essentially editorial. The material is presented directly, but the theatrical context in which it is presented provides emphasis and, at times, a secondary level of argument. A third level is found in the songs; written by Geoffrey Ursell, they counterpoint the narrative text with frankly subjective satire and sentiment. A typical example of the satiric voice is a sarcastic anthem which excoriates Otto Lang, the Saskatchewan member of the Trudeau cabinet whose responsibilities included the Wheat Board:

> Otto Lang, Otto Lang,
> He's a friend to the farmer, a friend to the worker,
> A friend to Trudeau, a friend to the railroad,
> Your friend Otto Lang.
> When we sing Otto Lang, we're singing two four letter words.

In keeping with Kramer's rejection of emotional appeal in the text, the songs supply the only note of sentimentality in the play. The show concludes, after a denunciation of international business practices and an update on the ongoing Canadian Agricultural Movement's boycott of local stockyards, with an emotional invocation:

earth, sunlight, water
give grain life to grow
bread for every table
if we want it so
if we want it so.

As the song indicates, the politics of *No. 1 Hard* are simple. The play is divided into four 'investigations,' focusing in turn on the history of grain capitalism in Saskatchewan, the federal government's current policies regarding wheat sales, Cargill's move into the Saskatchewan industry, and the role of the Wheat Pool. In *Paper Wheat*, the Wheat pool is celebrated as the heroic expression of co-operative populism, but in *No. 1 Hard* it is criticized as another form of capitalism:

POOL 2
An elevator agent with 18 years experience was ordered out of the elevator by his doctor. The pool was asked to give him rehabilitative training. They told the union: 'why would you expect from this company anything one goddamn bit different than you'd get from the Canadian Pacific railway.'
POOL 3
I've never belonged to a fucking co-op. I don't intend to belong to a fucking co-op, and I don't give a goddamn. This is just a job for me. (member of Pool management) (24)

The scene builds to a denunciation of the Wheat Pool for its refusal to admit the health hazards of grain dust. According to Kramer, 'The Co-op is simply mass capitalism – everybody gets a little richer. The grain dust scene ... tries to make the point that the problems are deeper than the distribution of capital.'[12]

True to its investigative purpose, *No. 1 Hard* does not try to provide solutions to the problems it identifies, although solutions are implied in the play's left-wing perspective. In the end, the play draws the conclusion that the problems of the grain industry must be blamed on greed, especially on the part of the multinational corporations. *No. 1 Hard* is premised on a political morality rather than a specific ideology; it appeals to the populism that it identifies as the victim of exploitation and betrayal.

As originally conceived, *No. 1 Hard* was to include satiric scenes written by Deverell to ridicule government policies and demonstrate the workings of the industry. In the end this idea was abandoned; as Deverell has written, 'the facts satirized themselves better than I could. (For example read the Foreign Investment Review Act.)'[13] This decision to exclude invented material reinforces the play's claim to documentary authority. There was, however, one such satiric scene in the original version. Designed to illustrate the mechanics of the grain futures market, the scene shows what happens when 'Farmer Brown' sells his next year's crop to 'Hungry the Baker.' The crop is sold back and forth between the various parties at changing prices until everyone but the farmer has made a profit. In the revised version, the scene was dropped in favour of extracts from a Royal Commission on the grain industry established in 1900 to report on the operation of the market. The replacement scene lacks the comedy of the original, but it adds to the textual authenticity of the play.

Although *No. 1 Hard* embraces the whole of the grain industry in an historical context, it is a highly selective examination, requiring a basic familiarity with the subject on the part of the audience. The play begins with an acknowledgement of the audience's expertise in the form of a preface delivered by Ed Partridge, champion of the co-op movement in the 1920s. An audience unfamiliar with the history of the movement and Partridge's role in it might well miss the significance of his opening speech, which provides an opportune bridge between the world of the theatre and the world of the farmer:

PARTRIDGE
Western Canada, to my mind, is marvelously well suited to be the stage and the people to furnish the cast for a wonderfully interesting politico-socio-economic national life-drama, having for its motif a great co-operative experiment; not a tragedy – the world has had enough of state tragedies – but a noble melodrama wherein the bad shall be discomfited, the good vindicated and things generally set right in individual and social life ... I'm the man from Sintaluta, I'm Ed Partridge. (1)

In *Paper Wheat*, Partridge is celebrated as the architect of a heroic and successful enterprise, but in *No. 1 Hard* his vision is presented as an ultimate failure. This fundamental difference in the historical analysis of the topic is one of the main factors responsible for the differences in form and presentation style in the two plays. *No. 1 Hard* argues the minority case, that the status quo is immoral, and that the heroic myth of the co-op movement is false. It is because the play is essentially iconoclastic that it is restricted to the presentation of concrete evidence. Invented material, such as the 'Hungry the Baker' sketch, weakens the apparent objectivity of the documentary evidence. In *No. 1 Hard* the actors remain subordinate to the material they perform, whereas in *Paper Wheat* the performance relies on the actors' personalities. Their charm made *Paper Wheat* a national success; in *No. 1 Hard* the personalities – and even the number – of the actors are immaterial.

Paradoxically, the simple structure of *No. 1 Hard*, with its distinctions between form and content, and between text and performance, allows for more narrative freedom than the more complex scheme of *Paper Wheat*. In the final segment of *No. 1 Hard* there is a brief scene in which a narrator tells the story of a grain trade fraud in the United States. The story is set to music from the American television detective series *Dragnet*, and the narrator speaks with the terse syntax of a police report. Three actors in trench coats mime the action. This gesture is typical of the play; it emphasizes the criminality of the fraud, and it creates a context in which documentary facts are made pleasing to the scene.

In the final version of *Paper Wheat* we find a similar scene, in which an episode of corruption on the Winnipeg Grain Exchange is presented as a comic parody of an old radio series. In *No. 1 Hard* the detective story gesture is typical of the relation of text to performance throughout the play. In *Paper Wheat* it stands out as an anomaly, because the form and the specifics of the detective motif bear no relation to the narrative pattern established to that point in the play.

In *No. 1 Hard*, the strict adherence to documented evidence permits the actors to move around the confines of historical reality to substantiate the evidence in performance. In *Paper Wheat*, because of its more relaxed attitude towards historical evidence and because of the emphasis on invented scenes, the actors must authenticate the historical material by the very fact of the performance itself. This places the weight of authentication on the narrative motifs and gestures the actors create, and this in turn requires that those gestures provide a meaningful context for the dramatic invention. The detective story gesture removes the material of the episode from the reality of the play because the context it provides is essentially false. In this sense, the two plays stand in opposition. *Paper Wheat* generally relies on the performance to authenticate the stories it celebrates, whereas in *No. 1 Hard* the performance simply indicates editorial attitudes towards material already authenticated in the narrative text.

No. 1 Hard analyses the grain industry as a political struggle in which the farmer audiences are still engaged. This is reinforced by the inclusion of up-to-date reports on topical current events and political discussions with the audience following the performances. Both of these are traditional agitprop techniques. In *Paper Wheat* the grain industry's struggle is presented as an historical event that has run its course. In the end, the two plays speak to the same audiences, but they define them differently. The grain industry is the source of bitter anger in *No. 1 Hard* but a cause for celebration in *Paper Wheat*. If there is a single reason other than the charm of the actors that may account for the success of *Paper Wheat*, it may be that the presentational form of the play is that of a heroic epic. In performance it celebrates not only the historical event, but the very telling of the story as well.

PAPER WHEAT

Although *Paper Wheat* is not a complex play (despite certain inadvertent complexities of structure), an analysis of it is complicated by the fact that it exists in three versions. The first production, conceived and directed by Andras Tahn, has never been published; the second version, published in the *Canadian Theatre Review*, is that of Guy Sprung's 1977 revision, and the final version, published by Western Producer Prairie Books, is Tahn's later emendation of Sprung's revision. This analysis will focus on the first and second versions, explaining their differences and examining the changes in the nature of the performance as it relates to the historical facts it describes.

The 25th Street Theatre began life in 1972 as a co-operative arts centre called 25th Street House, and from 1973 to 1975 it produced a series of Canadian plays, including several by Andras Tahn. When Paul Thompson offered to direct a show for the company in exchange for rehearsal space for *The West Show*, he introduced a cast of local actors (including Linda Griffiths and Layne Coleman, both of whom later became Passe Muraille regulars) to the techniques of collective creation in a revue called *If You're So Good Why Are You in Saskatoon?* As Don Kerr has described in his very useful introduction to *Paper Wheat: The Book*, Tahn was excited enough about the possibilities of collective creation to advertise a play tentatively called *The Co-op Show* for his next season.[14] At the end of the financially disastrous 1976-7 season, Tahn began recruiting a cast to bring his project to life. The original cast of *Paper Wheat* comprised four women (Linda Griffiths, Catherine Jaxon, Brenda Leadley, and Sharon Bakker) and two men (Bob Bainborough and Michael Fahey). They began researching the play in February 1977 in preparation for a March opening. The actors were all young and relatively inexperienced; for most this was their first attempt at collective creation. The process of research and creation was similar to that developed by Paul Thompson with *The Farm Show*. The troupe travelled to rural communities to uncover first-hand narratives of the homesteading days. It was not an easy experience. As Tahn told one journalist:

There was no expense money; people had to crash wherever they could find a bed or a couch. We didn't have a clue what we were doing. We went out and talked to anyone who would talk to us about homesteading and the co-ops. It was 'monkey see, monkey do' – taking what people told us and turning it into scenes.[15]

As the later crisis in the company would prove, the research process was frustrating for the actors, especially since they were not paid until the show opened. Two days before that opening, the actors had accumulated four hours of material and worked through through several hundred scene ideas. The lack of organization in the research reflected a deeper problem, one which would follow the play through all three versions. Although it was conceived as a play about the co-op movement, Tahn's aversion to political subjects and the actors' natural sympathy for anecdote and emotion moved the play towards the subjects of homesteading and the grain industry as a whole during the research phase. According to Bainborough:

The people we met on these forays were amazing. They let us into their homes, fed us tea and cookies and told us their life stories ... We were left full of warmth and awe for what they had begun and inspired by their ideals and humanity. The experience was like looking at a mountain. You didn't know whether to laugh or cry or run up it or take pictures of it or just stand and look at it.[16]

The research process was complicated by the fact that the actors, only half of whom came from Saskatchewan, knew little about their subject. Without the expertise to help them sift through the material and find a precise focus, the actors tended to respond to their findings emotionally rather than analytically. Together with the difficulties of uniting a cast around a thematic issue rather than a specific community (a difficulty which took Thompson until *The West Show* to resolve), this naïvety effectively precluded the possibility of a complex critical perspective in the play. It was this problem that Guy Sprung would attempt to solve, to Tahn's displeasure, in the revision of the following year.

Tahn had originally planned to open the play in Regina, but, as the scheduled opening neared, decided instead to open it in the rural community of Sintaluta as the first step of a five-town tour that would climax in Saskatoon. The decision to open in Sintaluta was fortunate, as Tahn has admitted:

I think if we had opened where we were going to open – Regina – we would have died. It would have killed the show – because it was a stumbling, awkward, little – you'll pardon the expression – quadruplegic.[17]

As the birthplace of Ed Partridge, who figures prominently in the play, Sintaluta offered a safe testing ground before a partisan audience. The enthusiastic response it received ensured the play's survival. Without it, the actors might well have given up. Two days before the opening, the cast staged what Tahn has called an 'insurrection'; the play did not yet have a form suitable for performance, and 'every actor had a scene that he created that he wanted in the show.'[18] As well, the cast shared serious misgivings about Tahn's artistic and administrative competence.

On the day before the opening Tahn realized that the play needed scenery. Volunteers from the community jury-rigged curtains from blankets to cover the exits in the community hall that served as theatre, and a phone call to Saskatoon brought a hastily painted vista of clouds and prairie, over which was superimposed the outline of the map of Canada. This backdrop arrived just as the audience was lining up for admission.

Tahn has described how he stood at the back of the hall during that first performance, embarrassed at the clumsiness of the play and certain that it would fail.[19] Instead it received a standing-ovation. There is no record of that first performance of *Paper Wheat*; the earliest extant version is that of the Saskatoon performance at the end of that first week, by which time the script had undergone extensive revision. In the days following the premiere, the play was trimmed of its more awkward excesses, including a monologue, delivered by Linda Griffiths, which described the history of the world as a stirring process culminating in the birth of Ed Partridge.

Although the version that dates from the end of that pilot tour is basically similar in general structure and outline to the later published scripts, it differs substantially in detail. According to Guy Sprung, the original made his revision possible, but they are essentially different plays.[20] In all three versions, the action is divided into two parts. In the first act the play follows the fortunes of a group of immigrants who take up homesteading on the prairie, and in the second it traces the political and historical events of the co-op and Wheat Pool struggles. If the first and second versions are substantially different plays, it is not only because they vary in detail. Sprung introduced major changes in structure and content, but perhaps more importantly, he altered the nature of the performance itself.

According to Sprung, the first version of *Paper Wheat* lacked coherence.[21] This judgment is supported by an analysis of the text. At first glance, the original play (the version dating from the end of the first tour) seems typical of the many documentary revues performed in the 1970s by young and enthusiastic actors on a bare stage. The opening scene is representative of the style and tone of the play. It begins with a woman singing a hymn in a thick German accent. In her hymnbook she finds a pamphlet which extolls 'the warm temperate climate' of Saskatchewan, and decides to emigrate:

All right kids, come on. We're going to Canada today. Look at the picture. We have to go first on the boat. Freddie. Freddie! Come on Freddie, here we go. Here we are on the boat. Ahh. It's so crowded on this boat. [Mimes action of boat.] Look at the sea. That's right. [Pause] Oh, after four weeks at sea and maybe a few storms it gets maybe a little bit boring ... [22]

The woman arrives in Saskatchewan to find a treeless, frozen expanse. The monologue ends with a gag when she gives the pamphlet to the imaginary Freddie to use as toilet paper. The scene, brief as it is, introduces two important themes of the play: the hardships of homesteading, and the false promises of a gentle land – promises ironically made true by the industry of the sod-busters.

The narrative technique of the scene clearly derives from Passe Muraille's excursion into the west; it was from Thompson that Tahn learned the theatrical power of an actor who simultaneously narrates and performs a story. The monologues also reveal the major problem with the play. It introduces its themes in the most superficial manner, as the steps in a joke leading to a punch line. Like the other historical scenes in *Paper Wheat* the monologue is at heart ahistorical. Instead of depicting the reasons behind the tide of immigration which this woman represents, the scene merely establishes the bare fact of immigration.

The next series of scenes describes a generalized picture of homesteading life: a Scotswoman is sent to Saskatchewan as a mail-order bride; a farmer from Ontario speaks of the unexpected vastness of the prairie; a British homesteader nervously proposes marriage to his housekeeper; and a Norwegian settler is cheated by a crooked grain elevator agent. The arrangement of these scenes is arbitrary. Like the opening monologue, the sequence describes situations as typical, but without the necessary historical perspective to give them deeper meaning. The act lacks unity: characters vary from scene to scene but reappear when required to develop the semblance of a continuous plot. The tendency towards recurring representative characters results in a hesitant performance style which wavers between the presentational technique of revue and the mimetic action of drama.

This can be seen in the 'Old Bessie' scene (found in all three versions), which begins as a sketch about the hardships of the farm wife burdened with an impossible list of chores. The sketch is the lead-in to a rousing ode. But it is the transition between these two performance modes, from narrative realism to presentational song, that is of interest. At the conclusion of the dialogue, a third character enters the scene with a guitar:

ERNIE
Hello, John
JOHN
Well, Ernie.

ERNIE
How's things?
JOHN
Busy, busy.
ERNIE
Not too busy for a song, I hope.
JOHN
Well, I see you brought your guitar.
ERNIE
That's right.

The ode follows:

Oh, Bessie, someday you'll be heaven bound,
You'll go to meet your maker, you'll be six feet underground.
But Bessie, until that day when you're free,
Get up old girl, and do your chores, you're working free for me.   (23)

This device of placing the song within the scene superimposes the demands of the presentational performance form on the invented world of the drama. It bridges the narrative and presentational modes, but that bridge is unnecessary and indeed detrimental to the play. It suggests an identification of actor and character that is not sustained in the play as a whole. The persona of the actor is suspended between narrative fiction and presentational reportage. The relation of these two modes is confused throughout this first version of *Paper Wheat*, and a measure of that confusion survives into the second version as well, despite Sprung's attempts to resolve it.

This confusion of fiction and documentary performance technique is only a minor problem when the play examines the rigours of homesteading and the necessity of co-operation. In these scenes the characters are clearly schematic representatives of thousands like them, and they are given a degree of commonality through the performances. The necessity of distributing a large number of characters among a small cast, however, leads to a problem with the historical thought at the core of the play. In the scene following 'Old Bessie' the necessity of co-operation is demonstrated by an episode in which a farmer with a broken plough swallows his pride and accepts an offer of help from his neighbour. That neighbour, because of the preponderance of women in the cast, is a single woman, homesteading on her own. The decision to portray the neighbour as a woman was an attempt to establish dramatic continuity rather than a practical necessity; elsewhere in the play, women take on male characters if required. The neighbour identifies herself as Jean Shirley, the Scotswoman introduced as a mail-order bride in scene 2. She explains her spinsterhood with a passing comment that 'the lad never showed up.'

For the sake of dramatic continuity, the scene sacrifices historical credibility. The circumstantial details required to explain Jean Shirley's presence in the scene argue against its historical validity as a typical incident. Such an incident may well have happened in real life; certainly it is not impossible. The play, however, has no means of authenticating it beyond its schematic structure – the very thing that argues against the story. The problem is one of execution rather than analysis. To accept the moral lesson of the scene – that a man must accept a timely offer of help if he is to survive – the audience must first accept the dramatic reality of a woman who is homesteading on her own and who cannot cook (she proposes to lend her plough in trade for meals), and a man who would rather face certain ruin than borrow a plough. In Sprung's version the scene is made probable by the simple device of changing the woman to a Ukrainian settler. The scene then becomes a political parable about the need to bridge cultural and linguistic gaps in order to survive. By providing the scene with a more probable dramatic and historical circumstance, co-operation is presented as an historical necessity rather than an ideological prescription.

This problem with the historical presentation of the subject is compounded when the play moves into the realm of historical fact with the rise of the co-op movement. The final two scenes of the first act in the original version describe the conditions that brought about the co-op struggle. In the first scene, the Norwegian farmer is cheated by an agent; in the second a group of farmers meet in a cafe to compare their experiences in marketing their wheat. They decide the situation needs changing:

JOHN
Well, we can't let this go on and on. I'm tired of it.
SVEN
I think we should have a meeting or something.
JEAN
That's right.
JOHN
We should find out what the rest of the farmers think about it. And maybe we can do something about it. (32)

At this point the play attempts to introduce the characters into the historical facts it celebrates. This final dialogue, with its promise of militant action, effectively recasts the preceding scenes as a lengthy prologue to the actual subject of the play. The first act charts the historical details necessary to an understanding of the co-op movement, but it does so in a manner that is perhaps too incidental to create the desired structure of cause and effect. The decision to take action is presented as an isolated incident because the preceding scenes are at once too specific in terms of character and too general in terms of historical analysis.

In the second act, the promise of political action that ends the first act is fulfilled but, in keeping with the simplicity of the historical statement of the play, the politics are not analysed. The act begins with a theatrical metaphor: a wrestling match between 'Grain Grower's Gertie,' 'Big Business Bertha,' and 'Government Gail.' Written and inserted into the play on the day following the Sintaluta premiere, the scene outlines the general facts of the co-op's origins in a quick series of match rounds. The metaphor reduces the historical process to a quick series of crises:

GOV'T GAIL
After the war the Wheat Board is dissolved. (G. grabs B's head, running to opposite corner, smashes it into turnbuckle.)
GERT
Fifty percent of Saskatchewan's farmers sign up for a Wheat Pool.
PROMOTER
Wheat Pool's a tough one, Bertha.
(B. gets up as G. runs for the ropes; they bounce off the ropes and collide centre stage, both wiped out.)
PROMOTER
Well, I don't know about you, but it looks like the depression to me.   (36)

In the end, the decision of the match is reserved until the next century and the promoter promises to return the play 'to reality.' This introduces a long sequence about Ed Partridge, whose attempt to understand the workings of the grain market is prefaced by a song and dance routine called 'The Grain Exchange Rag':

I got wheat to sell; it's not even mine
It's made of paper, and it's borrowed on time
I sell short; he sells high
We all end up with a big piece of pie.   (38)

This song performs the same function that the 'Hungry the Baker' scene played in the original version of *No. 1 Hard*, but whereas in that play the overt theatricality of the scene worked against the authenticity of the documentary, in *Paper Wheat* the song reinforces the political context – principally because, simple as it is, the song is no simpler than the play it embellishes. This first version of *Paper Wheat* has no real argument to authenticate, and the problems Sprung encountered when he tried to incorporate a dialectical argument in the second version suggest that the play works best when it reflects the prejudices of the audience. In that sense, the first version of the play may be described as an emotional agitprop which argues sentiment rather than ideology. This is perhaps most evident in the scene following 'The Grain Exchange Rag,' in which Partridge encounters a dense and arrogant British lord on a train. The scene serves only to reinforce prejudice, as the poorly educated farmer triumphs over the blithering aristocrat.

The next five scenes, approximately one-fourth of the play, take the form of a self-contained drama about Partridge. As in the first act, the play moves towards the development of a plot. The scenes owe more to pageantry than to historical drama; each depicts Partridge at a crucial point in his career. The incidents are iconographic rather than dramatic. According to Bob Bainborough, who played the role of Partridge:

I studied Ed Partridge. I met his sister, I read his book. I researched E.A. Partridge until I dreamed about him. The only thing I didn't want to do was play E.A. Partridge in the show – the co-op show that was now the wheat show. The rest of the cast thought that was ridiculous and I ended up playing Mr Partridge anyway. I don't know why I made such a fuss but I guess I felt he was larger than life and I was over-awed by him.[23]

In *No. 1 Hard*, Partridge is present as a choral figure who provides ironic commentary on the reportage. In both plays his words are taken from his own writings, but in *Paper Wheat* they are the basis of invented dialogue that allows him to express his ideals. Of particular interest is the intersection of Partridge with the invented characters from the first act; when Partridge addresses a farmers' meeting we once again meet the farmers who decided to take action earlier in the play. The historical reality of Partridge and his agitation for the co-op is contained in the world of the fiction established in the first act.

Following the Partridge scenes, the play returns to the narrative structure of the documentary. The penultimate scene describes the formation of the Wheat Pool in 1924. The scene is organized as a series of quick vignettes framed by the character of Aaron Sapiro, the American organizer. To an audience unfamiliar with the history of the movement, the chronology of the scene is confusing, and the distinction between the Wheat Pool and the earlier Grain Growers' Grain Company is unclear. As Sapiro argues the need for co-operative marketing, interspersed vignettes depict various humorous schemes used to induce farmers to sign for the Pool. The scene ends with cheers when the plan signs up the required number of farmers, and the play jumps to the present day.

The final scene is made up of a series of short monologues delivered by a group of old people sitting in a row of chairs. The scene acknowledges, but does not try to explain, the historical irony behind the play: the socialist settlers of the past are now affluent retirees who travel the globe. In form, this is the most traditionally documentary scene in the play, based as it is on recorded interviews. It provides an emotional retrospective of the co-op movement, thus uniting the historical material with the reality of the audience. The closing passage builds on that connection in a sentimental evocation of mythic grandeur. Significantly, this curtain speech was not collected from an authentic source, but written by Linda Griffiths. In it a sod-buster describes the beauty of the virgin prairie and the ordeals of homesteading in resounding, epic language. It ends with a celebration of heroic youth:

> You know, I'd give it all to be young again, I would. To hold my hands on the handles of a plough. To smell the warm earth and see it fall aside in waves, right to each side, smooth as water. I'd give it all to be young again and feel that I could change the world. (67)

This appeal to nostalgia is perhaps the most important reason for the success of the original production of *Paper Wheat*. Reviewing the show for the left-wing magazine *Next Year Country*, Bob Jeffcott argued that this nostalgic sentiment precluded critical intelligence:

Nowhere in the play is there mention of the sort of businesses the Co-ops and the Wheat Pool have become, or a glimmer of understanding of why this should be. The final statement of the play ... rings false to anyone who has ever had to work for or dealt with a present day Co-op, credit union, or the Wheat Pool. [24]

For his part, Tahn maintains that this absence of critical perspective was intentional: 'I wasn't interested in the events. They meant nothing to me. I was interested in the people.' [25]

Whether by design or, as is more likely, because of the short and difficult creative process, 'the people' in *Paper Wheat* are depicted in the simple terms of an historical pageant. Like the traditional Canadian patriotic pageant, *Paper Wheat* is a sentimental tribute to the heirs of a glorified tradition, and like most pageants it works best when it flatters the audience and embodies their prejudices.

It was this lack of critical perspective that Guy Sprung tried to rectify in his revision of the play. Sprung's version is a more clever piece of theatre,and it is more coherent in its internal logic, but it invites criticism when it attempts to replace the pageant-like elements of the original with a more complex view of history. Paradoxically, as Sprung tried to make the play into a dialectical statement, he added to it even more features typical of the pageant form.

PAPER WHEAT: THE SECOND VERSION

Tahn was forced to recruit another director to mount the second tour of *Paper Wheat* when his cast refused to work with him again. Although a popular success, the first tour of the play lost money, and was marked by frustration and acrimony because of Tahn's ad hoc administrative methods. Tahn's choice of Sprung was the single most important factor in the transformation of the play from a local revue to a national hit. Recently returned from Great Britain, where he had been one of the founders of London's populist Half Moon Theatre, Sprung had a demonstrated commitment to political theatre. As a free-lance director in Montreal he had received national attention for his work with David Fennario at the Centaur Theatre. Tahn's choice of Sprung was apparently motivated by a measure of personal interest as well: he hoped to elicit Sprung's interest in his own play *Jacob Kepp*. Sprung was hired on the condition that he would have control over script and casting, although according to Tahn there were to be 'no major changes.' For his part, Sprung felt no obligation to follow the original script. When he arrived in Saskatoon in the late summer of 1977, he had listened to a tape of the show and decided to begin the process of research and creation anew. To maintain a balance of continuity and originality, he decided to retain no more than two of the original cast, choosing Sharon Bakker and Michael Fahey. Sprung considered it 'ludicrous that a play about the west should not have a single ethnic actor,' and so brought from Montreal three actors who would give the show the necessary ethnic balance.[26] Skai Leja was of Latvian descent, David Francis, a Canadian trained in Britain, brought a convincing English accent to the play; and Lubomir Mykytiuk enriched it with his fluency in Ukrainian. This enabled Sprung to simplify the first act by giving each actor one principal character, so that instead of the confusing eleven main characters in the original first act, there were now five. Mykytiuk played Vasil Havryshyn, a Ukrainian homesteader; Fahey played Sean Phalen, an Irishman; Francis played an English immigrant named William Postlethwaite; Bakker played his wife; and Leja played Anna Lutz. According to Leja, her character was based on a real woman. The actual Anna Lutz had been German, but Leja made her into a Latvian because she found the German accent difficult.

As in the original version, the choice of characters is essentially schematic, designed to show an authentic cross-section of the settler population. With the ethnic differences removed, the characters are virtually the same: all are honest, industrious, and independent. They are obvious idealizations of the typical homesteader. This too is characteristic of the pageant form.

Sprung's retention of the pageant aspects of the play is apparent in his introduction of these characters in his revised opening scene. As the actors sing a lively song about Canada's need for settlers on the prairie, they portray a group of immigrants heading west on a train. Between verses each character in turn states his or her reason for coming to Canada. This parade of immigrants is reminiscent of the patriotic pageants of an earlier generation. In Minnie Williams's 1923 pageant, *The Romance of Canada*, for example, we find a similar scene of hopeful immigrants waiting for a train to take them west. As in *Paper Wheat*, they deliver short speeches that identify their ethnic origin:

ENGLISHMAN

I'm on my way to Regina. I shan't go far out. I'll take up a homestead, and with my trap and my dog, it's just the life I'm looking for.

SCOTCHMAN

I'm looking for a wee bit of land to put the wife and bairns on, but all the land here aboot is taken by some city folk. I'll have to gang farther west. [27]

The scene then introduces a comical Irishman and a family of Ruthenians who 'all look bewildered and jabber together.' If we subtract the song from Sprung's first scene, it is virtually the same as Williams's.

SEAN

I was over in Liverpool looking for work and I was walking down the street this one day, and I saw this sign. It said 'Come to Canada,' and in the picture they got these golden fields of flowing wheat. Well, coming from an Irish family of eighteen, I thought to myself ... I'll give it a try.

VASIL

I come to Canada alone. In Ukrainia I was youngest son. There were eight sons. We were ... poor. I could not even marry. I hear that in Canada there is land. I tell my father. My father says, 'You are young. You go, I'm too old.' So I go. [28]

By linking these speeches with a song, Sprung joined the technique of the pageant with the presentational fact of the performance. Much more than in Tahn's version, the telling of the story – the performance itself – is an essential theme in the revised *Paper Wheat*. From the start, Sprung had the advantage of a more experienced, and arguably more talented, cast than Tahn had. In addition, he asked Tahn to recruit a fiddler for the show. Tahn hired a retired farmer named Bill Prokopchuk, a champion fiddler who had performed with modest success in Nashville. Prokopchuk's presence in the play gave it a needed authenticity, bridging the world of the performers and the world of the audience.

Sprung's emphasis on the humour and theatricality of the ensemble performance gave the play the wider appeal it needed to attract audiences with no special interest in the subject matter. In his revisions of the play he worked towards simplifying its didactic elements, so that the character action of the first act functions more clearly as a necessary prelude to the political material of the second. To clarify the didacticism and enhance its entertainment value, he borrowed from the techniques of agitprop, the Living Newspapers, and Joan Littlewood. Throughout his version of the play, narrative content is reinforced with theatrical commentary. At its best, this takes the form of virtuoso theatrical gestures, such as this juggling sequence in the penultimate 'Togetherness' scene, in which Lubomir Mykytiuk demonstrates the workings of the economic market:

> For purposes of this demonstration, this rubber ball (SIS bounces ball to LOUIE) – thank you ... will represent a commodity on the open market. And this rubber ball (SIS throws again) – thank you – will represent another commodity on the open market. And this (SIS throws bread roll, which doesn't bounce, of course) ... This bread roll will represent one more commodity on the open market. Let's call it a loaf of bread. Now this (juggling three objects into play) ... is the open market. (A quick run through a few juggling techniques) Not bad for a Ukrainian, eh?
>
> (72–3)

By the end of the routine, the bread roll has been reduced to a morsel as each transaction takes a literal bite out of the farmer's profits. This juggling act is typical of Sprung's theatricality. The virtuosity of the performance and its reminder of the actor's personality embellish the relatively simple didactic statement. As in agitprop the scene reduces analysis to emblematic depiction.

Sprung's most effective theatrical innovations in the play tend to follow this principle. The substitution of theatrical demonstration for analysis is particularly notable in the 'co-op quickies' interspersed in the play. These short vignettes are yet another feature typical of the pageant form:

Four farmers wander on with small sheaves of wheat in their hands, and sorrowful
expressions on their faces. They look at each other and back at their wheat, then an
idea hits them. Slowly, one by one, they put their individual sheaves together.
Their expressions change as all that wheat becomes one large sheaf. A sign appears
from the foot of the stage: It reads: GRAIN GROWERS' GRAIN COMPANY 1905.   (59)

This pattern of reductionism extends to the narrative structures of the scene
themselves. In most cases, the scenes take their narrative shape from the fact of
performance itself (in the case of songs and direct monologues) or from the
research process (especially in the case of the final 'Old Folks' scene). The
significant exception is the scene that parallels the 'Dragnet' scene in *No. 1
Hard*. In this case, the theatrical gesture tends to isolate and simplify the
material it expresses.

In the course of their research, Sprung and his actors came across the story of
a Winnipeg journalist who sold his services to a group of grain tycoons. On their
orders, he wrote a series of pseudonymous letters to the Winnipeg newspapers
ridiculing the Grain Growers' co-op. The episode is a revealing but minor
glimpse into the business practices of the day. In the play, however, it is singled
out to typify the co-op's entire experience on the Grain Exchange. The incident
is presented as a radio drama, using techniques similar to the radio scenes in *Ten
Lost Years*. The actors recreate a sound studio on the stage and parody the
methods of radio production. The stage direction describes the theatrical context
of the scene:

A not yet invented CBC radio studio in the 1910s. General confusion as the mikes
are set-up and the actors come in talking about last night's parties and the
general bad state of the profession. An assistant floor manager yells, 'Fifteen
seconds to airtime!' and deposits a box of sound effects on the table. The wrong
sound effects. Panic reigns, improvisation ensues: a washboard for typewriter
noises, kazoos, blocks of wood, whatever.   (59)

The narrative gesture of the radio drama transforms the facts of the historical
event into an entertaining theatrical statement, but it does not provide a
meaningful perspective by which the event may be understood. The 'radio
drama' is a parody of a popular American series of the 1940s:

WHISTLER
(Approaching footsteps, then whistling) I am known as The Whistler. I see into
dark corners, through the silent shadows and behind the closed doors that
hide the unknown activities of this thriving metropolis, WINNIPEG! ...   (59–60)

There is no analytical relation between the historical event and an American radio program which post-dates it by three decades. In effect, by imposing a metaphor drawn from the 1940s, the scene removes the incident from its historical context and places it in a generalized past. Like the 'co-op quickies,' it simplifies historical complexities which the play elsewhere defines as dialectical.

In his revision of the dramatic and political content of *Paper Wheat*, Sprung attempted to impose a logical structure of cause and effect on the original, so that the form of the play would manifest the polemic content. To this end, he retained the general outline of the first act, but gave it a more coherent dramatic unity. Following the pageant-like opening scene, the act begins with Vasil as he purchases a wagon and homesteading supplies on credit. Vasil cannot speak English and the outfitter cannot speak Ukrainian, but they manage to conclude the deal successfully. The point of the scene is delivered in the outfitter's final speech to his assistant:

> Well Charlie, he looks like he might make a go out of it. But don't worry, the odds are in our favour. That's the fifth time we've sold that stuff. (40)

There is no reason to suppose that Vasil will fail; *Paper Wheat* is a celebration of success, and this is one of the few references to the possibility of failure. The scene establishes the frequently contradictory interests of the farmer and commercial business. Whether Vasil succeeds or fails, the businessman will profit. The small outfitter of this first scene prepares the way for the crooked elevator agent later in the act and the multinational businesses in the second act.

The scene is followed by a monologue, taken from the original but wholly rewritten, in which Anna Lutz describes her first impressions of Swift Current in terms of the smells that hit her when she stepped off the train. The speech brings Anna into the action, and provides a theatrical transition. Her description of a crowded town filled with hopeful immigrants places the previous scene in a wider picture and prepares the way for the following scene, 'Squeezing the Land.'

Again taken from the original (although edited considerably), this scene stands as one of the most effective uses of theatrical metaphor in the play. As Bill and Elizabeth Postlethwaite describe the hardships of their life on the land in terse sentences, 'they tell the story of their land by folding, furrowing and squeezing a rough grey blanket on a table.' The effectiveness of the metaphor is obvious when the scene is compared to its counterpart in the CBC adaptation of the play. In that version, the couple deliver the lines sitting over tea, without the blanket. Without the metaphorical image, the abbreviated style of the dialogue seems inane.

The simple theatricality of the scene is followed by a lyrical ballad about prairie winds. Like the Anna Lutz monologue, the song serves as a presentational transition to another mimetic scene. It is in this next scene that Sprung's decision to give his characters specific ethnic identities finds dramatic as well as historical justification. In the original version, a farmer enters his home for lunch and, while eating, proposes marriage to his housekeeper:

JOHN
In the last little while we've been getting to know each other fairly well.
ELIZ.
Yes.
JOHN
We get along pretty good.
ELIZ.
Yes.
JOHN
We don't have many arguments to speak of.
ELIZ.
No.
JOHN
Well, ah ... I'm just wondering if it isn't time we ... we ... ah, you stopped working here and maybe we got married.
ELIX.
Yes.
JOHN
You want to get married?
ELIZ.
Yes, if you want to. (11)

In Sprung's revision, the scene takes place between Vasil and Anna Lutz. The lines are virtually identical but the effect is very different:

VASIL
From time to time, you work here, I know you, you know me.
ANNA
Ya.
VASIL
Well, we get along alright.
ANNA
Ya.

VASIL
We don't argue.
ANNA
No.
VASIL
I thinking to myself. Vasil, maybe Miss Lutz not work for you no more. Maybe
you ask Miss Lutz ... to marry you.
ANNA
Ya.
VASIL
You want get married?
ANNA
Yes, if you want to. (45)

With the addition of the dialect, the scene is not only more humorous but
more complex. It is as much about the problems of communication and survival
as it is about the social conventions demanded by homesteading life. It is at this
point that the characters introduced in the first scene begin to converge, as they
continue to do for the remainder of the act.

Of the ten remaining scenes in the first act, five are new to this second
version. These new scenes clarify the dramatic structure, but, more importantly, they give the act a more balanced rhythm and enhanced sentimentality.
They include two songs: 'Homesick Blues,' in which the characters recall their
homelands; and Sean's 'Toiling in the Broiling Sun,' a humorous work shanty.
The other additions are a short anecdote by Sean about 'baching' it on the
prairie; the first of the 'co-op quickies' (in which two farmers try to haul their
wagons out of the mud and discover they must co-operate); and a scene between
Elizabeth Postlethwaite and Anna Lutz.

This dialogue scene replaces one in the original in which two women, living
on neighbouring farms, introduce themselves and discuss the perils of dust
storms. Sprung's scene keeps the premise of two neighbouring farm wives who
seek each other out for companionship, but here they discuss the corrupt
elevator agents who cheat their husbands. It is in this scene that the historical
facts of the co-op struggle are first mentioned. Elizabeth asks Anna, 'Did
you hear about that meeting tonight? The Territorial grain growers' meeting?'
They agree that action is necessary, and it is Anna Lutz who proposes the
solutions:

Well, why don't we get together. Put all our grain together and ship it away. We'd
get better prices than we're getting now. (53)

In the first version, the idea of political action is invented spontaneously by the discontented farmers in the final scene of the act. In this revision, the mention of a meeting refers to political action independent of the characters we have met. The scene implies that Anna Lutz is not the first to invent the co-op solution, but significantly we first hear of it from an uneducated farm wife. The co-op struggle is thus introduced as a truly populist movement.

The five scenes from the original version are retained with varying fidelity. The 'Broken Plow' scene is virtually unchanged. It takes place between Vasil and Bill Postlethwaite, and the difficulties of communicating across linguistic and cultural gaps give the scene a more stable dramatic logic than the original. Similarly, Sean's monologue in which he encourages two stubborn oxen to pull his plough differs from the original only in the ethnic details. In the original, the farmer was Scottish and the oxen had Scottish names; in this case they are Irish. The elevator agent scene is identical to the original, except that now it is Sean rather than the Norwegian Sven who is cheated. Only the 'Old Bessie' scene survives without significant changes.

The final scene of the act received the most attention. Instead of the discursive conversation of the original, which leads to the spontaneous decision to take political action, the revised scene brings the three farmers together logically. In the Elizabeth–Anna scene we have been informed that Bill and Vasil have gone to town to sell their grain; in the elevator scene we have seen Sean do the same, and now the three meet to compare notes. They discover that they have all been cheated and argue about the merits of the aforementioned meeting. They decide to attend, but in the interim, they will visit the agent, and in Vasil's words, 'get little bit of exercise.' The ideological militancy that closes the act in the original is reinforced here by the physical militancy of the angry farmers.

Sprung's revisions in this first act compressed the action into a more logical dramatic fable. By defining the characters more closely in terms of background, language, and relations to each other, he strengthened their individuality, and in doing so made them more plausible as representatives of their epoch. In that sense, Sprung made the characters more historic, and at the same time he prepared the audience for the second act by containing the character action in a presentational frame of songs and monologues.

As in the original, the first act of the revised *Paper Wheat* is the human basis of the second. It anchors the broader political canvas in an established sense of community. In the revision, however, Sprung strengthened the distinction between these two perspectives by eliminating any reference to the first act characters in the second act, and by dismantling the self-contained Ed Partridge drama. Six of the eleven scenes in Sprung's second act are new; of the other five, three are virtually unchanged from the original and two are radically revised.

In both versions of the play the second act covers the historical ground from the co-op struggle to the present day. In the original, the final 'Old Folks' scene is a coda attached to the historical account. Sprung on the other hand attempted to bridge the gap between historical time and the present by expressing the great changes in the nature of the co-op movement as an historical contradiction. In Tahn's version, the final scene depicts the relative prosperity of today's wheat farmers as proof of a battle won; Sprung's version attempts to unite past and present in a more complex dialectical framework.

Like the original, Sprung's second act is divided into three general parts, dealing respectively with the co-op struggle, the Wheat Pool campaign of the 1920s and the ensuing radicalism of the Depression, and the present day. Sprung reshaped the relative formlessness of the original by clarifying the transition between scenes and punctuating them with songs and 'co-op quickies.'

The act begins, appropriately, with Ed Partridge as he awaits a train at the Sintaluta station. Sprung solved the problem of the Partridge scenes in the original by having him speak directly to the audience. Partridge is thus established as a narrator (much as he is in *No. 1 Hard*); his direct address also establishes the presentational style of the act. In this scene, Partridge is about to board a train to Winnipeg, there to learn about the Grain Exchange. He is depicted as an affable farmer with a folksy wit and a passionate conviction that 'we farmers are going to change the world.' Partridge's research into the workings of the market is summarized by the 'Grain Exchange Rag,' taken intact from the original. In Tahn's version, the Rag was followed by the brief 'Lord Snidwell' scene, in which Partridge bests a bigoted aristocrat, and the weighty 'Meeting' scene, in which he addresses the characters from the first act. In the revised version, the Snidwell scene disappears and the meeting is compressed into a lengthy monologue. Addressing the audience as a meeting of farmers, Partridge outlines his plan to buy a seat on the Grain Exchange. The success of the plan is announced immediately in a 'co-op quickie' (the wheat-sheaf vignette described earlier). It is at this point that the narrative structure of the act changes abruptly with the 'Mystery Theatre' scene. As discussed, the radio drama metaphor bears no relation to the historical subject, but it does provide a sense of performance consistency: the two Partridge scenes are both followed by ensemble scenes that emphasize the fact of performance.

The 'Mystery Theatre' scene is followed by the last of the Partridge scenes. As the 'radio studio' is cleared away, Partridge is discovered at his desk. His opening comments re-establish his narrative function:

ED PARTRIDGE
Yes? (Looks up at audience from his desk) Say, didn't we meet ... at a railway

station, 1905 ... I was on my way to Winnipeg ... that's right, that's right. I
was just doing some reading and writing, I'm writing a book. Excuse me, I was in
the middle of a sentence when you dropped in ... [29]

This deictic technique gives the scene a quality of documentary realism,
functioning much as it does in *The Farm Show*; the difference here of course is
that the speech is invented. The dramatic fiction of the first act has given way to
a documentary style which tends to reduce the distinctions between actuality,
didacticism, and invention in the play.

In this speech, Partridge alludes to his retirement from the Grain Growers'
Grain Company, and describes his vision of 'Coalsamao,' a 'separate Co-
operative Western State.' He concludes the monologue with a reading of a
doggerel parable, written by a contributor to his book, about 'a Neolithic
man/An enterprising wight' whose prophecies of future civilization meet with
scorn from his peers. At the end of the verse, Partridge excuses himself and
returns to his work as the rest of the cast eulogize him in a sentimental song
taken from the original.

The emotionalism of the Partridge scene is followed by a quick change of
mood. Partridge is replaced on stage by 'Farmer Leo,' a knee-slapping cynic who
scoffs at the idea of a Wheat Pool. The year is 1924, and the Pool needs to sign up
50 per cent of the seeded land in Saskatchewan. As Leo pours doubt on the
undertaking, the actors perform a series of quick sketches, taken from the
original, which purport to show various humorous subterfuges used to enlist
farmers. These vignettes are delivered as quick intervals in a fiddle reel.
Typically, a woman bribes a farmer with a piece of chocolate cake, and a
seamstress promises to raise hemlines if the men sign up for the Pool. As each
device brings in more signatures, Leo's scoffing turns to guarded, and then
enthusiastic, endorsement. Finally, the Pool needs one more signature – his –
and its success is announced in a 'co-op quickie,' in which two actors, each with
one shoe, try to tap-dance and succeed only when they join together.

In the original version, these vignettes are connected by the character of
Aaron Sapiro in a simple counterpoint structure. Sprung's version of the scene
is more sophisticated in its theatrical structure than the original. By framing it
with a humorous skeptic, containing it in a musical structure, and reinforcing
the humour of the vignettes with exaggerated performances (Leo is played by a
woman; the seamstress by a man). Sprung transformed the simple didacticism
of the original into a celebratory retelling of the event. Ironically, as the scene
gained in theatricality, it lost in information. In the original, Sapiro connects
the vignettes with quoted excerpts from his writings on co-operative marketing.
The fact that Sprung's version seems more effective supports the argument that

in *Paper Wheat* the telling of the story is more important than its actual details.

The final three scenes of the act bring the historical record up to date. The first of these, following the 'Leo' scene, fills in the Depression years. An 'entertainer' opens the scene with a feeble joke about drought, and gives the platform to the fiery co-op organizer, Louise Lucas. She is not mentioned in the original version; here she is included as a representative figure of an important period in Saskatchewan's history, and, it would seem, as a militant woman to counterbalance Ed Partridge. Her speech, although lengthy, is included not for its information, but for its emotional appeal. She condemns the iniquity of the Depression and makes an urgent plea for a co-operative future.

This is the signal for the play to move into the present. From Lucas to the present day is a leap of almost fifty years, but from this point the act abandons its chronological structure. The loud chords of a 1960s rock band announce the shift with a song that answers Lucas with a modern point of view:

> Saskatchewan is really getting to me.
> Take me Big City, I want to be free.
> Gimme, gimme lots of Free Enterprise
> I've had it up to here with socialist lies.
> Now don't tell me I'm trying too hard
> The only Pool I want is in my backyard. (70)

It is in the subsequent scene that the differences between Tahn and Sprung are most obvious. Sprung devised the 'Togetherness' scene to comment on the political economy of the grain market; when Tahn re-edited the text for the Western Producer edition, he revised the scene substantially to remove what he called 'this political crap.' In Sprung's version, the scene opens with a satiric reference to the loyalty the co-ops command in Saskatchewan. A 'typical' family sits down to supper:

MA
Have some co-op milk, Louie.
LOUIE
Oh, Ma!
MA
Pass the co-op pickles, Fred.
DAD
Wait just a co-op minute ...
MA
Are we going to Arizona this winter, dear?[30]

The conversation establishes the fact of material prosperity, and introduces four contrasting attitudes towards the co-op movement. The first is a short statement from Dad, who complains that co-ops have an unfair business advantage. Ma answers him with a long parable about a pig farmer caught in 'the big Cost-Price Squeeze' when 'Mr Con Glomert' manipulates the market. The third perspective is supplied by Mr Otto Gill – a thinly veiled reference to Cargill – who enters the scene and delivers an actual speech defending private enterprise in the grain trade. Finally, Louie supports his mother's point of view with his juggling act. The scene as a whole attempts to provide a balanced picture; it shows what the co-ops have become but does not explain how this state of affairs came to be. Although the scene is weighted in favour of the left-wing argument, it does not answer the specific critique of the co-ops raised by Dad and Otto Gill. The prosperity of the family testifies to the historical success of the co-op movement, but at the same time it suggests that the co-ops have served their purpose. Having raised the issue, the scene lets it rest as an unresolved contradiction.

In his later revision of the scene, Tahn eliminated the Con Glomert and Otto Gill sections and inserted three short speeches, given to Sis and Ma, which summarize the changes in the co-op movement. To Tahn's mind, this resulted in a more objective scene: the co-op is still the favoured choice, but its practices are criticized. The scene mentions, for example, that the co-op's peas 'are Libby's rejects with a co-op lable slapped on them.' On balance, Tahn's version benefits from the absence of the Con Glomert story and suffers from the loss of the authenticity of Otto Gill, but its final effect is similar to that of Sprung's version. The problem is described but not analysed. In both versions the scene is followed by the nostalgic sentiment of the 'Old Folk' scene from the original.

In the final analysis, Sprung's revision of *Paper Wheat* is, like the original, a celebration of a heroic movement. By clarifying the historical account, drawing out the dramatic fable and stressing the ensemble performance style, Sprung gave the play the context it needed to speak to audiences outside Saskatchewan. Although Martin Knelman, reviewing the show for *Saturday Night*, criticized it for 'waving the flag of regional chauvinism,' critical response across Canada was invariably enthusiastic.[31] Even Quebec's left-wing theatre journal, *Jeu*, responded with grudging admiration:

Donc, le show est bien fait, bien pensé mais trop bien huilé et on sort de là en se disant que s'ils ont trouvé un nouveau pays, nous autres, ici, les Québécois, on n'en fait sûrement pas partie. (Mais ça c'est pas grave, c'est le but de show.) C'est très Canadian, if you know what I mean.[32]

Paper Wheat is commonly seen as a triumph of regional culture in Canada, but significantly, regional sentiment is only partially responsible for its appeal. Compared to *No. 1 Hard*, which is premised on an analysis understandable only to its regional audience, *Paper Wheat* appeals to a broader romantic sentiment. In the body of Canadian documentary theatre, it is an anomaly: it is the least documentary of the plays in this study, but, along with *Ten Lost Years*, the most successful. Like *Ten Lost Years* it is a nostalgic hymn to the past, but in *Paper Wheat* fact and fiction flow into each other to define a heroic myth.

5

The Political Documentary:
Buchans: A Mining Town

In 1974, the Mummers Troupe of Newfoundland introduced a new element into the form of community documentary pioneered by Paul Thompson. Under the direction of Chris Brookes, the Mummers lived for eight weeks in a bunkhouse in the central Newfoundland mining town of Buchans, where they created a documentary at the invitation of the local union of the United Steelworkers of America. Like *The Farm Show*, *Buchans: A Mining Town* is a collectively created compilation of oral history and folklore which incorporates the process of research into the performance text. Because of this basic similarity of the two, critics have tended to overlook the significance of *Buchans* in the development of Canadian theatre. When Brookes took the show, under the title *Company Town*, to Toronto in 1975, Urjo Kareda, reviewing it for the *Toronto Star*, dismissed it with the comment that '*Company Town* seems built to a documentary drama formula, and the exercise now seems tired and stiff.'[1]

Although it may appear to conform to a Passe Muraille 'formula,' *Buchans* embodies radically different assumptions regarding the nature and purpose of documentary. Like Thompson, Brookes was impelled by a nationalist commitment to indigenous theatre, but his nationalism was directed to Newfoundland, not Canada, and it was combined with a militant socialist ideology. *Buchans* is more than a portrait of a community: it is a partisan documentary of a controversial labour conflict, devised as a tool of community animation. In it Brookes developed a form of political theatre unique in English Canada, and clarified the techniques that would earn the Mummers Troupe a reputation as Canada's most radical theatre. As the text of *Buchans* has not been published, this discussion will outline those techniques through a close examination of the process by which the play was created and a detailed description of the performance as it was seen by its target audience in Buchans.

The unique features of *Buchans* grew out of two related features of the

Mummers Troupe's early development. The first of these concerns the influence of agitprop and traditional folk theatre on Brookes's theatrical aesthetic, and the second has to do with his attempt to reconcile his commitment to an artistic collective with the problems of establishing professional theatre in Newfoundland.

The work of the Mummers Troupe for the most part is the work of its founder Chris Brookes, who gave it its characteristic style, hired the actors, and in the main selected the projects it undertook. A native of Newfoundland, Brookes had studied at the Yale School of Drama, following an undergraduate degree in engineering, and had worked with John Juliani's experimental theatre at Simon Fraser University. After a year in Toronto's fledgling alternative theatre scene, Brookes made his way to Newfoundland in 1972 with his partner Lynn Lunde by performing Punch and Judy puppet shows on university campuses.

Like the early Passe Muraille, Brookes had been influenced by the contemporary radical American theatre; in St John's he and Lunde decided to form a 'street theatre' that would be 'highly eclectic in style, able to work, indoors or outdoors, as flexible and mobile as possible.'[2] With this in mind, Brookes established a non-profit corporation with himself, Lunde, and John Doyle as principal officers. Known as Resource Foundation of the Arts, it remained the legal parent of the Mummers Troupe until 1979.

The new troupe's first venture into political theatre was a hastily improvised puppet show called *The Coronation of Cecil B. DeMille*, produced in support of striking cinema projectionists. Performed in a shopping mall, it was, according to Brookes, a failure: 'Passers-by thought we were just another bunch of hippies doing silly street theatre. They were right.'[3]

The troupe's evolution from 'a bunch of hippies' to Newfoundland's principal theatre began later in 1972 when Brookes, Lunde, and Doyle revived the traditional Newfoundland Christmas play of St George, which had died out in the early years of this century. Newfoundland was the only part of Canada where the ancient British mummers play has been known to be performed, and its combination of ritual (the combat of St George and the Turkish Knight embodies an ancient winter solstice ceremony of resurrection) and antic theatricality appealed to Brookes's delight in popular theatre forms. Brookes revived both the play and its traditional manner of presentation, travelling through the streets and dropping in unannounced at parties in private homes over the Christmas season. It was after this revival that the company began calling itself the Mummers Troupe. The annual mummers play became a constant in the work of the troupe, and it brought Brookes much favourable publicity in a society proud of its folk traditions.

Although the mummers play had died out in living memory, it was only one aspect of mummering (as mumming was known in Newfoundland). In its more common form, mummering consisted of house visiting in disguise over the twelve days of Christmas, similar to the Hallowe'en traditions of the mainland. Although more widespread than the mummers play, the house-visiting tradition too has died out in many parts of the province. In an unpublished paper on the history of popular theatre in Newfoundland, Brookes argues that mummering provided a cultural precedent for socially active theatre in the province. Mummering was technically illegal, having been banned in the nineteenth century because of occasional violence. In reviving the mummers play, Brookes maintained that he was rehabilitating a popular tradition that had been suppressed for political reasons:

[As] they marched from house to house, the mummers were considered to have the power to commit gross breaches of social decorum and to wreak retribution against persons who had over the year incurred the wrath of the community.[4]

The original mummers, according to Brookes, exemplified a 'degree of anarchic socialism,' with bands of working-class mummers threatening the property of the mercantile class that dominated Newfoundland's economy for most of its history. In his analysis, mummering 'nourished a collective class consciousness' until the government outlawed the practice in 1861.

For Brookes, the mummers play was a touchstone to Newfoundland's cultural past, and a reminder of the ritualistic origins of theatre. In this he found a lesson for modern political theatre:

Any political theatre which intends to really move its audience (I am referring to activism, not emotionalism), over the long term and on a wide social level, must find a language not just of issues and ideology, but of ritual and ceremony rooted in a sense of collective belief beyond language, integrating the lives of the spectators through traditionally symbolic performance invoking a mass for secular salvation.[5]

Whether Brookes succeeded in finding this 'language of ritual' is a moot question. In less abstract terms, the influence of the mummers play on his theatrical technique is clear. The annual productions of the mummers play reveal Brookes's basic theatrical principles: an apparent disregard of formal staging; a boisterous improvisational humour; and a serious attempt to create an 'event' with an audience. The mummers play demanded a presentational acting style that would enable the actors to enter any space and use it to their advantage. The troupe would travel the streets of St John's during the twelve days of Christmas and drop in unannounced on parties according to the traditional custom. They also performed in public places, including ships in the harbour, city buses, and, on one notable occasion, on the baggage carousel at the St John's airport. The impromptu humour and ribald clowning that emerged in these performances developed as integral features of Brookes's later work.

It was Brookes's belief that, with its commitments to traditional culture and political activism, the Mummers Troupe could evolve as Newfoundland's authentic 'regional' theatre. Unlike the other Canadian provinces, Newfoundland lacked an established theatre company subsidized by the Canada Council. By 1974, the Mummers Troupe was one of three professional theatres in the province; the others were Codco, a comedy troupe (which had been formed in Toronto at the suggestion of Paul Thompson), and the Newfoundland Travelling Theatre, which toured plays from the international repertoire around Newfoundland with university actors. An indication of the prevailing attitude towards indigenous theatre in Newfoundland can be found in a 1973 report to the Canada Council, in which Dudley Cox, director of the Newfoundland Travelling Theatre, recommended a merger of the three companies:

I suggest that if one-third of Newfoundland Theatre is presenting a carefully-conceived, adventurously and skilfully played theatre programme to schools, and the remaining two-thirds of the company is engaged in producing traditional proscenium theatre, with a cautious leaning towards indigenous works, then here is the way to begin professional theatre in Newfoundland.[6]

This recommendation was endorsed in May 1974 by Keith Turnbull, who had been commissioned by the Canada Council to report on the situation of Newfoundland theatre.[7] By that time, the Mummers Troupe had already completed its first year of work and was preparing for the trip to Buchans.

Brookes's aspirations to professional status for his troupe were frustrated by the hostility he provoked in the provincial government, which for most of the troupe's life refused to provide funding. (Prior to 1975, the Mummers subsisted on occasional project funding and Brookes's salary as artist-in-residence with Memorial University's Arts Extension program.) The popular image of the Mummers Troupe can be seen in a report to the Canada Council which describes its work as 'anarchist ... agitprop political warfare type productions.'[8] In the years following the success of *Buchans*, the Canada Council would become the troupe's major patron, despite one official's judgment that Brookes's theatre was 'political rather than creative.'[9]

Brookes's difficulties in securing the funding to support a full-time company were compounded by his difficulties in finding trained actors who shared his commitment to political theatre. For most of the company's life, St John's was too small a city to support a community of professional actors, and because the troupe did not have continuing financial support, Brookes could not afford to hire a full-time ensemble. For the first three years casts were hired on a per show basis, until in 1975 Brookes initiated a 'core group' policy which put a small number of actors on a full-time payroll. After 1975, the problems of keeping an ensemble together were made more difficult by Brookes's decision to hire Newfoundlanders almost exclusively. Few Newfoundlanders had professional training and, in consequence, Brookes found himself relying on a small pool of actors who came to consider themselves charter members of a true collective.

Despite his ideological commitment to a collective structure, Brookes was unwilling to surrender his proprietary control of the troupe. In 1976, cast members of (*What's That Got to Do with*) *The Price of Fish* presented Brookes with a manifesto in which they declared their reasons for leaving the troupe: 'We cannot condemn the evils of capitalism and then find ourselves working under a capitalist structure.'[10] The manifesto argued that members of the troupe had been deceived into thinking themselves part of a genuine collective:

Now we, as workers, feel cheated and deceived. Each of us has contributed significantly to the growth and reputation of the Mummers' [*sic*] Troupe but we worked under a false premise, the premise that we all owned the company, which we do morally, but unfortunately legally it lies in the hands of Resource Foundation for the Arts.

Brookes for his part tried to create a structure that permitted 'participational democracy' while maintaining institutional stability. From 1975, when the cast of *Buchans* first challenged Brookes's control of the troupe, to its final days, the history of the company was a complex process of redefinition complicated by personal arguments. Reflecting on the issue after the company's demise, Brookes wrote:

Perhaps if the Mummers Troupe had begun in 1972 as a permanent collective it would have developed a more collective sense of responsibility. As it was, by 1976 it was a product of its own evolution: Lynn and I had carried the company on our backs for four years, and the tree had grown as the twig was bent. It was difficult for new members to appreciate past company lessons without having experienced them first-hand, and Lynn and I were loathe to repeat already-learned mistakes time and again with each new production and each change in the collective status quo.[11]

In the end, this organizational conflict led to two crises from which the

Mummers Troupe never recovered. In 1978, a group of 'core' actors left the company in the wake of an acrimonious dispute over Brookes's management and formed Rising Tide Theatre, which eventually emerged as the principal theatre in St John's, with the blessing of the provincial government. In 1979, controversies over Brookes's management of Resource Foundation for the Arts, which by that time had acquired a theatre in a converted union hall, forced a separation of the Mummers Troupe from its parent foundation. In the division of spoils, Brookes kept legal title to the Mummers Troupe, and a publicly elected board of artists assumed control of Resource Foundation and its assets.

These conflicts had their origin in Brookes's inability to create an administrative structure that could give the company stability and at the same time allow it the freedom to create its productions as immediate responses to political events. It is a measure of Brookes's accomplishment that, despite this failure and the obstacles of insufficient funding, internal strife, and a high turnover of actors, he was able to refine his techniques of political documentary in a series of productions that remain unique in Canadian theatre.

Brookes's first successful venture into popular theatre was a history show variously called *Newfoundland Night, Cod on a Stick, Newfoundland Dress-up*, and *Regular Weekly Entertainment*. It was conceived as a popular history of the province along the model of Léandre Bergeron's radical *Petit Manuel d'histoire du Québec*. Created collectively, the show toured Newfoundland in the summer of 1973 on a grant from the Canada Council's Explorations program.

Newfoundland Night is a satiric revue which presents the highlights of the province's history from a populist, anti-capitalist perspective. Its politics are simple: each episode demonstrates how once again the rights of the working class and the Newfoundlanders' dreams of independence are suppressed by the merchant class which supports the crown. The various episodes are given continuity by a narrator. The performance structure of *Newfoundland Night* introduces the techniques that would become instrumental in Brookes's later work; it combines documentary evidence with puppetry, stand-up comedy, mime, and lampoon. In his later productions these elements would be applied to more specific purposes but they are already evident here in rough.

Newfoundland Night's assault on the orthodox versions of the province's history begins with a comic scene in which John Cabot and his son discover the island while seeking 'cheap pizza spice.' The humour is crude, relying heavily on puns and topical references. As a parody of conventional teachings, the play contains little in the way of information. Its importance is to be found not in the text itself, but in the performance it documents. Brookes has written that, while touring the show around the south coast of Newfoundland by boat, 'it occurred to me that the usefulness of the tour lay not just in bringing to people a show about their own history. It was important that we came at all.'[12]

Although the play is mostly satirical, it also contains Brookes's first tentative uses of documentary material. The episodes outlining the genocide of the Beothuks, the rise of William Coaker's Fishermen's Protective Union, and the great sealing disaster of 1914 juxtapose authentic documents (letters, newspaper reports, and speeches), direct narration, and non-realistic staging which conveys meaning through choreography and mood. At this point in Brookes's development, the influence of the confrontational radical theatre of the 1960s was still in evidence. He was just beginning to find his own theatrical style.

The theatrical techniques of *Newfoundland Night* also contain clear references to Thompson's work at Passe Muraille. Brookes had seen *The Farm Show* and *1837: The Farmers' Revolt* in Toronto the previous winter, and both plays are quoted in *Newfoundland Night*. The 'Bond Head' metaphor from *1837*, in which the actors form a giant face as a visual pun on the name of the governor who provoked the rebellion, becomes a fishing admiral in Brookes's play, and the 'tractor pull' from *The Farm Show* reappears as an engine pull between 'the Coaker six horsepower make and break engine,' representing the union, and the 'Water Street combination' engine, representing the St John's merchants.

The inclusion of documentary material suggested to Brookes a technique of ironic montage that would later emerge as a major principle in *Buchans*. The opening of *Newfoundland Night* provides an example. In a dig at the provincial Arts and Culture Centre, which prefaced its performances with the 'Ode to Newfoundland,' Brookes began the show with a recording of the anthem as performed by the university choir. Between the lines of the song he spliced the recorded voice of an old fisherman, who describes the oppressive poverty of the traditional credit economy that kept fishermen in perpetual debt to the merchants. His voice interrupts the anthem eight times, so that the music becomes an ironic motif to a bitter indictment:

SAM
... And we damn near starved that winter.
[CHOIR]
God guard Thee ...
SAM
We never had a thing.
[CHOIR]
God guard Thee ...
SAM

They treated the fishermen, those merchants, something like Hitler treated the
Jews!
[CHOIR]
God guard Thee
Newfoundland![13]

In *Newfoundland Night*, documentary fact is merely a means of introducing a polemic. As Brookes later wrote, 'Stage images stay with an audience
long after individual lines of dialogue have been forgotten, and I wanted our
symbols to suggest a way of seeing the historical material.'[14] The use of documentary material in the play is one technique of revising history. It has no
substantial value of its own, and its authenticity is announced rather than
demonstrated.

While touring the play around Newfoundland's west coast, the Mummers
found themselves in the small outport of Sally's Cove, shortly before the final
ceremony that would incorporate the village, along with five others, in the
newly established Gros Morne National Park. The protocol agreed upon by the
federal and provincial governments called for the gradual relocation of the
communities.

The Mummers' arrival on the scene was opportune, for Brookes had
proceeded with the *Newfoundland Night* tour in the hope that just such a
situation might present itself. The Sally's Cove situation made an agitprop
intervention not only possible, but practical. When the troupe arrived, the
villagers were already organizing a protest, and they welcomed the assistance of
the actors. In their attempt to provide 'useful theatre' for the community, the
Mummers found themselves inventing a documentary form by necessity. *Gros
Mourn* (the title is an obvious pun on the park's name) was put together in less
than two weeks, and as Brookes's published diary of the process reveals, there
was little time for theoretical and formal exploration. In its style, *Gros Mourn*
derives directly from *Newfoundland Night*. It used the same set (a scaffold),
and the satiric tone is essentially the same. Unlike *Newfoundland Night*, which
parodies received teachings of history, *Gros Mourn* reflects upon an immediate
and material issue. It was made with the specific needs of the local audience in
mind. As Brookes has written in his article on the play:

[This] sort of theatre should not be interpreted simply as political 'outside agitation.' It is
mirror-oriented, along a certain axis of course, but not necessarily designed to rouse the
community to action ... The political aspects of the piece were not so much a result of the
process (of involvement with the community) as of our being there at a time of crisis for
these people.[15]

This identification with a community in struggle is the key to *Gros Mourn*. It was plannned from the beginning as a partisan intervention. In his diary of the process, Brookes noted that 'the government's view is adequately published; our show will need to deal with the people's view of their future.'[16] The actors found themselves accepted by the community, but their intervention created expectations. Brookes refers to an old couple 'who are militant about their situation but think that we should have the answer to their problems.'[17] By intervening in the community, the Mummers implicitly promised expertise and support that they were in the end unable to deliver. In later projects, Brookes would work closely with a local activist group committed to an ongoing program. In Sally's Cove, however, there was no such organization; there were merely the determined efforts of a few citizens who welcomed any help that was offered.

The Mummers approached the Sally's Cove problem emotionally rather than critically. *Gros Mourn* relies heavily on satire and sentimentality to build its case, with no pretense of objective analysis. The play offers the villagers' subjective perceptions of the issue. The first performance in Sally's Cove, according to Brookes, was like 'an act of love.'[18]

Considered as a partisan intervention in a political conflict, *Gros Mourn* may be understood as a play of signs and signifiers. The principal iconographic sign is the set itself, consisting of the scaffold and a Gros Morne Park banner with its emblem of an arctic hare. The outline of the hare's head is cut into a flap, so that an actor's head might appear in its place. Costumes, as in *Newfoundland Night*, consisted of regular clothing (Tee-shirts and jeans), with indicative props (such as a mortarboard to signify a pedantic professor).

Other signs include visual and verbal puns, announced headlines, and sound effects. The 'animated Gros Morne News' is typical. Derived from the techniques of 1930s agitprop, the animated newspaper consists of a large representative 'page' with hidden holes through which the actors stick their heads to deliver announcements.

The most complex signs extend into dramatic gestures, as in the two recurring 'vaudeville' routines. The first introduces 'Freddy Federal' and 'Percy Provincial,' who appear like human puppets, announcing their presence with children's noisemakers. Their routine parodies the style of CBC news broadcasts:

FREDDY
Good evening, I am Freddy Federal.
PERCY
And I am Percy Provincial.
FREDDY

And tonight we have some good news and we have some bad news. But first the good news.

PERCY

People of Sally's Cove, there has been a change in government policy. You don't have to move. And now the bad news.

FREDDY

Your children do.[19]

In the second routine, two Newfoundland politicians are portrayed in the manner of a minstrel show:

MAYNARD

Mr Doody, Mr Doody, I wonder if you could tell me who was that cute bunny I saw you out with last night.

DOODY

Why, Mr Maynard, that was no bunny that was my arctic hare. (Forced laughter ...)[20]

Both of these routines are best understood as gestures that give theatrical form to satiric comment. Their value lies not in the quality of the performance, but in the audacity of their conception. The Doody-Maynard scenes mark the first time that living Newfoundland politicians had been attacked on the stage. It was a radical step for Brookes to present them as a pair of low (and humourless) comedians. It was this, along with a savage caricature of federal cabinet minister Jean Chrétien, that gave the Mummers a reputation as trouble-makers and agitators. Press coverage of the citizens' demonstration at the park's signing ceremony, at which Chrétien was present, blamed the troupe for leading a 'mob' in 'booing sessions.'[21]

The polemical structure of *Gros Mourn* depends on emblematic illustration, with the actors addressing the audience directly. The theatrical signs and gestures provide the real argument, which is verified by documentary material in the form of found dialogue and short monologues. The actors in *Gros Mourn* play themselves, and the performance is informal. The fact of the performance, with its implicit message that the crisis in Sally's Cove merits the attention of artists, is its substantive value. This is evident in Brookes's description of the discussion which followed the first performance:

Eventually most of the discussion adjourns to the bar, retelling the show's jokes and images. Do I imagine that there is a pride in all this talk, a pride that they and their community have been the fabric of a good piece of theatre?[22]

Later, after the park demonstration, Brookes noted that 'our show has crystalized a terminology for many of the demonstrators. They use metaphors drawn from the play's imagery as they present their case.'[23]

For Brookes, *Gros Mourn* demonstrated the effectiveness of documentary as an animation technique. For the most part, actuality in *Gros Mourn* is either narrated or presented as a theatrical gesture. Found material is placed within theatrical quotation marks, such as the animated newspaper. Although Brookes had equipped the actors with tape recorders, 'because it may be important to remember precisely how people speak with us,' the actual words of the community are included only to verify the argument advanced through the montage.[24] The performance of the documentary material identifies the actors with the community. In the following year, in Buchans, that identification would become the starting point of the play itself. Judged by its theatrical techniques, *Gros Mourn* is not the mirror that Brookes had in mind. Rather, it is a reduction of the issue. The brief process of creation did not allow the troupe sufficient time to discover the form of the play in the specific culture of the community it documents.

Gros Mourn was a landmark in Canadian political theatre, but it was more significant to the later development of the Mummers Troupe than it was to Sally's Cove. For Brookes, the experience proved that theatre could be used as a vehicle of political action, and the angry response it earned from the government funding agencies demonstrated clearly the problems of trying to create political art in a system that depends on government subsidies – problems neither the Mummers nor the arts councils would ever resolve to mutual satisfaction. *Gros Mourn* was for Brookes an object lesson in the delicacies of press coverage and publicity, in theatrical technique, and in the methodology of intervention theatre.

BUCHANS: A MINING TOWN – THE PROCESS

While touring *Newfoundland Night* in 1973, the Mummers arrived in the mining town of Buchans near the end of a bitter six-month strike. After talking to the striking miners, Brookes resolved to return after the tour was completed to create a picket-line agitprop. In the end, because of the Sally's Cove experience, Brookes postponed the Buchans project until the following summer. Instead of an agitprop, he decided to create a full-length documentary on the community.

Located in the geographic centre of Newfoundland, Buchans is an anomaly in the province in being one of the few communities removed from the ocean. Founded in 1926, the town was completely owned by the American Smelting and Refining Company (ASARCO). Most of the workers and their families lived in company-owned housing, although a minority owned their own homes in an adjoining townsite. For most of its history, Buchans had been free of labour strife, but in 1971, the union, Local 5457 of the United Steelworkers of America, called a strike over wages that lasted five months. Technically, the strike was a success, and the union won a modest increase. But two years later it rejected a further wage offer and called another strike. This one would last six months. Behind the matter of wages there lay a more serious problem. By 1973, Buchans's deposits of copper, lead, and zinc were close to depletion, and the continued survival of the community was in question. That uncertainty underlay the labour situation.

Brookes returned to Buchans in July 1974, with a cast of six actors that included Allen Booth, Donna Butt, Lee J. Campbell, Howard Cooper, Bembo Davies, and Connie Kaldor. Of the cast, only Brookes and Butt were Newfoundlanders; Brookes had hired the rest of the group in Toronto. They were paid a salary of sixty-five dollars per week each, out of which they had to pay the cost of room and board in the ASARCO bunkhouse.

The preponderance of mainlanders in the cast introduced a complexity into the process of making the play. Buchans, with a population of 2,000, was considerably larger than Sally's Cove; mainland accents would be noticed immediately. The cast would have to struggle to win the confidence of the community. Brookes saw this as a potential advantage:

I thought we could make our outside-ness work for us. I wanted to grasp this built-in situational alienation and make it work, not negatively but positively, in the Brechtian sense. We had the chance which would not [sic] suck Buchaneers into identifying with the performers, but which would allow them to analyse, from a distance, what we were saying about their community. It would be their show, not ours. [25]

This theoretical alienation did not offer a solution to the problem of accents. In a letter written the following year, Brookes made the point that 'an acted accent is usually noticeable ... one unavoidably makes a statement to some extent by *being* a white man *acting* the part of the Indian.' [26] In Newfoundland, more than any other part of English-speaking Canada, a person's accent is an emblem of belonging. In the end, the actors successfully imitated the accent, if not well enough to disguise their origin, then at least well enough to reduce the importance of the issue.

When the company arrived in Buchans, it was without a clear sense of what the play would be. Prior to their arrival, Brookes had defined four basic principles to guide them through the process. The actors would rely wholly on tape-recorded interviews with townspeople: 'Where invention was necessary, we would adopt a more obvious presentational style of performance so that the audience would know that we were inventing on our terms, not theirs.'[27] Secondly, the play would be a people's history, 'as much a history of union sensibilities as of the community.' Thirdly (and least defined), 'we would be careful of our impact on the community.' Finally, the actors would live in 'total immersion.' It was for this reason that Brookes arranged with ASARCO for the cast to live in the company bunkhouse. The mine management also agreed to allow the actors to accompany underground work shifts for research.

For the actors to create a 'people's history,' they had to become, in a very short time, experts on the history, sociology, and industry of Buchans, and they had to find, at the same time, a theatrical form to express that expertise. Even as they put the play together, the cast had to explore and experiment with dramaturgical techniques that would permit them to express, and on a deeper level to formulate, what the play would say. They had to learn to perceive the life of Buchans from the point of view of the residents, and, in the process, abandon their own misconceptions. As with accents, 'outside-ness' was a liability; just as the mainlanders in the cast had to adjust to the realities of Newfoundland, the cast as a whole had to overcome their preconceptions about industrial labour. An ingenuous entry in Brookes's rehearsal diary offers a case in point: 'Went through the mill today – it's like *Modern Times*. Rube Goldberg mechanical all over. Funny little machines for measuring out chemicals.'[28]

As the actors began to learn the basic facts of the community, they also learned to work together. The actors had been hired on the basis of their abilities and appearances, rather than their political attitudes, and consequently there was no ideological consensus within the group. Brookes worried about the problems of finding a 'group language,' and he worried about the actors' class attitudes. To the actors, Brookes's political purpose was never in doubt, but the lack of political unity in the group manifested itself in the end in a general statement of pro-union sentiment.

Buchans is on the whole an effective and unified play, but it overlooks or sidesteps issues crucial to its argument because of the lack of consensus. It is political in its general scheme, but cautious in its specifics. Controversial issues, especially those that question the union's actions, are ignored. Union sponsorship brought with it an implicit censorship. More comfortable with emotion than analysis, the actors naturally tended towards the kind of realism that Brookes had hoped to avoid:

We must *never* improvise scenes where we pretend to be Buchaneers. Only scenes which *clearly* are our own expressionistic comments as *actors* on Buchans. We must not take their lives away from them, give them mainland accents and graceful movements – and actions more dramatic – because their's are not good enough for our stage.[29]

Yet, this is exactly what happened in *Buchans*. The play works best when the actors authenticate the documentary material with realistic representations of familiar and typical characters, although there is no attempt to impose plot or dramatic action on these characterizations.

In *Gros Mourn* the actors admitted their status as outsiders in the performance because of their overt intervention in a political crisis. This time, however, that approach could not work. Despite Brookes's desire for 'alienation,' it would contradict the very nature of the community documentary. To distill a portrait of the community from their experience, the actors had to achieve an accurate quality of direct imitation. The validity of the performance would rest upon a portrayal that would convince the persons portrayed. By necessity and training both, the actors approached their subjects realistically, and because the process required that they experience, however briefly, the living conditions of the community, they soon developed an emotional sympathy for the people they were documenting. Because of this sympathy, there is little in the way of 'expressionistic comment' in *Buchans*. The implicit self-censorship of the process and the lack of political consensus resulted in a performance that was necessarily sentimental in its appeal.

Their immersion in the life of the community gave the actors material for improvised scenes with typical characters. These scenes serve as frames that provide context and continuity to the monologues that are the meat of the play. The show required that each actor represent numerous characters, some but not all of whom would be identifiable to the audience because of their speeches. Only rarely do the actors imitate a recognizable personality. The natural tendency towards realism and the need for a coherent structure resulted in scenes of 'typical' dialogue and banter which gives *Buchans* a performance continuity. In effect, the actors take on the roles of typical Buchaneers who re-enact the history of their town. These roles are not as defined as they are in *Ten Lost Years*, but as in that play, the range of personalities in the cast suggests a typical cross-section of the union membership.

As the actors began to make contacts in Buchans, as they began to isolate particular aspects of life in the community, their uncertainty about the structure of the play became an obvious problem. Throughout the process, Brookes kept a diary, which would later form the basis of his memoir of the Mummers' history. Two weeks after arriving in Buchans, he noted in it:

Several good ideas this week for the pre-1914 period. 30s movie scene, square dance factory process

The group finds visual imagery – the handling of visual material – difficult. I think that the group is lost as per dealing with the overall material – we're at that fuzzy point where I think we must (I must?) structure part of the stuff to give us a base, a see-how-it-can-be-done demonstration, and get at least part of our material safely tucked away out of our overloaded minds.[30]

But if the play was to be a true 'people's history,' it could not be formed on first impressions. A governing structure was required to focus the research. As Brookes's diary shows, by the end of the first two weeks the structure was apprehended only in vague chronological terms. The compression of research and rehearsal time meant that the structure of the play would have to take form even as the actors were sorting out their first impressions of the community.

The actors would spend the mornings and evenings researching, which usually entailed conversing with various townsfolk and transcribing taped conversations. They would meet in the afternoons in the school gymnasium that served as rehearsal hall to share what they found and to try out scene ideas. If an idea seemed workable, it would be put aside until there were enough scenes and ideas to suggest a solution to a particular segment of the play.

The use of a chronological structure gave the actors a beginning point in rehearsal, but it also presented a new problem. Some chapters in the town's history were either more colourful or better documented than others, and some of the major areas of attention (such as the experience and culture of working underground) were essentially ahistoric. It was obvious that the play would have to move both chronologically and thematically. The descriptions of the various aspects of life in Buchans had to be integrated into an historical structure, although the actors' experience of these aspects was obviously contemporary. The dramaturgical problem, then, was to find in each period the typifying factor that would advance the overall thesis of the show. Certain periods suggested suitable choices, such as the harsh living conditions of the Depression years, or the first expressions of labour unrest in the 1940s. When the actors could not find a representative story or incident for a period, they would use that segment of the historical overview to describe an aspect of community or working life. Consequently the play does not always follow a logical progression. There is no logical reason, for example, why the sequence on women and domestic life should fall into the 1950s segment.

At the end of the fourth week, Brookes noted:

By now we have accumulated masses of material and individual scenes but have not yet edited or structured long sequences. I sensed that we had a 'handle' on the show, but some of cast were losing faith, unsure whether any structure is possible from the material

... There was a showdown over working methods, the question of improvisations. The sequences must be made 'more dramatic,' some said, and more character invention would help.[31]

The compromise that emerged from this showdown was a modification of Brookes's initial idea. The actors' comments on the material would be presented 'through the staging (with puppets, etc.) and simply by the editing process itself.' In practice even this solution was modified. In the end the play would comment on the material through Brookes's typical theatrical gestures, as in *Gros Mourn*, and through realistic character improvisation.

Brookes's tendency to conceive scenes as theatrical metaphors appears to have met with resistance from the cast. This conflict suggests one of Brookes's major limitations as a director. Despite his desire to produce a 'people's history,' his artistic response to the material was still coloured by his agitprop experience with its delight in broad gesture. After the troupe watched a softball game between teams from Buchans and Grand Falls, Brookes had an idea 'to structure the '73 strike as a union vs company softball game.'[32] The idea was never developed, but it was the kind of device that Brookes would later use more appropriately in his political revues.

The final structure of *Buchans* is a synthesis of Brookes's tendency to think in terms of issues and political relations, and the actors' inclination towards the representation of sympathetic personalities. As a result, the play operates on two levels of meaning: the meaning of each vignette and monologue, and the gradually developing ideology of the play as a whole. The specific thought in each vignette is attributed by the authenticity of the performance to the informant who supplied it, but its significance is made clear by the unfolding narrative of the play. It is in this unfolding that Brookes's sense of theatricality is crucial.

The theatrical devices in *Buchans* solve immediate problems in the play as well, especially by providing transitions from one unit to another. More importantly, they give the documentary its structural language. The worry, debate, and frustration of the process became a source of creative strength to the cast, and their growing commitment to the community resulted in a play of perhaps unexpected dramatic intelligence.

BUCHANS: A MINING TOWN – ANALYSIS

The text of *Buchans* exists in three versions: an audiotape and typescript of the first performance in Buchans on 30 August 1974; a videotape of a performance in Halifax in October 1974, and an audiotape dated 19 June 1975 of the revised version which played for two weeks at Toronto Workshop Productions under the title *Company Town*. In this discussion I will refer to the typescript of the original performance. The actors will be identified by their first names, as they are in the typescript.

In the original version of *Paper Wheat*, a prologue described the entire history of the world as a prelude to the grain co-op movement. That same progression from the general to the specific is found in *Buchans*, although on a less grandiose scale. Beginning with the discovery of ore deposits in 1926, the play recounts four decades of history, which culminate in the 1973 strike. That strike is identified as the summation of the community's history and a necessary precondition of its future. The history of the town is significant only in so far as it describes the evolution from mining camp to community, an evolution made possible by growing union militancy.

Buchans is a pro-union play but, despite Brookes's avowed socialism, it is not anti-capitalist. It condemns ASARCO while admitting that without the company there would be no community to celebrate. ASARCO is not personified in the play, and management personnel appear only briefly as witnesses in the 1973 strike sequence. Nowhere in the play do we hear the authentic voices of those who make the decisions. The play's perspective is essentially that of the union itself, to whom the company may be an oppressive but necessary fact of life.

The exclusion of the management voice was of course implicit in the troupe's identification of the union as the expression of the community. This does not mean, however, that *Buchans* casts ASARCO as a melodramatic villain. Rather, because the play attempts to document the workers' perceptions of their history, the company is depicted as an impersonal force. By describing the growth of union sentiment in the town, the play argues that only by challenging that force could the people of Buchans win acceptance as a community. The community is the collective hero of the play, but it is clear that it consists exclusively of the unionized workers and their families. In the end, *Buchans* defines community in terms of economic class rather than culture.

The emphasis on the subjective experience of the community is reinforced by the use of folklore and popular legends in the play. After listening to the stories of a retired trapper and guide named Charlie Perrier (who had guided the original ASARCO geologists), Allen Booth became, according to Brookes, 'fascinated with [Perrier's] idiosyncratic "d' you believe that?" which we thought made a nice leitmotif for an oral people's history.'[33] Two-thirds of the way through the process, Brookes noted in his diary, 'the idea of stories barging all through the play is heavy on my mind.'[34] In the folklore of tall tales, stories, and ballads, the actors found what amounted to a popular mythology of Buchans.

Significantly, *Buchans* begins with myth rather than sociology. Brookes imitates the sound of the mine's shift whistle with a penny whistle to signal the start of the performance. Allen Booth enters as Charlie Perrier, recounting a tall tale about the discovery of the ore deposits. This prologue establishes that the perspective of the play to follow is rooted in subjective experience:

> I have a very dangerous story to tell you. This story is so dangerous that I cannot even tell it. So I will tell you another story. This story is not so dangerous but it starts out the same way ... [35]

The story describes how as a young man, Charlie Perrier guided the American geologists to the site of the ore deposits. The first tests were negative. In order for the local men to keep their jobs, Charlie performs a 'magic trick,' shaving copper from the bottom of a kettle:

> I say, look now it's ore, on it. Well, the men they thought I was crazy, but I sent the powder to the company and three days later I got a special delivery letter from the company. 'You have found copper. Keep working!' Well now, we kept working and we worked all that winter and we work all that summer and we never lost our job. D'you believe that? (1)

This apocryphal introduction is immediately given a realistic context by the entrance of the next actor, Bembo Davies, who refutes the tall tale:

> When I came here there was only Lucky Strike, and the old mine down there, right down there below in the valley. And it was discovered apparently by an Indian, Matty Mitchell, a Micmac Indian, no true blood Indians in those days, only the Beothucks and they were killed off years and years before that. And he discovered it a long, long time before that.

Nowhere in the play is there a factual account of the discovery of the ore deposits and the founding of the town, athough that information could have easily been researched. The discovery of the mine is presented as pre-history. Actual details are of less importance than popular consciousness.

The 'D'you believe that?' motif draws our attention to the fact that these are living memories. It is used three times in the play: after a ghost story in act 1; after a rambling demonstration of the putative presence of alcohol in orange peels at the beginning of act 2; and again at the close of the play. After the final scene, Allen Booth re-enters as Charlie Perrier and ends the play with a reference to the prologue:

> Well now, we have told you a story. We could have told you a very dangerous
> story. You know that.   (53)

After the first performance, this last line was changed to 'D'you believe that?'

Throughout the play we are reminded that we are witnessing popular history in the making. Unlike *The Farm Show*, *Buchans* rarely incorporates the process of research directly into the performance, but the monologues that make up most of the play nevertheless retain a sense of the original interviews with rhetorical questions and verbal indicators ('well now,' 'you know,' 'you see'). In *The Farm Show* these deictic techniques create a mirror image of the original meeting of actor and informant. They remind the audience that the play is a subjective report of what the actors discovered. In *Buchans*, these techniques have the opposite effect; they reinforce the actors' roles as typical Buchaneers. The verbal indicators serve to disguise, rather than emphasize, the actors' 'outside-ness.'

The identification of the actors with the community is reinforced by the set, which consists of the Mummers' familiar scaffold and a 'square-set' of mine-shaft shoring timbers borrowed from ASARCO. A sheet printed with mess-hall rules and regulations serves as a backdrop and a silent reminder of the constant presence of the company. The square-set is an open cube of heavy timbers, used variously as a picture frame, a platform, and, of course, a mine shaft. For the miners in the Buchans audience, it was a familiar object of everyday life. In Buchans, the performance took place in a school gymnasium, with set and audience on the same level. There was no curtain, and as the audience took their seats, their first impression of the play was that of the square-set, removed from its context and transformed into a sign of itself. The square-set functions as an emblem of the actors' affinity with the workers, and as a declaration of documentary authenticity.

That claim to authenticity underlies the relation of characterization and theatricality throughout the play. Characterization in *Buchans* is essentially theatrical rather than dramatic. It comprises the specific devices the actors employ to give their monologues context, and to provide a narrative coherence to the documentary material. The actors conceal their mainland origins with assumed accents, and establish consistent performance personalities. They make no attempt to disguise themselves: they wear on stage the same clothes (work shirts and jeans for men and women) as when they met their audience as researchers. When an actor assumes a specific character (as when Allen Booth becomes Charlie Perrier), the change in character is made clear to the audience.

Rather than proceeding from the text, as with mimetic drama, characterization in *Buchans* originates in performance; it can be found in the text only as isolated moments of improvised dialogue and in the verbal structures of the monologues. A reading of the text cannot fully reveal the quality of characterization that unites the dialogue and the monologues into a single coherent personality.

The characterizations are established in the play at the same time as the community is introduced. Following the prologue, the actors enter individually; their brief monologues create a quick collage of first impressions of Buchans in its early days. More importantly, the actors are introducing their personae. Bembo is the clown of the show, somewhat nervous and abstracted; Lee is more typically 'salt of the earth,' conveying a sense of solid determination; Howie is short, intense, and emphatic. Donna is aggressive and fierce, while Connie is somewhat more sentimental and 'typically feminine.' The women have in common a defiance that is in part typical of the women of Buchans, and in part a reflection of the problems they found in asserting a woman's role in a male-dominated issue – and a male-dominated cast. Allen Booth has the least specific persona. He is the musical composer in the show, and he delivers most of the factual 'bulletins.' He also takes part in Bembo's clowning.

Because these characterizations are performance patterns that provide a continuity of individuality through the show, the monologues are semi-autonomous. Their relation to the characterizations is most clearly apparent in the improvised bunkhouse and underground scenes that form the centre of the first act.

Following the introductory sequence of first impressions, Allen produces a fiddle and announces, 'Ladies and Gentlemen, the Buchans Reel!' The dance that follows is more than a folksy change of tempo; it was conceived as a metaphor for the basic sociological fact of life in Buchans. Allen sings out, in cadence:

There's a mine beneath your feet
Just rock to you but it's cash to me
We've got the capital, do you a deal,
Come on in, do the Buchans reel. (9)

After the first tour of the play, Booth wrote to Brookes: 'The square-dance – mildly amusing but it doesn't do what we want it to do i.e. show that the Company calls the tune ... the caller should tire the dancers out somehow.'[36]

If the reel does not succeed as theatrical metaphor, it does provide the first example in the play of the unity of theatricality and character. At the end of the song, the dancers spin off in pairs:

We'll build the town 'cause we know best
A miner needs a place to rest.
We've got: uptown [Two dancers spin off]
We've got: downtown [Two more spin of]
We've got: the bunkhouse.

On the last line, the last pair of dancers, Bembo and Howie, spin to find themselves in each other's arms. A horrified double-take completes the transition: the actors are now identified as miners in the bunkhouse. The reel begins as a theatrical gesture and concludes as a character gag.

This takes the action into the bunkhouse scene, but it is delayed by a brief monologue from Donna, who describes the difficulties of finding work in Buchans in the Depression, and by the first of what will become a recurring series of financial bulletins. The lights go to black (in keeping with the principle of making the process of art visible, the actors control the lighting themselves), and the backdrop is lit from behind. The actors, in silhouette, sing a song taken from an ASARCO promotional film, as Allen shouts the details of ASARCO's 1934 financial report. He completes it with the statement that 'the life expectancy of the Buchans mine in 1934 was eight years.' The announcement of revised life expectancies recurs throughout the play, reminding the audience that the town has always been living on borrowed time.

The bunkhouse scene is a collage of monologues, songs, and improvised banter. As this is the 1930s unit of the play, most of the monologues reflect the Depression years. The theatrical gesture of the bunkhouse is the context in which those years are described, but the scene is equally about the qualities of camaraderie out of which a sense of community developed.

Howie begins the scene with a monologue about general conditions in Buchans in the 1930s, when the only means to and from the town was the company's railroad. The other men take up positions in the scaffolding as he speaks, and for the first time in the play narrative monologue overlaps with action in the theatrical present:

HOWIE
... Now, I lived in the bunkhouse meself, and they put in a miserable time. I know they did, cause time and time again you'd see 'em sitting on their beds in the bunkhouse and you'd go in and say somethin' to 'em and they'd hardly even notice ya. [TO BEMBO] 'Hi buddy.' You see what I mean. So they were t'inking about it. Their families back home and all that. You know there were men who used to live for to get a letter and I seen 'em take that letter and they read it four or five times.

BEMBO
Hey Buddy! You read my letter for me?
HOWIE
You want me to read the letter for you?
BEMBO
Yeah, I can't read.

(4)

It is by means of this technique of overlapping time that character improvisations are integrated into the historicism of *Buchans*. The actors embody both past and present; because their characterizations extend over the decades, they emphasize the continuity of the community.

The overlapping of time is the theatrical equivalent of a cinematic dissolve. When Howie 'steps back' in time to help Bembo read his letter, the mood of the scene changes, and our attention is directed to the letter itself. The men exchange comic banter as Howie deliberately misreads the letter as a joke. Lee takes it and begins to read it aloud. As he does so, Connie takes a seat in the frame of the square-set and becomes the far-off wife writing to her husband. Lee and Connie alternate in the reading, and the men supply realistic bantering interjections. When the letter is completed, Bembo mimes the donning of a coat and exits. Once he is out of sight behind the set, he announces statistics of the housing shortage in Buchans in the 1930s. Lee, still on the scaffold, delivers a monologue describing the scarcity of women in Buchans. He ends with a nostalgic note about the old movies, 'the best place of 'em all' to take a date.

This is the cue for a piece of comic business that has no real value in the play, except as an antidote to the sentimentality of the letter scene. It does however provide a good example of Brookes's anti-illusionistic staging. As Lee finishes his monologue, he places four chairs, in two rows of two, in front of the scaffold and facing the audience. Bembo and Connie hang a sheet in front of the square-set, switch on a light behind it, turn on a portable tape recorder, and to the tinny sound of melodramatic piano music, act out in silhouette an exaggerated silent movie love scene. The other actors enter and sit in the chairs: Lee sits with Donna; Howie interferes; Lee chases Howie from the scene, and Allen exits hand in hand with Donna. Although the 'cinema' seats are placed beside rather than in front of the 'screen,' so that the audience can see both simultaneously, the gesture indicates the actual situation.

When the shadow play ends, Bembo and Connie step forward and stand in an embrace. We are once again in the temporal context of the bunkhouse scene. They speak about the trials of long separations and the difficulties of meeting again after months. Donna enters and speaks to the same theme, recalling the time her husband arrived home on Christmas eve. Once again, Brookes illustrates the monologue with the overlap of time: in the middle of the monologue, Lee enters and embraces Donna while she continues speaking in the past tense. As the two couples maintain their embraces, Allen delivers a monologue about his father showing up like Santa Claus (implicitly referring to Lee and Donna), and Howie caps the scene with a strong denunciation of ASARCO's practice of firing men when they were on holiday.

The sentimentality of the scene culminates in a plaintive song as the men drift back to the scaffold 'bunkhouse.'

> I went to see the doctor
> Cause the bunkhouse was cold
> My son, he said, that winter air
> Puts iron in your soul,
> I said I don't need iron, with copper and lead.
> A coat of paint is all that keeps
> The sheets from freezing off my bed.
> I need a lullaby, need a lullaby ...   (8)

When the song ends, Allen steps forward and very obviously assumes a new character, bringing his hands across his face as if donning a mask. He delivers, with appropriate demonstrative gestures, an anecdote about the use of carbide lamps to combat bugs in the bunkhouse. When he finishes, the actors clear the stage, except for Bembo, who produces a triangle and strikes a tentative note. There is an answering note from a euphonium offstage, and he begins to sing off key:

> There is a place in Buchans town
> You goes right in and you sits right down
> Take a cockroach on your knee
> Till you turn your head and he's in your tea.   (9)

Lee enters, banging on a bass drum with a mop, and joins him in the second verse. Howie enters next, tapping his hardhat with a drumstick, and finally Allen enters with the out-of-tune euphonium for the fourth and last verse. In most performances, depending on the audience reaction, the men would follow this with a short but lively bunkhouse song. They bow formally and exit, leaving Howie on stage alone. Still with his hard hat, he tells a rambling story about mess hall conditions. This is the first – and as yet, incidental – mention of the union in the play:

Well, eh, being a union member see, they'd have us down to the messhall to see
what things were like and then we'd go to the company, see, and eh, when we went
– well, they were really bad ...   (9)

He begins to describe, not without relish, the horrors of cockroaches
dropping into the food. Eventually this leads him to reminiscing about 'khaki
dodgers,' a kind of hard tack much in favour as a missile. The other men enter
stealthily:

... Now, my wife, she'd bake me a bun or a pie or somethin' but these khaki
dodgers, they were everyday. You know they'd be throwing them?
LEE
No, you're kiddin'.
HOWIE
Yeah!

As Howie sticks to his story insistently, the others bombard him with khaki
dodgers. The pandemonium is silenced by a blast of the shift whistle (once
again, Brookes with the penny whistle). It is time to go to work. The men enter
the scaffold and 'descend' into the mine as the lights change. One of the actors
shakes the scaffold, creating the rhythmic mechanical sound of an elevator.
When the actors step out of the scaffold, we understand that they are now
underground.

The dramatic weaknesses of the bunkhouse scene are representative of the
play as a whole. It is perhaps too long, and it builds to a false climax in the
'lullaby' song. The exigencies of the creative process are apparent in the
subordination of thematic logic to the theatrical rhythm of the montage and the
definition of the characterizations. The scene establishes the empathic base
upon which the play's ideology rests. We are introduced to the historical
conditions of early Buchans through the subjective experience of these
characters, and, while this makes the later sequences in the play possible
(especially the culminating 1973 strike scene), it does so at the expense of
genuine historical analysis. This may be a necessary consequence of a 'people's
history' in which experience speaks louder than analysis. Nowhere in the play,
for example, do the actors give us precise information about the founding of the
union. What matters is not historical fact, but the growth of a sense of struggle.
The historicism in *Buchans* is essentially naïve, defined in the general terms of a
hard past leading to a militant present.

It may be, in fact, that this naïvety contributes to the success of the play, as
theatre and as community document. Given a choice between dry fact and

colourful anecdote, the actors invariably choose the latter. But even this does not account for the major weakness of the scene: the depiction of women as ancillary characters.

The depiction of women in the bunkhouse scene is typical of the play as a whole, despite the 'women's scene' in act 2. As one of the actors told an interviewer: 'The women's role is just as strong in the early bunkhouse scenes, just because it feels so goddamned weird that they're not there.'[37] Although the miners' forced separation from their families gives the bunkhouse scene its structure and pathos, the women are in fact incidental. They embellish the reality established by the men in the scene, but they have no individual presence. It is only in the one scene in the second act that the two women in the play have the opportunity to define their characterizations with improvised dialogue.

The bunkhouse and underground scenes comprise two-thirds of the first act of *Buchans*, and together they form the longest unit of continuous narrative action in the play. Although the play as a whole is unified by the narrative devices of characterization and theatricality, these two scenes are clearly separate, with their own internal logic of montage. Nowhere else in the play do we find so much material expressed in such specific dramatic terms.

This is in large part a consequence of the research process itself, for the underground scene is the only part of the play that documents observed behaviour rather than oral history. The bantering of this scene is based on the unique humour of the two-man 'buddy' system that Lee and Howie observed when they spent a shift in the mine. The 'straight man–funny man' exchanges they witnessed there give the scene its structure. The banter establishes the working relationships of the miners, and it provides the context for the monologues. Even more than the bunkhouse scene, the underground scene operates on two levels of theatrical reality: the narrative level of the monologues, and the theatrical 'present' of the work shift. These two levels are integrated in the performance. We accept that these miners are telling their stories directly to the audience even as they are working:

ALLEN
... How about turning on the air and the water.
BEMBO
O ya. Right. I'll go down and do it now.
(Steps out of square set, pauses with audience.)
BEMBO
Hey, did I ever tell you about the time that, eh, buddy and I was drilling raises, eh? And we drilled along, driving up from the seventh level up to the sixth level and,

eh ...

ALLEN

Hey buddy. Turn the air and the water on.

BEMBO

Oh ya. Oh, it's broken. All shagged up. I can't get it working.

ALLEN

Fix it then.

BEMBO

Ya, I'm working on it. And uh, so we are drilling up this raise, eh, and all of a sudden we comes across this rather peculiar smell in the air ... (17)

The scene proceeds with alternating units. We first see Howie and Lee as they enter the shaft; when they leave to get some more tools, Allen and Bembo enter, moving the scene to a different place in the mine. The two teams then meet in the lunch-room, after which they return once more to their alternating places of work. The montage is indicated verbally as well as physically:

LEE

... Well this isn't gettin no work done. Come on let's go get some blocks.

HOWIE

[Sings] Well, I love me mother and me sister too ...

(They exit.)

(Allen and Bembo enter.)

BEMBO

[Sings] ... but I wouldn't love you ... (17)

Because *Buchans* is a play about struggle and not about work, the underground scene examines the rewards and costs of mining, rather than the actual methods of work. The banter informs us that these are men comfortable with each other and their jobs:

HOWIE

... What are you doin' now?

LEE

I beg your pardon?

HOWIE

I say what are you doin' now?

LEE

What's this I got in me hand?

HOWIE

A hose.
LEE
What do you do with a hose?
HOWIE
You water down the stope.
LEE
So what do you think I'm doing?
HOWIE
Waterin' down the stope?
LEE
No, I'm here with your wife havin' a shower.   (14)

It is through exchanges like this that the actors describe to the audience the actual business of mining. The monologues fill in the texture, describing the colourful details ('Now a lot of the boys, I did, wear their long johns underground ... ') and the folklore of the mine. The emotional core of the scene occurs in Howie and Lee's first episode:

(The sound of small rocks falling. Lee stops.)
LEE
What's that?
HOWIE
You know, I loves this ... second to my wife. And I'll tell you the way it is. I'm contented at my work. I'm really contented at my work ... watch out buddy!
(A piece of ground falls.)
LEE
You know there was more men killed from the time the mine started ...   (15)

Lee's 'fall of ground' speech redefines the scene; beginning as a generalized portrait of miners underground, it becomes at this point a specific tribute to the heroism of the Buchans miners. The speech is an emotionally powerful litany with a reverential tone:

LEE
But since I've been here, oh there's been a lot of minor accidents, but there's been well, there's been a few deaths too. Maddie Mercer was killed by a fall of ground. Mike Kelly was killed by a fall of ground. And it's all falls of ground that caused most of the deaths here. Stan Bartlett was killed with a fall of ground. Mike St. George had his two legs cut off with a fall of ground. I walked out the drift behind him ...   (16)

These names were all familiar to the Buchans audience, many of whom faced these same risks every day, and indeed would return to them immediately after seeing the play. The reverence of the scene is heightened by the performance: as Lee speaks the names, they are echoed by Howie sitting behind him. The deaths are a part of life in Buchans, and there is no attempt to blame them on the company, as the silicosis described in act 2 is blamed.

By reviving the memory of this shared grief, the actors pay homage to the community, and this in turn endows them with authority to speak for that community. The fall of ground speech is the emotional centre of the first act, just as the 'twenty-five year watch' speech with its condemnation of the company's disregard for the ravages of silicosis is the centre of the second.

When the men retire to the lunch-room, the scene reverts to the banter with which it began. The men exchange jocular insults, swap lunches, and tell jokes. The lunch-room scene exists only to introduce the women's perspective. As Howie begins to tell a joke about a travelling salesman, the men freeze and Donna enters with an improvised monologue. She describes, patiently at first and then with growing hysteria, the number of sandwiches and lunches she makes every week. As she piles detail upon detail, the tempo increases until the speech disintegrates into incoherent hysteria. In substance, it is similar to act 1, scene 10, of *The Farm Show*, in which the much-put-upon Marion turns into a squawking chicken under the pressure of her daily routine. Donna's speech reflects the ambivalence of the women's roles in the play. It is an ironic compliment to the stamina of the women of Buchans, but is nevertheless extraneous to the scene itself; it is a comic interlude rather than a serious expression of a condition of life. In effect, it is a depersonalized comment, at odds with the carefully developed individuality of the miners.

The scene returns to the lunch-room; Howie completes the punch line of his joke (understandable only to those who know the whole joke); and the men return to work. Ostensibly, the underground scene coincides with the 1940s segment of the play, but it is atemporal: the chronological placement of the scene is vague. When Lee at one point refers to the old days, Howie responds: 'To hear you talk about it buddy, it's a wonder you're still here.' The scene is about the past, but its perspective is that of the present. The technique of overlapping time that introduced the bunkhouse scene has given way to a continuous present that recalls the past.

Theatrical comment in the bunkhouse and underground scenes is limited to the 'editing' of the montage and the interplay of monologue and dialogue. Only in the silent movie scene do we find the agitprop theatricality that becomes so crucial to the second act of the play. The bunkhouse and underground scenes establish firmly the human context that makes the theatricality acceptable as an expression of the community. This is evident in the introduction of puppets in the 1941 strike scene that concludes the act.

Both acts of *Buchans* close with a strike, but whereas the 1973 strike is depicted as a desperate struggle, the 1941 strike is celebrated as the first occasion of labour militancy. Again, the scene develops through montage. When the miners leave the workplace, the lights dim and we hear the sound (created by the actors) of exploding dynamite charges. The actors hum the ASARCO tune as Allen delivers a financial bulletin for 1941. As soon as he finishes, Donna enters and calls out the list of union demands. Underneath the demands the other actors hum the tune 'Solidarity Forever,' and Lee delivers a monologue describing the causes of the strike.

The story of the strike is presented through monologues and visual emblems. The major prop is a large banner, with 'Strike' printed on one side and the ASARCO logo on the other. This banner serves initially as a symbol of the strike but with its ASARCO side showing becomes both a company railroad car and a curtain for the puppets Brookes introduces into the scene.

The puppets, which caricature governmental authority in the form of policemen and members of the arbitration board, emphasize the actors' functions as narrators. This is a revival of the Punch and Judy techniques of *Newfoundland Night*, but the *Buchans* puppets are more abstract in design, with simple cartoon-like features. They are as simple as it is possible for puppets to be, mere papier mâché heads stuck on the ends of sticks.

The puppets here perform a more specialized function than they had in Brookes's previous plays. They embody the obvious comment on depersonalized authority (with the implicit suggestion that the servants of government are controlled by their masters), but the puppets are obviously manipulated by the actors, not by invisible authority. We see the puppets first as policemen arriving by rail to break the strike:

BEMBO
And, eh, by and by, when the train come in, not a soul. But you'd see a scattered head looking out the window – policeman. [A puppet peeks hesitantly over the banner.]
LEE
Boo! [The puppet disappears.]
BEMBO
And, eh, by 'n' by, you'd see a scattered fella'd know someone here, he'd come out talking to 'em. [More puppets appear.]   (26)

The actors' manipulation is made even more clear when the puppet policemen begin drinking with the strikers. The puppets 'disembark' from the train, and as Bembo describes how the police and the miners would walk down the street together, he acknowledges with a friendly pat the puppet peering over his shoulder.

The police are followed by an arbitration board, in which the actors take on the qualities of puppets. Allen, Connie, and Howie (holding a stick puppet to round out the group) wrap themselves in the banner and hobble forward, singing the 'Rule Britannia' parody Brookes had previously used in *Newfoundland Night*. The board members speak with exaggerated British accents, and Connie has tied her long hair in a knot in front of her face to indicate a walrus moustache. These transformations are made in full view of the audience. Unlike the police puppets, the arbitration board is clearly a political cartoon; the actors become puppets to underline the board's pro-company decisions.

The second, and more pointed, use of a human puppet closes the act. With Bembo standing beside him silently, Lee tells the story of Les Forward, the man who organized the strike. When the strike was over, the company promoted him foreman, which entailed his leaving the union. They then fired him. The story is then retold as a puppet demonstration:

ALLEN
The Les Forward Story.
LEE
Les Forward joins the union and gets his union card.
BEMBO
Thank you. [He stands framed by the square set and mimes the actions.]
LEE
Les Forward is elected president of the union. (Clapping.)
BEMBO
Thank you.
LEE
Les Forward wins the 41 strike single handedly.
BEMBO
Thank you.
HOWIE
Les Forward is offered a job with the company as mill foreman.
BEMBO
Thank you.
HOWIE
Les Forward passes over his union card. [Bembo walks forward out of the frame.]
ALLEN

Foreman do this.. [He makes a face; Bembo imitates him.] Foreman do this. [Another face.] Foreman do this. [Another.] Foreman do this. [Allen waves; Bembo imitates. The others wave back.]

EVERYONE

Bye Les. [Bembo is left alone on the stage.] (29–30)

The act ends with a blast on the whistle. Bembo announces an intermission, and the stage is left empty. The first act of *Buchans* has delineated the human value of the mine and the community that has grown around it, and ends with a recognition of the union struggle. This final scene shows the union as a natural response to the company, but it has not yet been shown to be a political necessity. The final note of the first act is an indication of the political focus of the second.

It is perhaps the greatest structural weakness of *Buchans* that the second act recapitulates the general progression of the first. Rather than building from the angry irony of the Les Forward scene, it begins by restating the general sense of community. The dramatic and emotional weight of the act centres on the silicosis scenes and the 1973 strike. But the original chronological structure of the play necessitated a sequence about the 1950s. Just as the 1930s and 1940s sequences provided the place for the bunkhouse and underground material, the 1950s sequence details the social life of the town, and although it contains material invaluable to the play, its location retards the development of the theme.

This first third of the second act is the least unified part of the play. The original working structure of the rehearsal process is most apparent here – material is grouped more for convenience than for thematic development.

The act begins with Howie's rambling demonstration of alcohol in orange peels. It starts as a parody of the prologue:

HOWIE

I have a story to tell you. It's a very dangerous story. It's about a fellow I heard about, used to live in Buchans ... (31)

As Howie tells the story, he acts it in gesture, and as he describes how the man used to drink hair tonic with beer, he becomes progressively 'drunker.' According to Brookes:

I think Howie and Bem brought it [the story] in with some others told to them by [an] old geezer over in the townsite who had his lawn decorated with old hot-water boilers, the novelty of which rather struck Bem ... Howie made it into more of an experiment to see if the [orange] peel really would flare.[38]

The monologue turns into an actual demonstration:

HOWIE
Could we have the beautiful blonde lady out here please? This is the beautiful blonde lady. This is a match. Now, if there is in fact any alcohol in the orange peel, when put in contact with the lit flame – something should happen. Lights. Did you see that? Proof. There is actually alcohol in the orange peel. Now. Do you believe that?

The piece has no real value in the play and indeed was cut in the 1975 remount. It does, however, begin the act with a recognition that the play is as much an entertainment as a didactic history. The two are more effectively combined in the 'Christmas of '49' recitation that follows soon after. (In the remount, this piece was moved to the top of the act.) Following a brief clown interlude in which Allen attempts to assist Bembo in wounding himself so that he can catch the train out of Buchans, the recitation describes an incident when the miners, angry at the company's refusal to provide transport out of town on Christmas, rioted in the mess hall. The piece had been written as a song by one of the miners, but Brookes felt it would work better as a recitation in the traditional Newfoundland style. The decision to change modes is in keeping with the general treatment of found material in the play. There are only two instances in Buchans where the actors sing songs written specifically for the play (in the bunkhouse scene, and the women's scene that follows the 'Christmas of '49.') In general, the music of the play is taken from actual sources: the ASARCO theme song is used to signal the corporate financial bulletins, and the striking miners in the last third of act 2 sing refrains from actual strike songs. The two songs written for the play are something of an inconsistency, for otherwise the actors do not impose their own music to enhance the material, as happens in *The Farm Show* and *Ten Lost Years*.

That the song in the women's scene may be necessary to the scene is perhaps an indication of its arbitrary nature and placement. Connie and Donna enter as soon as the recitation finishes; they hang up washing on a line strung across the square-set and trade observations on the living conditions of Buchans. They describe the poor construction of the houses, the lack of recreational facilities for children, and the impossibility of improving the general appearance of the town. Their monologues are short, to give the scene the narrative structure of a dialogue. This is the most awkward use of characterization in the play, for the dialogue is clearly organized to present information, rather than to validate the impersonations of the actors. Because the scene is set apart from the rest of the play, it suggests a division of experience between men and women in the town, but this idea is not explored. In fact, the women's song indicates that the opposite was intended:

> Who says we don't work by the whistle, with us it just don't show.
> Yes, you got to have dinner ready my dear, before that whistle blows.   (37)

The last minute problems of finding a workable shape to the play is evident in this and the scenes that follow, in which structure is little more than format. The women's scene leads into a short sequence of monologues about religious differences between Catholics and Protestants, and a general series of vignettes illustrating life in the 1950s. Here the lack of integration inherent in the original chronological structure results in a self-contained series of tableaux, 'The Buchans Photo Album.' Played in the frame of the square-set, the scene presents 'snapshots' of social life, not unlike the 'Picture Frame' scene of *The Farm Show*. The actors take turns describing the pictures of various parties, hockey teams, 'young duckies' at the dam site, and line-ups at the store on pay night. The final photograph leads into one of the most striking uses of visual montage in the play:

BEMBO
There's a picture of a herd of moose just about to leave Buchans before the 1955 strike.
(Photo: Moose stampede.) [The actors imitate a herd of moose and vacate the frame. Allen remains, standing silently and looking at the audience.]
BEMBO
[Pointing to Allen.] And here's a picture of the 1955 strike! ...   (41)

This capping line transforms Allen into an icon of Buchan's labour history: the portrait of the angry miner. Allen steps forward and delivers a brief monologue about the strike, which failed because only the miners went out, while the surface workers stayed on the job. The play now moves into the final segment about the labour troubles that brought the Mummers to Buchans.

The 1973 strike sequence uses the techniques of agitprop, in which dramatic sense depends on the audience's partisan involvement with the issue. As in *Gros Mourn*, that involvement means that the actors need merely indicate the actual event. The interpretation is more important than the representation. Rather than describing the event in full, the scene outlines a causality to which the intended audience of Buchaneers might bring their own memories. Without that sense of personal participation, the effect of the scene is lessened. In his review of the Toronto run, Urjo Kareda said that it 'makes almost no impact and the interesting event – the community politicizing itself – is only hinted at, not developed.'[39] The true impact of the scene is a function of the relationship between the actors and the Buchans community. The scene depicts only as much as is necessary to create its argument.

To this point in the 'people's history' the play has emphasized the growth of a distinct community; now, before showing the historical consequence of the conflict between community and company, the play must demonstrate the absolute necessity of the strike. It is here that Brookes's ideology is clearest. The strike is presented as a conflict between company and union, but although the company is the same impersonal force that we have seen throughout the play, the union is the aggregate of all the subjective experiences that the audience has shared in the play. That is why the strike is not introduced as a matter of contracts, but as an issue of human dignity and survival.

The necessity of the strike is demonstrated through the human cost of the mine operation. The strike scene is prefaced by a sequence of monologues about silicosis, 'that dread disease that every miner dreads.' These recollections are followed by a brief reminder of ASARCO's profits, an updated life expectancy bulletin for the mine, and a clown routine in which Bembo 'magically' turns Buchans ore into American dollars. The magic act is included as an ironic symbol of the miners' alienation from the financial realities of the multinational corporation.

These two themes of human wastage and the impersonality of the company are brought together in the piece that precedes the actual strike scene. This is the emotional centre-piece of the play, based on an incident that occurred at the beginning of the second week of research. Brookes had the idea of including a scene in which the company's practice of presenting a gold watch to miners who have completed twenty-five years of service would become an ironic reflection of corporate indifference. The improvisation took place in the union hall, observed by a retired miner:

We began our 25-year watch improv. One by one the actors of our group entered the presentation scene, refused to accept their watch and demanded to speak. The scene was not working. The improvised speeches sounded false, unlike what a real miner would say. Peter [Noftle, a retired miner], sitting in the back of the bar, suddenly came forward, entered the scene, accepted the watch, and politely asked the 'company manager' for permission to speak. I switched on the tape recorder, and I suspect the remarkable speech which followed had been rehearsed for many years in Peter's mind.[40]

This was a breakthrough for the actors, the first occasion in the research process in which they were forced to admit the obvious superiority of documentary material. Brookes incorporated not just the speech but the whole incident in the play. The scene begins with Allen as the 'company manager' about to present a watch. He calls out a name, and Brookes interrupts, stepping into the play to describe the incident in the union hall. Brookes's intrusion in the play parallels that of Peter Noftle in the rehearsal: an outside element changes the substance and the context of the established structure. In the language of semiotics Brookes, by interrupting the scene, 'foregrounds' the making of the play, and his description of the rehearsal incident reminds the audience that the play is a result of a genuine process of intervention. The foregrounding of the process by which the play was created embodies the political ideology of the play itself.

The speech is delivered in the play just as Peter Noftle delivered it that day in the union hall. This is one of the few points (along with Allen's Charlie Perrier speech) where the actors create a recognizable impersonation. The speech lasts just under four minutes; its tone is earnest and its style is naively rhetorical:

> ... I came here when I was 33 and in the prime of life. I gave the best years of my life to the American Smelting and Refining Company. After 25 years I am given a watch. Now, it is not my intention to criticize or ridicule the Buchans Mining Company. Many will say: you made your living here, you raised your family here. I grant you that. But in the over 25 years of hard and honest service, American Smelting and Refining Company never gave me anything I never worked for ... (43)

The speech builds to a refusal of the watch – not because of a hatred of the company but because the watch itself is an insult, insufficient compensation for and recognition of the sacrifices the miners have made. Peter Noftle refers to his own loss of hearing, and to the incidence of silicosis in the mines. He ends with a powerful tribute to the miners:

> But to you my fellow workers, I want to say this: we have worked hard together, we have worked underground, in dangerous places and I do not care where you go today – you of the company will have to agree this, that you will not find anywhere a harder working nor a more steady people than what you have had here working underground for you over the years. Thank you.

This speech is a summary of the play's emotional argument, but it is more than that; it is a ratification of the entire process of community intervention theatre, an authentic voice of the community made possible by the play. Its placement in the play is crucial, for it is the pivot on which history turns into politics. Significantly, it is the only speech in the play attributed by name. As Lee exits, Allen says, 'Thank you Mr. Noftle.' The audience is reminded once more that they are hearing their own voice. The emotional impact of the scene was not limited to the Buchans audience. David Billington, the drama critic for the Southam wire service, saw the play two months later at the Miners' Museum in Glace Bay, Nova Scotia:

When the speech ended, the audience broke into long, heartfelt applause. But the clincher came when, at the play's end, the miner himself, Peter Noftle, stood up and thanked the Mummers on behalf of all the Buchans miners ... And there, in that museum with the walls hung with the picks and hammers of soft-coal miners long gone, with a real miner giving a short impromptu speech, theatre ceased to be an imitation of life and became life itself.[41]

Following the speech there are two brief monologues, one an anecdote illustrating that ASARCO's authority was a 'bluff' that could be challenged, and the other indicating the reasons for the increased militancy of the 1970s: younger men starting work in the mines, 'who had seen what had happened to their fathers and said they'd be damned if it would happen to them.' The historical reasons for the strike are never described in full; the substantial reasons have already been made clear by Peter Noftle.

Two more monologues outline in brief the unsuccessful 1971 strike, significant only in that the lessons of that failure were invaluable two years later. These short pieces provide information, but more importantly, they bring the entire cast on stage. As Donna concludes her bellicose reading of a letter to the editor of the St John's *Evening Telegram*, the actors step forward as a group and shout 'We're on strike!'

The strike scene is divided into four main episodes: the rejection of the company's offer; the strike vote; the court injunction; and the subsequent violence, in which company offices were ransacked and property damaged. By the standards of industrial violence, that of Buchans was not particularly notable, but it was a shock for Buchans, and the scene attempts to justify it as an inevitable expression of popular anger. When the play was created the memory of the strike was still fresh, and the issues upon which it was predicted were still a cause of worry. By admitting the violence, the Mummers placed it into an historical context for the community.

The strike scene is developed through a montage of authentication devices which call attention to the levels of documentary reality. The monologues rest upon the authority that the actors have developed through the play, and they are juxtaposed with more obvious documents: strike songs, visual icons, and quotations (affidavits, letters to the editor). The result is a montage similar to that of the Living Newspaper.

The principal image of the scene is the picket line, with the actors standing in line abreast across the front of the set. The monologues are punctuated by short refrains from actual strike songs, and the actors carry actual picket signs. Because the scene as a whole is basically iconic, dramatic tension is indicated through verbal emphasis and rhythm. Short staccato speeches, shouted interjections, and overlapping voices create an impression of urgency and emotional violence. The actors provide a collective narrative voice, and continuity is expressed by means of spoken titles ('April 9, 1973 – 27 days into the strike!'). In places, monologues are broken down and divided among several speakers for effect. We see this in the moment of greatest tension, when an unseen RCMP officer approaches the picket line:

CONNIE
He tried to stop us on the road.
ALLEN
We got up around the staff house.
HOWIE
He stood in the road and he put out his hand and he tried to stop us.
LEE
We just pulled right in around him.
ALLEN
He said what's the trouble. He was scared.
DONNA
The man was really scared.
CONNIE
He knew he was after making a blunder. (50)

As in the 1941 strike scene, the narrative is illustrated with theatrical gestures, but the puppetry of the earlier scene here gives way to essentially realistic depiction. Once again the ASARCO banner represents rolling stock, this time a caboose placed in front of the plant gate by the miners. There is no attempt to dramatize the actual incidents. The staging makes physical the relationships described in the narration, depending primarily on the technique of overlapping time.

The climactic violence is first introduced in retrospect. The confrontation with the RCMP officer culminates in a verbal threat of violence from the miners, followed by a blast on the whistle. The actors freeze, the lights go to black, and the backlight comes on behind the screen. After a significant pause, Bembo steps forward and speaks quietly:

> I'm not a violent person by any means. That day you know I thought about what
> I done that day and I just – I didn't feel bad about it ... (50)

He describes the frustrations that fed the violence, in which the offices were turned over and the caboose burned. When he finishes, the other actors knock the screen out of its place and with a crashing noise rearrange the planks on the scaffold to indicate violent disorder. The scene continues with a heated description of the violence, but the tone is quickly muted, becoming more reflective as the actors reform the picket line. The RCMP arrive in force, but they are invisible to the audience; we see them reflected in the fearful faces of the strikers. The tension is released as the actors describe how the RCMP commander approached the line – only to ask permission to inspect the damages.

At this point, the history is complete; no mention is made of the eventual settlement of the strike. The actors remove the strike banner and deliver their final summations in a quiet, direct address to the audience. This final segment exists in two forms, having been completely rewritten for the 1975 remount. In the initial version, each actor steps forward and delivers a comment on the town's future. Howie reaffirms the necessity of the strike, and hopes it need never be repeated; Donna calls for the union, government, and company to discuss the life expectancy of the mine. Bembo scoffs at the reports of a limited life expectancy, Lee points out the ominous lack of exploratory development, and Connie suggests that 'this place is going to be a boom town' while admitting she is a 'dreamer.' It is at this point that Allen reappears as Charlie Perrier, closing the play with a reminder of its origins.

In the 1975 version, the ending is more pointedly political. When the strike scene ends, Allen picks up one of the wooden blocks that rest at the corners of the square-set and places it at the front of the playing area. In a conversational tone, he begins to tell the audience about his decision to build a new basement in his house. The other actors in turn deliver their statements about the future, and, between each one, Allen brings forward another block, telling us a little more about the basement. The monologues are similar to those that ended the original version, but as a year has passed they are updated. The order is rearranged to emphasize the town's increasingly desperate situation. Speaking last, Donna informs us that the company's lease has only a year to run, and that the government has established a task force to study the future of Buchans. It is Allen who has the final word:

> Some people think that I'm crazy to be building now, but, uh, I'm not saying
> that everybody should be building now. I'm not sure that I should. But I can't wait
> forever for somebody else to decide how I'm going to live.[42]

This ending is perhaps more definite than the original because it is written for a Toronto audience. In the first version, the conflicting points of view that close the play direct the questions of the town's future back to the audience. The actors cannot pretend to answer those questions for them. In the revision the ending expresses the determination of the townspeople to maintain their community; it is a message from the town to the outside world.

With the assistance of the Buchans union, the Mummers toured the play to other mining centres in the province and Nova Scotia in the fall of 1974. The 1975 Toronto run was intended as the first leg of a tour to mining towns of Northern Ontario and Manitoba, sponsored by the national office of the Steelworkers' union. Ironically, this breakthrough in labour support of the arts was aborted when the Steelworkers received a complaint from Actors' Equity, who objected to union funding of a non-union theatre.[43]

The union's interest in *Buchans* points to the major problem with Brookes's attempt to intervene in a political situation. As a theatrical portrait of a community, *Buchans* is an unqualified success, but judged in terms of its political purpose, its effectiveness must be questioned. The play had no tangible effect on the subsequent history of the town; in the late 1970s, the mine ceased operation, and the community was reduced considerably in size. By its very nature, interventionist theatre must be judged by its political results. It is significant that the most effective moments in *Buchans* are those which, like the Peter Noftle speech, appeal to heightened sentimentality, rather than critical analysis. The value of *Buchans* is in the end propagandist rather than actively political. As Brookes later wrote: 'We didn't supply in the show the vehicle for accomplishing a change in that situation. We sort of said, "this is what should happen and how brave the union is." We didn't plug into an activist vehicle.'[44]

In the plays that followed *Buchans*, Brookes attempted to work as closely as possible with sponsoring agencies. To involve his theatre with ongoing social and political programs, he moved away from the adherence to documentary actuality that is so important to *Buchans*. In the years after *Buchans*, Brookes produced only two more community documentaries (*East End Story*, 1975, sponsored by the Community Planning Association of Canada; and *Weather Permitting/Silekapet Kissiane*, 1977, sponsored by the Labrador Resources Advisory Council). The main thrust of the Mummers' later work was the propagandist revue devised for general audiences. In such plays as (*What's That Got to Do with) The Price of Fish* (1976, sponsored by OXFAM) and *They Club Seals, Don't They?* (1977, sponsored by the provincial government), Brookes combined documentary actuality with satiric invention to express a political analysis of a topical issue. The Buchans experience led Brookes to the belief that politically effective theatre must be created in consultation with a political organization. With *Buchans*, Brookes established the Mummers Troupe as the most actively political theatre in English Canada; at the same time the experience of the play demonstrated the limitations, both inherent and imposed, of interventionist theatre.

6

Documentary and Audience Intervention: It's About Time

So far I have defined two general approaches to the relation of the actor to documentary material. In *Ten Lost Years, No. 1 Hard*, and *Paper Wheat* the actors bear an arbitrary relationship to an autonomous and essentially literary text. There is no direct relation between the matter of the play and the particular actors in a given performance, even though those actors may have contributed to the making of the play. In *The Farm Show* and *Buchans*, on the other hand, the relation of actor, material, and text is direct, and the text is essentially non-literary. The significance of the performance depends on the audience's recognition that the actors are reporting their own experiences and findings, and that the process of making the play is part of its meaning.

It must be recognized that the distinction between these two approaches applies only to the original productions of the plays in this latter category, even though the direct relation of actor and material may be built into the text. There have been several productions of *The Farm Show* by other theatres in the decade since it was first performed, and even *Buchans* was picked up (under the title of *Company Town*) by Ottawa's Great Canadian Theatre Company in 1978. In these productions the text is transformed into an autonomous entity to which the actors bear a relation that is no less arbitrary than in a play such as *Ten Lost Years*. This condition suggests that these two general approaches find a common factor in that the play survives the performance.

This objectification of the text is the main tendency in Canadian documentary theatre but it is not the only one. In Edmonton, Catalyst Theatre has developed an alternative approach to documentary in which there is no final performance text but rather an ongoing process of improvisation and audience participation. One of the most important experiments in this new form was the performance of *It's About Time*, a 'participational theatre event,' created and performed from summer 1982 to February 1983.

Developed with and for inmates of penal institutions and half-way houses in Alberta, *It's About Time* changed substantially in every performance, according to the specifics of the host institution and the needs of the audience. In its attempt to reconcile the flexibility necessary for an improvisational performance with the constraints of a coherent dramatic structure, Catalyst evolved a form of documentary performance that is radically different from that of the plays discussed so far.

This form of participational documentary is unique in Canada, but it has important parallels elsewhere. The reasons for its development can be found in Catalyst's evolution as a social animation theatre but an appreciation of it is best arrived at in the context of three pioneers of 'intervention theatre': the Viennese psychotherapist J.L. Moreno, who founded psychodrama in the 1930s; and two Brazilians whose work over the past two decades has had vast international influence, director Augusto Boal and adult educator Paulo Freire.

In Moreno's theory of 'sociodrama,' first proposed in the 1930s, we find the earliest application of participational documentary techniques and in Boal's 'Forum Theatre' we find the first use of the interactive techniques that characterize Catalyst's work. Both Boal and Catalyst were influenced by Freire's radical theories of adult education, which provide the theoretical justification for audience intervention in the performance as a means of social analysis.

Catalyst's unique development was made possible by its paradoxical origins, for the company grew out of a university course devised for students who did not plan to enter the professional theatre. Catalyst was formed in 1977 by students working under David Barnet, a professor of improvisational drama at the University of Alberta. Barnet had begun to explore collective creation and documentary performance while teaching at the Manitoba Theatre School in the late 1960s. He found that documentary theatre based on oral history and improvisation was an effective means of teaching non-professional students 'to act well, act with complete involvement, without teaching them technique.'[1]

In his classes at the University of Alberta, students were required to research and perform a short documentary play. In 1977 one such group improvised a cautionary tale about alcoholism entitled *Drinks before Dinner*. Conventionally dramatic in form and style, the play depicted the problem of alcohol abuse through representative characters based on real models. At Barnet's suggestion the actors approached the Alberta Alcohol and Drug Abuse Commission (ADAAC) to inquire about a grant to subsidize a short tour of the play. Impressed with the play, ADAAC offered to sponsor a province-wide tour, funded by its Sponsored Projects Branch. Under the name of The Intimate Theatre of Alcohol Awareness, the students took the play to fifty-nine communities during the summer of 1977. The tour was a success; ADAAC commissioned a follow-up show, and other social agencies expressed interest in similar projects.

On that basis, Catalyst Theatre Society was founded by Barnet in 1977, and in 1979 Jan Selman, a recent graduate of the University of Alberta's Master of Fine Arts program in directing, took over as artistic director. Selman was an opportune choice for the job; although relatively inexperienced she demonstrated the intelligence and imagination needed to transform Catalyst into a self-sufficient professional company. By 1982 Catalyst was operating on a budget in excess of $400,000 a year, of which half was provided by ADAAC and the rest by other commissions and private fund raising.

Catalyst promoted itself as a social service agency, and although the company began to perform for general audiences in 1979 (with topical collective creations and occasional scripted plays, such as David Freeman's *Creeps*), most of its shows have been sponsored by social agencies for specific audiences. It is fair to say that Catalyst accepted the implicit censorship of such sponsorship, for while the company's theatrical technique became increasingly political, in so far as it dealt with strategies for individual and collective action in response to social problems, the plays adhered to the ideology of the sponsor. Like the Mummers Troupe, Catalyst was committed to a 'useful theatre,' but because it did not work towards a declared ideological goal, it won quick acceptance in Edmonton's social welfare community. Its sponsors have included, among others, the Alberta Law Foundation, the United Church, Edmonton Social Services, and the Canadian Addictions Foundation. According to the Catalyst newsletter:

A Catalyst project always involves some kind of in-depth relationship with the audience for which it is created – through research, discussion, direct participation and pre and/or post production activities. Actors have worked in virtually every setting imaginable – on the streets, in group homes, town halls, conference rooms, school gymnasiums, classrooms, hospitals and, occasionally, in a traditional theatre.[2]

From the beginning, Catalyst explored methods of involving the audience directly in the performance. In *The Stress Show* (1978), the actors 'justified' their decisions to the audience by engaging in discussion while remaining in character. *The Stress Show* consisted of short sketches depicting common stressful situations. After each scene, the principal character would turn to the audience and defend his or her choices. Each performance included a scene created for that specific audience, including a taxi drivers' union meeting, the students of a hair-dressing school, and workers in a downtown office.

By the standards that Catalyst later developed, these 'justifications' were limited in their capacity to draw the audience into a critical discussion of the issues of the play. The audience was invited to respond to the characters, but that response could not affect the direction or outcome of the scene. By questioning and criticizing the characters of the play, the audience could express their attitudes towards the action and the problems it depicted, but the scene could not in turn respond to those attitudes. The 'justification' technique precluded a synthesis of the discussion at hand.

In 1978 Catalyst began to explore more direct methods of audience participation with *The Black Creek Project*, an AADAC-funded performance for high school students. To explore the problems of alcoholism and work, the students were invited to 'apply' for various positions on a pipeline project. The Catalyst actors became the 'crew supervisors'and introduced the dramatic problems as the students built a model pipeline with plastic sections. The exploration of participation techniques continued in a series of workshop projects for young audiences. In *Name of the Game* (1980), the students moved around a giant game board to 'explore life decisions.' In *Project Immigration* (1980), the students acted as immigration officers who had to interview five potential immigrants to Canada. The immigrants, played by the Catalyst actors, represented a variety of ethnic and educational backgrounds. The students had to choose the successful applicants and defend their decisions publicly.

These performances certainly qualify as theatre, but even though they incorporate invented characters, they cannot be considered drama, and their relation to documentary is incidental. The situations they describe are based on actuality, but they are selected for their representative nature. The actors and audience assume roles made necessary by the event itself; by participating in complex decisions, the students are encouraged to examine their own prejudices. The event itself is the object of the performance. Although these performances lack a text, other than that created by the participants, they have a fixed structure that governs the audiences' freedom to affect the outcome of the action. The audience is invited to make choices, but has no voice in formulating the basic problem upon which the performance is based. In this regard, the school workshops are an exception to Catalyst's principle of developing the project in close consultation with the target audience.

The desire to involve the audience in the development and performance of the play rests upon the assumption that this involvement will enable the participant to use the play as part of the process of changing the reality it describes. This theory is similar to that advanced by Augusto Boal, and like Boal's, it derives from the work of Brazilian educator Paulo Freire.

In his *Pedagogy of the Oppressed*, Freire advances a concept of adult education predicated on a Marxist analysis of the process of social change, which posits that an oppressed class is denied the ability to determine the conditions of its existence. Freire calls for a 'problem-posing education' consisting of 'acts of cognition, not transferals of information.'[3] This education is a process of 'decoding' reality; the educator entering a community must decode what he discovers, codify it again (in a photograph, a play, or a drawing), and use this as a catalyst for discussion. For Freire, true education is a process of political analysis; his work in the slum barrios of Brazil led him to the conclusion that education is of value only if it leads to material change. By decodifying reality as a basis of critical analysis, Freire argues that 'men discover each other to be "in a situation"':

Only as this situation ceases to present itself as a dense, enveloping reality or a tormenting blind alley, and men can come to perceive it as an objective-problematic situation – only then can commitment exist. Men *emerge* from the *submission* and acquire the ability to *intervene* in reality as it is unveiled. *Intervention* in reality – historical awareness itself – thus represents a step forward from emergence, and results from the *conscientizacao* [conscientization] of the situation.[4]

For Freire, the process of 'conscientization' rests upon two related principles. Education, he argues, must lead to action, 'an authentic praxis': 'To achieve this praxis … it is necessary to trust in the oppressed and in their ability to reason.'[5] Praxis in turn is the 'new raison d'être of the oppressed,' which leads inevitably to revolution. Freire's work in Brazil led him to a revolutionary conclusion, but his theories are not necessarily revolutionary, and although he depends upon a Marxist analysis of society, his methodology is not inherently Marxist. For Catalyst, the 'oppressed' might be the mentally or physically handicapped, or prison inmates – any group that finds itself disadvantaged or isolated from the mainstream of society.

Freire's concept of 'conscientization' provides the basis for a model of political theatre that is antithetical to agitprop. In reference to Catalyst, it might be more exact to speak of 'sociological theatre,' but a play like *Project Immigration* defines human beings as political beings; the student participants are asked to engage in a process of political reasoning. In this sense, political theatre need not be overtly ideological. It suffices that the theatre be committed to an understanding of the relation between individuals and social structures in such a way that those structures are defined as subject to change. In this model, the political effectiveness of the theatre is a function of form, which embodies a political analysis.

Catalyst's most important work is premised on Freire's belief that the oppressed can change their own situation by a 'critical intervention in reality.'

In theatrical terms, this requires a change in the way a play is researched. Instead of studying an issue and then transforming the conclusions into a theatrical text as in *Drinks Before Dinner*, or a theatrical game as in *Project Immigration*, the actor is required to function as an intermediary who helps the audience formulate the theatrical problem – Freire's concept of 'decoding' – and 'codify' it as drama.

Catalyst's first experiment in this vein was *Stand Up for Your Rights* (1980), commissioned by the Alberta Law Foundation and the Alberta Association for the Mentally Retarded as a vehicle to discuss the legal rights of the mentally handicapped. According to Jane Heather, one of the actors in the project, the company discovered three major difficulties:

- how to make a show really participational for this target audience without everything getting out of control
- what is really 'out of control'
- learning to trust the audience[6]

Stand Up for Your Rights was performed in three versions: the initial production from January to May 1981; a remount the following year; and a television adaptation broadcast on the CBC on 11 November 1981.[7] The performance in all three versions consisted of a series of scenes depicting common problems the actors had identified in their research. The scenes followed two main characters, Shelley and Frank, both mentally handicapped adults in their late twenties. The television version, which is the only one now available, presents four scenes, although in performance the number of scenes and the issues they depicted would vary. In the first scene of the television version, Shelley's parents refuse her permission to marry Frank; in the second, Jane, a young handicapped woman, encounters discrimination when applying for a job in a greenhouse; in the third, Shelley defies her parents; and in the fourth, Frank loses his job. In each scene the action is structured to end at a moment of decision that touches on a question of legal rights.

The actors performed the scenes in a close-up realistic style, and the audience (consisting usually of twenty to thirty persons) was invited to intervene. According to David Barnet, who adapted the show for television, 'we were very nervous, we didn't want to fail on the stage, we didn't want any handicapped person to fail, so we controlled it tightly.'[8] The performance was controlled by a referee who introduced the action as a game. The audience was invited to stop the action whenever a character needed help, or when someone was treated unfairly. In practice the referee would often take the initiative of stopping the action with his whistle when he perceived a response in the audience, or when a response was desirable. The actors had to learn to trust their audiences:

> In the second production we tried to be more daring with participation. We attempted to utilize all reasonable suggestions from the audience not just the ones that fit our notion of how the scene should go. We also attempted to allow a scene to continue as long as the target audience had ideas to contribute. In the first show we had been arbitrary in cutting off the scene when it was over.[9]

According to Jan Selman, the television version was too 'protective' of the audience because of the limitations of the format. The restricted time and the awareness that the program would be broadcast to the general public resulted in a performance that was more closely supervised than usual. In a normal performance, the actors could find themselves spending two hours on one scene. Whenever possible, the audience was invited to step into the role on stage, to demonstrate how the actor might have responded to the problem more effectively. This is where the question of trusting the audience became crucial. The handicapped participants could not always maintain the thrust of the scene; they could freeze or lose focus. The very nature of a play which advocates legal rights for the mentally handicapped led to a paradox that could only be resolved by great sensitivity on the part of the Catalyst actors. The audience had the right to reshape a scene as required, but could only do so with the assistance of the actors, who had to repress their natural inclination to instruct the participant.

The special circumstances of the mentally handicapped audience led Catalyst to develop a form almost identical to that created by Augusto Boal in Brazil in the late 1960s. The similarity was not entirely coincidental. Selman had read Boal's writings, which outline his theoretical ideas, but it was not until the summer of 1983, two years after *Stand Up for Your Rights*, that an opportunity for comparison presented itself, when Quebec's Théâtre Sans Détour brought to Edmonton a 'Forum Theatre' performance based on their work with Boal.

Boal's ideas of 'popular theatre' are derived directly from Freire, and Boal acknowledges his debt in the title of his own book, *Theatre of the Oppressed*. From Freire, Boal took the basic principle of coding and decoding to enable the audience to intervene critically in their reality and, like Freire, Boal works towards a goal of popular revolution.

Boal begins his discussion with a critique of Aristotle, in whose *Poetics* he finds a recipe for a 'very powerful purgative system, the objective of which was to eliminate all that is not commonly accepted, including the revolution, before it takes place.'[10] Boal blames Aristotle for the invention of a 'coercive system' of tragedy that saps individual initative. He proposes instead a poetics in which the audience become the 'transformers of the dramatic action':

Aristotle proposes a poetics in which the spectator delegates power to the dramatic character so that the latter may think and act like him. Brecht proposes a poetics in which the spectator delegates power to the character who thus acts in his place but the spectator reserves the right to think for himself, often in opposition to the character. In the first place, a 'catharsis' occurs; in the second an awakening of critical consciousness. But the poetics of the oppressed focuses on the action itself; the spectator delegates no power to the character (or actor) either to think or act in his place: on the contrary, he himself assumes the protagonic role, changes the dramatic action, tries out solutions, discusses plans for change – in short trains himself for real action.[11]

Boal's polemical interpretation of the Aristotelian concept of catharsis serves a strategic purpose. It provides him with a defence against the hypothetical detractor who might dismiss his work as sociological role-playing rather than drama. Boal attempts to integrate his work into the larger body of dramatic theory; this in turn provides the basis of his argument, following Freire, that his theatre is the only form that allows the oppressed to express their own reality in drama. The interactive theatre embodies the Freirean concept of dialectics: the theatre can be a forum in which the oppressed can clarify and advance their historical 'emergence,' and as an aesthetic form, it is uniquely their own, repudiating received cultural forms.

In his Arena Theatre in Sao Paulo, Boal explored a number of techniques, including a variant of Living Newspaper. His major invention, the Forum Theatre, evolved from the introduction into classical texts of a referee figure called the Joker. The Joker represents the author in the text; 'he is polyvalent: his function is the only one that can perform any role in the play, being able to replace the protagonist when the latter's realistic nature prevents him from doing something.'[12] In effect, the Joker began as a method of formalizing polemical interpretation of a text. In the Forum Theatre, the Joker is a master of ceremonies and referee.

Boal's Forum Theatre has developed into a strict formula. The actors create a scenario in consultation with the target audience; the play is performed once in its entirety and then repeated. The scene is organized around single example of oppression leading to a contradiction which defeats the oppressed character. The Joker explains the rules to the audience. A participant may replace the oppressed character at any point in the action when the scene is repeated. If that person suggests an unrealistic solution, the audience is asked to stop the action by calling 'magic!.' This leads to a discussion, and eventually the audience will discover a solution to the dramatic problem.

In its basic structure, this is virtually identical to the form Catalyst invented in *Stand Up for Your Rights*, and it shares a major weakness. Although the scenes are developed in consultation with the audience, there must be an implicit 'correct' solution. In *Stand Up for Your Rights* Shelley has only one choice when her parents refuse to let her marry. She can surrender, or she can leave her home. Surrender is unacceptable, for it closes off any other possibilities. If the performance is honest, it will reflect the consciousness of the audience, who will see on stage the consequences of their own decisions. When this technique is put at the service of a specific political ideology that prescribes theoretical solutions, it can be manipulative. In Théâtre Sans Détour's performance, which was modelled on Boal, the scene depicts a saleswoman who is to be laid off her job unless she agrees to date her manager. She is caught in a contradiction when her husband perceives this as an opportunity to achieve his desire to keep her at home. The only admissible solution to the problem is unionization. This solution is made evident in the scene by the mention that several other women are in the same situation.[13]

It is in this issue of honesty that the concept of interactive theatre returns to documentary. The audience can intervene freely only if they accept the problem on the stage as absolutely authentic and pertinent to their own lives. The actors therefore must learn not only the specifics of the social problem, they must learn the authentic response of the person who lives the problem to avoid what Boal calls the 'magical' solution. The actors must retain their expertise while accepting, and in a sense documenting, the consciousness of the audience. When directed towards specific ideological ends, the actors must avoid making an implicit critique of that consciousness. In performance, this touches on variables that are not easily controlled. Theatrical elements, such as costuming, stage movement, and the physical appearance of the actor, add a level of implicit comment. Even in a play like *Stand Up for Your Rights*, which is directed towards sociological solutions, this can be a problem. How far, for example, may the actor playing Shelley's mother go in her attempt to persuade Shelley and, through her, the audience? The very nature of theatrical performance may in fact preclude an objective representation of a situation. In performance, a general situation is made specific, and this brings into play variables which the form may not be equipped to handle.

For Catalyst this problem is resolved by an increased reliance on the specific details of the target audience. In *It's About Time*, the dramatic situations are not formulated with a solution in mind. This was not so much a conscious decision as it was a reflection of a necessary condition, for prison audiences live in a reality that cannot be transformed. The prison walls fix the boundary of possible action. Consequently, the play deals more closely with the problems of individual adjustment to an unchanging reality. Given this restriction, the idea of interactive theatre touches on the concept of psychodrama.

As the term was first applied by J.L. Moreno in 1911, psychodrama referred to a specialized technique of psychoanalysis, but in common usage it has come to describe any application of theatrical techniques to psychological health and adjustment. This would appear to be far removed from the concerns of Catalyst, which examines individual problems in terms of social structures, and even farther from those of Boal, but the differences are those of orientation rather than technique. When asked to explain the difference between his Forum Theatre and psychodrama, Boal answered only that, 'the oppression scene multiplies so that all the participants share the same oppression and the problem is everyone's.'[14] Boal and Catalyst share the belief that the problems they depict can only be resolved by collective action.

The techniques of 'intervention theatre' had been anticipated by Moreno when he sought to extend his idea of psychodrama to group therapy. Moreno defined psychodrama as 'a deep action method dealing with interpersonal relations and private ideologies,' and he compared it with 'sociodrama': 'a deep action method dealing with intergroup relations and collective ideologies.'[15] His tentative experiments in sociodrama, beginning in the 1920s in Vienna and continuing over the next two decades in the United States, included an early form of Forum Theatre and a precursor to the Living Newspaper, a concept which he claimed to have invented and which was 'trivialized and distorted' by the Federal Theatre Project.[16]

It is significant that, like Boal, Moreno begins his theory with a critique of the Aristotelian catharsis in order to claim aesthetic as well as psychiatric validity. The Aristotelian catharsis is experienced by the spectator because of the 'conserve' of the drama, which confines the actors to an imitation of reality. But in psychodrama,

the protagonist is challenged to respond with some degree of adequacy to a new situation or with some degree of novelty to an old situation. When the stage actor finds himself without a role conserve, the religious actor without a ritual conserve, they have to 'ad lib,' to turn to experiences which are not performed and ready-made, but are still buried within them in an unformed stage. In order to mobilize and shape them, they need a transformer and a catalyst, a kind of intelligence which operates here and now, *hic et nunc*, 'spontaneity.' Mental healing processes require spontaneity in order to be effective.[17]

For Moreno, that spontaneity is the product of a 'mental catharsis' experienced by the actor. Moreno's techniques were devised to provoke the actor-patients 'to be on stage what they are more clearly and explicitly than they appear to be.'[18] Spontaneity is a necessary condition for healing but it is also a desirable state in itself. Stanislavski intimated this, seeking ways to 'make his actors more spontaneous in the acting of conserved roles.'[19] In fact Moreno's ideas of spontaneity have been justified by the experimental theatres of Antonin Artaud in France between the wars and Jerzy Grotowski in post-war Poland, both of whom shared Moreno's concept of an actor's catharsis and made it the preoccupation of avant-garde performance. It is equally true that both Artaud and Grotowski were able to apply essentially psychodramatic techniques to theatre by freeing the concept from the rigid structure that Moreno prescribes. His system calls for a presiding analyst and a clinical staff of trained 'auxilary egos' to flesh out the actor-patient's scenario.

Moreno realized that 'there is a limit ... to how far the psychodramatic method can go in fact-finding and solving interpersonal conflicts. The collective causes can not be dealt with except in their subjective form.'[20] Sociodrama posits a psychoanalytic solution to social problems, on the assumption that a 'collective catharsis' will lead to a deeper understanding of the 'life roles' of different cultures and groups.[21] This is in keeping with the idea that human and cultural relations could be understood as a science, which Moreno called 'sociometry.'

In his protocol for a sociodrama based on 'the Negro-White Problem,' Moreno describes the technique as it was applied in a seminar at an unnamed American university.[22] He asks a black couple from the audience to step onto the stage. They introduce themselves and begin to re-enact a typical evening in their home. Conscious of their audience and the subject of discussion, the couple's conversation centres on race relations. They are interrupted by 'Mrs. White,' one of Moreno's 'auxilary egos' in the role of a hostile white women who bursts into the apartment looking for the black child who hit her son. After her exit, the couple discuss their reaction to her racist attitudes, at which point she enters again in a conciliatory mood and invites them to dine with her. Initially the couple decline, but change their minds after Moreno's intervention. He asks them if this is a believable situation; this leads to an analysis of their attitudes and behaviour in the scene. Moreno then asks them to play a scene in their life as they envision it ten years in the future. They project a future in which they have 'gotten rid of Jim Crow' and in which the problems of racism have been modified greatly. At this point, Moreno turns to the audience and asks them to decide whether the couple acted in an 'appropriate manner.' He cautions them that they must vote with an awareness of the sociological implications of the scene. After the vote, Moreno calls for volunteers to replay the roles as they deem fit; these attempts form the basis of his concluding analysis, in which he charts the 'structure' of the audience in terms of its several responses to the scene. Throughout the session, Moreno is very much the clinical teacher directing the audience towards specific principles:

Sociodrama is introducing a new approach to anthropological and cultural problems, methods of deep action and of experimental verification. The concept underlying this approach is the recognition that man is a role player, that every individual is characterized by a certain range of roles which dominate his behaviour, and that every culture is characterized by a certain set of roles which it imposes with a varying degree of success upon its membership.[23]

Moreno and Boal both outline a structure in which audience intervention is permissible only within specific guidelines. For Moreno, the intervention enables the audience to arrive at a collective understanding of social reality; this understanding will enable the audience to correct their own deficiencies. For Boal the intervention enables the audience to understand their own abilities to change their reality. In both cases the theatre forum is a model of objective conditions, although in Boal's terms Moreno compounds Aristotle's 'coercive' system, and by Moreno's terms Boal is a propagandist more committed to action than understanding. Boal as a Marxist and Moreno as a psychoanalyst share a belief in the scientific analysis of human action, and this empiricism is reflected in the rigidity of the theatrical structures they propose.

Like Moreno and Boal, Catalyst seeks to use theatre as an analytic tool, but there is no science in its philosophy. *Stand Up for Your Rights* and *It's About Time* are based on systematic research, but they rely more on subjective understanding than scientific or ideological analysis on the part of the actors. The actors in turn do not claim the supervisory expertise that is essential to the techniques of Moreno and Boal. In *Stand Up for Your Rights*, a referee figure is necessary to explain the process to the mentally handicapped audience, but he is not a spokesman for a specific interpretation of the action. In *It's About Time*, a supervisory figure is unnecessary, because the play is devised to elicit an emotional rather than analytical response from the audience. In the process of developing the play, the Catalyst actors found that the less rigid and controlled the performance, the more effective was the intervention. The primary task confronting the actors in developing the play was that of inventing a form that could allow that freedom while retaining its coherence and dramatic structure.

IT'S ABOUT TIME: DESCRIPTION AND ANALYSIS

An analysis of *It's About Time* must be approached in terms of the problems that Catalyst confronted and resolved in the process of deciding upon the final subject and format of the project. Those problems are not easily delineated because in the process of researching the subject of incarceration, the actors and director were forced to re-evaluate and revise their initial goals. As was the case with the Mummers in Buchans, the Catalyst actors had to become experts on the subject even as they documented it from a position of presumed expertise. As they began to research prison life, they found that only by admitting the impossibility of achieving that expertise could they begin to understand the subject. This realization became the opening statement of the play, delivered in the manner of a prison 'rap':

> When we started out we knew fuck nothing
> Now we know fuck all.
>   It's About Time.
> We were fish and we were caught
> We want to do a play we thought
>   All about time.
> So armed with paper, pens and questions
> We began to get suggestions.
>   It's about time
> The system sucks most people said.
> And all we really need is bread
> And others said it's suicide
> To try and do a show inside.
>   We said/ it's about time
> We waded in we thrashed around
> We swam a bit began to drown
> We looked for answers to explain
> The simple ones went down the drain
> Sometimes we got badly burned
> This show's about the things we learned.
>   It's about time ... [24]

This opening rap was one of the few constants in every performance of *It's About Time*. As this analysis will show, the problems described in the rap required a form that could adjust to the specific situation of any institution in which the play might be performed. The text of the play exists only in a typescript of early versions of some of the scenes, all of which changed continually in performance. As there can be no authoritative version of the play, this analysis will refer to the typescript, as well as to an interview with Jan Selman and a public seminar on the show given by Selman, Anthony Hall, and Jane Heather.

It's About Time was conceived as a play about the problems prison inmates encounter when they are released into society. As in *Stand Up for Your Rights* the performance was intended to create a situation in which those problems could be analysed. This was the first such project Catalyst had initiated without a sponsor to provide guidelines and direction, and although this meant that the company was free to follow its own ideas, the absence of imposed goals meant that the actors had to define the purpose of the project themselves. This fact, combined with the special nature of prison audiences, forced the actors to reconsider their preliminary assumptions about the play. According to Jan Selman, who directed the project:

Previously, all the people we had worked with were people who thought they had a problem, and were willing to discuss it and engage in some kind of dialogue about it. Inmates don't think they have any problems. So why are you going to talk to them about their problems? Who are you and what are you up to? That was the first major problem we had to look at in a different way to do the research. Problem or no problem, they do not need you.[25]

Catalyst believed, and the prison authorities who gave the company permission to enter the prisons agreed, that the project had value. The actors' initial meetings with inmates revealed that the original idea of a play about the problems of readjusting to society was inappropriate. There were two reasons for this. The first reflects the nature of prisons themselves. The project took the actors to every kind of penal institution in Alberta, from the federal penitentiary at Drumheller, to short-term minimum security provincial institutions, and half-way houses. The actors discovered that if the idea of an interactive performance for prisoners had validity, it would have to deal with the very different conditions obtaining in the different types of institutions. In Selman's words: 'What we found out very quickly was that there's no point in talking to a guy who's got two years more before he gets out about the problems of getting out.'[26]

The second reason for the change in topic had to do with the nature of the research process. The actors began by meeting with inmates in various institutions. In these preliminary sessions, the actors tried to overcome the prisoners' suspicions and establish the rapport that would encourage the prisoners to relate experiences and insights not normally told to outsiders. When the actors asked the inmates what they thought the play should be about, the invariable response was that it should describe prison conditions for outside audiences. Selman has observed that had this been the direction the play had taken, the inmates 'wouldn't have told us the right stories ... no way.'

The eventual success of It's About Time testifies to the actors' abilities to develop a rapport with the inmates and obtain the 'right stories,' but that rapport was achieved with some amount of difficulty because of two factors. The most obvious was the intrusion of the realities of prison life. Selman has described one instance when the actors were taken on a tour of Drumheller after a fruitful session with an inmate group: 'Any sense of "personalness" we had developed that day was of course dispelled because now we were on tour and people were told to be in the cell where we could look in.'

At the same time, the actors had to confront their own attitudes towards criminality. Selman gives the example of a young parolee with whom the cast had established a rapport. On a return visit to his half-way house, they were told that he had been arrested again for the rape of a sixteen-year-old girl. The actors had learned to communicate with inmates as individuals, but they could not ignore the fact that many of the inmates with whom they were working had committed reprehensible crimes. It may be a reflection of the actors' personal attitudes towards the subject of crime that most of the offences mentioned in the play are crimes against property rather than crimes against persons. This may have helped modify the actors' personal reactions to criminality, but the very fact of criminal violence ensured that the play could not become a prison version of *The Farm Show*:

We were kicked around emotionally so hard by this stuff. You deal with where you stand with this stuff ... We could never be cons – we could never really know – we couldn't get closer, couldn't go and work in the barn for a day.

The actors' response to criminality may have been a factor affecting the research of the play, but it was not a serious problem. More difficult was their response to the prison system itself, for the research led to issues that the play was not designed to discuss. The actors began to learn the real issues of prison life when they asked the inmates what they would say in a show made for other inmates. This invited comments and issues that could only be dealt with in a critique of the penal system itself. To be successful as an analytic forum, however, the play could only focus on issues over which prisoners have some control or responsibility. In retrospect, Selman saw the play as a political act: 'They [the inmates] have their criminal consciousness; if [we] could move from there to the bigger things, we would be doing more than personal therapy.' In this, Selman echoes Boal's distinction between forum theatre and psychodrama. For Catalyst, however, the 'bigger things' were limited by the prison walls. The opening rap expresses the frustration the actors felt as a consequence of this limitation:

One thing everyone agreed
A chance a change is what we need

Long overdue
If I could be Robert Caplan [*sic*]
I would really make things happen
It's about time
But we're just us and us alone
You move a mountain stone by stone
Together we can move it faster
Take a step avoid disaster.

It's About Time avoids criticism of the penal system just as it avoids judgment of the crimes the inmates committed. This avoidance is a necessary condition of the project, but in the end it calls into question the efficacy of an interactive play designed to examine the problems of prison life. The inmates, and by Selman's admission the actors as well, attributed many of those problems to what they perceived as injustices in the penal system, but the play is predicated on the assumption that the inmates can assume responsibility for the social patterns they create within the system. The inability to reconcile that assumption with the necessary avoidance of the perceived sources of the problems is perhaps the most serious criticism of *It's About Time*. The optimistic assertion in the rap that 'you move a mountain stone by stone' is unsubstantiated in the play.

By the end of the research period, which lasted from mid-summer to December 1982, the actors had clarified the three basic principles that define the shape of the play. It had to address issues of prison life rather than the problems of adjustment into society; it had to restrict itself to those issues over which inmates have some control; and it had to reconcile the requirements of a show that speaks to the specific conditions of each prison with the need for a general structure and scenario applicable to prisoners in every type of institution.

In practice, the research process began with workshops with paroled residents of half-way houses, and continued with four sessions at Drumheller. These visits consisted of conversations with inmate volunteers; in their final visit the actors played some rough scenes, stopping frequently to ask the inmates to criticize and comment. This process provided the actors with necessary information, and it gave them documentary material in the form of case histories and short monologues that would be worked into the final play. In all of the workshops the inmates and parolees were asked to step into the scenes and improvise; in this manner the actors were able to test their own perceptions against the authentic response of the prisoners. Through this process the actors were able to define the basic issues of the play. According to Selman:

By the end of the rehearsal process ... we said, number one, the real issue is that a whole bunch of cons, especially young beginners, don't understand the system they're in, they can't even use what few benefits and what few routes there are. They don't even know how to use them. We got – to some extent – caught in that. That's what they were going to tell us, and so that's what we could then put out, and that was easy. But when we took that from experienced cons and ran into very green cons, new arrivals in an institution, it was a very important education kind of function: what is this system? How does it work? How do you get things out of it?[27]

The areas of investigation the actors defined in the research phase became the four basic units of the play. The first unit, 'The System,' introduces the particulars of the host institution and deals with the problems of adjustment to prison life. The second unit. 'Inside – Cooler,' is subtitled 'How to Make the System Work for You.' It looks at the problems of daily prison life: the difficulties of obtaining telephone calls to the outside, job changes, and visits. The third unit, 'Inside – Close,' asks the critical questions: 'Who am I? What do I want? How do I get it?' Here the issues are more complex; they examine relations with outside family and lovers; the complexities of dealing with other inmates and the obligation patterns that develop inside prison; and the larger question of inmate solidarity. The final section, 'Outside,' looks at the issues Catalyst had initially intended the play to examine.

Finding a suitable dramatic structure was only part of the complexity of the process. The actors also had to prepare the scenes with audience participation in mind. The scenes had to be structured in such a way as to invite audience comment and intervention without the leadership of a supervisory character. Most of this development occurred when Catalyst took a rough version of the show to Drumheller in December 1982 for five performances. At this point the actors were concerned with finding ways to 'open' the scenes to the audience. The experimentation with various techniques of drawing the audience into the scenes continued throughout the course of the project. Initially, the intervention techniques owed much to those used in *Stand Up for Your Rights*. The actors would ask the audience members to step into the scene, invite them to give the characters advice, or challenge the actor directly. The pronounced emphasis on characterization in the play is a direct result of this experimentation. For the audience, the dramatic characters gave the play authority; for the actors, the adherence to essentially documentary material reduced the possibility of error. According to Selman, 'we would constantly go back to a more presentational form, because often in animation you can start dreaming about "this person can become anything I want if I tell him what to do."'

For Moreno and Boal, the animation – that part of the performance that invites or provokes the audience to intervene – must be supervised by the clinician or the Joker, who directs the audience to an understanding of the analysis. Catalyst found that with prisoners the animation worked best when it proceeded from emotion rather than analysis. 'The best animation was the riskiest animation ... it challenged what the audience had given it with emotion, because the minute you pulled away they had all their reasoning and cons [deceptions] in place faster than you could move.' The actors found that prison society is 'a world of fast challenges and knife points.' Consequently, after a volatile scene, 'the actor and his character have the right now, because he's gone through that experience with [the audience] to challenge them. And that gets the fast answer back, which is then in the air, whether the guy retracts it or not, it's in the air and must be dealt with.'

The discovery that the play would work best when it provoked the audience to an emotional response was made possible by the decision to develop the performance around realistic characters, and in turn it seems to have justified that choice. In order for the play to be accepted as authoritative, the actors had to deny their opening statement of inexpertise by acting the parts of believable inmates with precise attention to detail. This is supported by Selman's example of a scene in one performance that did not work because the actor was wearing a belt in a situation in which belts would be prohibited.

Characterization is the key to the structure of *It's About Time*; it provides the authority necessary for the play to work, and it provides a method of adapting a general structure to very different audiences. Each of the three actors created a 'base' character, of whom the most relevant to a particular institution would receive the most 'airtime.' Robert Winslow played Mike, an older con who had been in and out of prison often, and is now incarcerated in a federal institution like Drumheller. Ed Lyszkiewicz played Jim, a 'fish,' imprisoned for the first time in a provincial institution. Jane Heather played Cindy, a woman with a long history of incarceration, now in a provincial institution.

A given performance would focus on one of these three characters, with the other two actors playing subordinate roles. In addition, the other two 'base' characters might appear in their own scenes. The exact structure of the performance depended on the actors' judgment. They would begin the performance by talking informally with the audience as they entered the playing area. These prefatory conversations established an informal atmosphere, and they gave the actors the chance to verify the conditions of the prison in order to avoid errors. In one show described by Selman, the actors were well into a scene about the problems of obtaining telephone calls when they discovered that calls were readily come by in that institution.

Depending again on the audience, each scene could be played in one of several variations. *It's About Time* exists then as a basic scenario which may be applied to any one of three central characters, for whom each scene exists in several different versions. The actors must follow the route through the play they judge most suitable for each particular audience. In traditional theatrical improvisation, the actors improvise the specifics of a scene on the basis of a set structure; here the opposite is the case. The scenes fall into two categories, character monologues and dramatic episodes. The monologues provide character exposition, as well as giving the play a direct presentational style necessary for the prison audiences, which in Selman's opinion had 'quite a strong lack of acceptance of theatrical convention.'

The performances usually took place in prison common-rooms or chapels, attracting any number from 15 per cent of the approximately five hundred inmates of Drumheller, to 75 per cent of the inmate population in some of the smaller minimum security institutions. Catalyst made an effort to keep the performance space as small and close to the audience as possible. The audience sat on two sides of the room, and portable flats screened off the remaining two sides. The set consisted of a table and two chairs. In half-way houses, where the play was usually performed in the audience's living room, the arrangement was even more casual.

It's About Time begins with the introductory rap cited above. The rap serves two related functions. The use of rhyme indicates to the audience that they are about to see a theatrical performance, and at the same time it 'demystifies' the performance by explaining the process by which it was made. It is also a frank admission that the actors have entered a world for which they are unprepared. The opening couplet of the rap is an ironic admission of inexpertise:

When we started out we knew fuck nothing
Now we know fuck all.

It is significant that *It's About Time* begins with a reference to the process formulated as a colloquial pun. According to Selman, the audiences found the rap very funny. The humour in *It's About Time* is one of the principal authentication devices of the play. Generally it is the humour of recognition; it demonstrates familiarity with the ways of prison life. The same principle holds true with the use of prison argot and vulgarity.

In the rap the actors introduce themselves as outsiders who nevertheless know their way around the prison system. Despite Selman's comment that the actors could not pretend to be prisoners in the same way the actors in *The Farm Show* could become the farmers they portray, they found in the course of the project that they needed to balance the realism of the scenes with even more direct reminders that they are performers and outsiders. Selman has suggested that future revivals, if any, might achieve this by adding more music to the show. The perceived need for an even more pronounced theatricality does not mean that audiences failed to appreciate the performance values of the play. A review of the play published in the Drumheller inmates' newsletter suggests the opposite:

High energy, fast rappin' rhyming with rhythm left no one dozing when this show began. The players moved like a team of pickpockets working the audience for all cash and valuables on hand, the audience paid with attention and were given performance with power to spare ... [28]

The rap is followed by a further demonstration of theatrical skill in a sequence called, in the shorthand of the play, 'High risk for actors.' In this test of improvisational skill, the actors ask the audience to suggest a topic. Two actors speak extempore on the topic (commonly, sex or drugs) while maintaining eye contact with each other. They then repeat the exercise, this time looking at the audience. The exercise establishes the actors' ability to improvise, and it demonstrates at an early point in the performance that the audience has some control over the direction the show will take.

The actors complete the opening segment of the play with short monologues introducing their characters. The typescript contains only one example:

I'm Cindy Lambert. I'm 23. I spent about half of the last four years in one joint or another. My last worker said to me, Cindy, you're institutionalized. She made it sound like a disease – once you get it you're dead. Cancer can be beaten.   (f 13)

The three 'base' characters are supplied with detailed histories that emerge later in the play as required. At this point, it is sufficient to establish that the three actors play three distinct but familiar personalities.

It is after these opening statements that each performance of the play begins to follow its own course, with the 'Make the system work for you' sequence that begins the 'Inside – Cooler' unit of the play. This sequence would normally examine one or more of three common prison problems: obtaining a telephone call, a change of job, or a visit from the outside. The actors play the scene so that the character fails to obtain his objective. The scene is then turned over to the audience in the first animation of the show. Because the scene describes a specific issue arising out of a technical procedure, the audience could be expected to respond easily. The responses produced by the animation provide the basis for further attempts at the scene, until the actors judge that the topic has been exhausted.

Following the animation, the performance moves on to one or two improvised scenes falling under the general heading of 'Reading people.' Again, these scenes focus on issues specific to the host institution, but this time the scene is presented as a problem in relating to other individuals such as guards, living-unit officers, and inmates.

The 'Inside – Cooler' section looks at typical problems from a structural or sociological point of view; in 'Inside – Close' the issues are defined in terms of specific characters. It is at this point that the character biographies are delivered in greater detail. The central character of the performance delivers a monologue that explains his history and the circumstances of his arrest. A typical example is that of Jim, the central character when the show played in provincial institutions such as Fort Saskatchewan, where the audience consisted of younger men serving sentences of less than two years, who were in Selman's words 'very noisy, rangy, wild.' Jim begins his monologue with a lengthy anecdote from his childhood, and goes on to describe his failed attempt to rob a drugstore. The language and tone of the monologue are typical of the show:

> ... Went down to Manpower. Holy Fuck! These fuckin' putrid colours, lime
> green, purple, shit banana. Yechh! And everybody in there looks like they just
> failed every test they'd ever written in the whole world.
> I waited in line for twenty minutes. They tell me to wait in another line – and they
> speak so loud, like in front of everybody else: 'Oh Mr. Smith, we see you've
> fucked up your life pretty bad. Dear me aren't you a failure!'
> Fuck off assholes. I went into a 7/11 on the way home and ripped off two skin
> magazines. (Pause) I'll fucking work all right! I started casin' out a drugstore
> ...
> (f 9)

Jim's monologue is based on an actual inmate's history, but it was written in three versions: the story he tells the prison authorities; another that he tells his fellow inmates; and the one he tells himself. These distinctions proved to be unfeasible in performance. According to Selman, 'their [the inmates'] consciousness is the Big Story that they tell each other, how you bend that to tell your kid [catamite]. But the real one – not admitted.' She gives the example of a performance at Fort Saskatchewan in which the actors felt it important to tell the final version, the story that Jim tells himself and no-one else. The audience took the story as another fiction; consequently, they were 'very disappointed' in the character and refused to accept him as one of them.

The versions could differ radically. In the story Cindy tells the authorities (a version used only once in performance), she describes a meeting in a Vancouver hotel with a salesman to discuss a possible job. The hotel is raided by the police who find hashish in Cindy's purse. She maintains that she was set up by the salesman. But in the version she tells her peers, she is caught in a major drug deal in Vancouver, and there is no attempt to apologize for her complicity. The versions are differentiated in performance: the version told to fellow inmates is delivered directly to the audience, while the typescript version of Cindy's story for the authorities indicates that it was spoken to another actor.

These monologues serve a structural purpose in the play by bringing the 'open' scenes back to the reality of the dramatic characters. They are however designed to elicit audience response as well. This ultimately led the actors to what amounted to a rediscovery of literary values, when the documentary reality of selected monologues was enhanced by the introduction of metaphor. This is most clearly seen in Jim's 'Mocked Turtle' speech, which comes towards the end of the 'Inside – Close' segment. In this particular monologue, Jim speaks from the perspective of an inmate who has been in and out of prison several times, and who has always served his full sentence without parole:

> This is how I fuckin' walk in here. Fuckin' turtle, right? And the worst thing is, I like it! I like walking like this! I like shufflin' along like a fuckin' turtle. Stick my head out, look around, pull it back in. You wanna know somethin', it's usually in. Fuckin' shutdown man! Lyin' around in the shop, walkin' up and down the unit, playin' (raquetball), it don't matter what the fuck I'm doin'. It's all the same.
> 'We got word your mother's dyin' back East. Take some Mellanil (bug juice) and cool out.' I fuckin' did too! Walked around doped up for two days, not a tear.
> You can throw me around, put the boots to me even, my head's in – no problem. Do any of you know, like when a turtle's head and legs are in and you throw it into the water – does it float or sink?
> When I'm chucked back outside, what will I do?
> (Pause, laugh)
> Into the watery waves of the world – *will I float?* – or will I sink? (f 34)

According to Selman, the response of most of the inmates to this monologue used the terms of the metaphor; typical responses were, 'You'll sink, man,' or 'Depends, did you get your legs back out or not?' As the Mummers found in Sally's Cove, the metaphor provided a focus for discussion. Perhaps more importantly, the introduction of metaphor seems to have offered a solution to the problem of 'the Big Story' by adding another level to the reality of the character.

If the monologue is made more effective by the introduction of a metaphor that allows the actor to express inner thoughts and attitudes, then it would seem to follow that the use of character action should be even more effective.

Characters in conflict can demonstrate a difficult situation as a complex of motivations and constraints, but the actors found that their first tentative efforts resulted in 'closed' scenes which resolved the problems without audience intervention. This tendency for scenes to 'close' dramatic problems in terms of fiction is similar to what Moreno identified as the 'role conserve,' and it underlies the initial critique of dramatic structure that impelled Boal and Moreno, as well as Catalyst, to experiment with intervention techniques. For Catalyst this seems to have resulted in a contradiction: dramatic scenes reveal character more thoroughly than monologues, yet at the same time they reduce the possibilities of intervention, especially in the absence of a supervisory figure. In *It's About Time*, most of the scenes follow the pattern set in the improvised scenes that follow the introductory unit, and although they seem to have been successful in provoking responses, they do not resolve this contradiction. In two scenes, however, Catalyst experimented with narrative techniques that suggest a resolution. They merit a closer look, for they touch on the larger question of dramatic form and documentary authenticity.

The first of these scenes is recorded in a typescript entitled 'Obligation/Alter Ego.' In it, Jim, as a 'fish' new to the system, asks Mike for help in filling out an application for temporary absence. Mike agrees, and although he offers his help in a friendly manner, a second actor playing his 'alter ego' verbalizes his actual thoughts.

MIKE
You don't read so good, do you kid?
ALTER EGO
He might be good for something.
MIKE
Fuck. Alright.
ALTER EGO
For a price.
MIKE
Got a smoke?
JIM
Sure man take the whole pack.
ALTER EGO
At least he's learned something.
JIM
Look I really appreciate this.
ALTER EGO
Save your thanks. You owe me.   (f 34)

Mike helps Jim even though he knows that the application will not be approved. Jim does not realize that he is being used, that he is now in debt to Mike, and that in the prison society that debt is binding.

The 'alter ego' was added to the scene initially to show the manipulation behind the words. In the language of traditional drama, it objectifies the subtext of the scene. After the scene was performed in Fort Saskatchewan, the actors dispensed with the 'alter ego' because the audience response indicated that the scene was 'doing their work for them.' Introduced as an anti-illusionistic device, the 'alter ego' in fact achieved the opposite effect. To elicit audience participation, the scene had to return to a conventional realistic style. According to Selman,

we placed it in a show in a situation where it was already established that it was anyone's show to get into, to participate, and he [Mike] simply at each decision point waited for the audience to tell him what to do with this guy, how to use him, whether to help him or not, what the implications of helping him were.[29]

The scene then became one of the most successful in the project, in part because it now required the active intervention of the audience throughout, and in part because of its volatile topic. In Drumheller, the scene provoked a rare discussion of homosexuality in prison:

They were willing in the drama to verbalize the fact that they would never verbalize in our research, about their use of each other ... When they came up for air at the end of the scene they rejected it all. 'Uh we were just putting you on.' But that group as a group had for those five minutes publicly admitted the social structure and their obligations.

The technique of waiting at each 'decision point' for audience direction reconciles the need for intervention with the structure of realistic drama. In effect, it returns to a more traditional form of improvised drama, in which the actor invents the specific direction of the scene within an established scenario. By following the directions of the audience, the animation could then force the inmates to assume responsibility for their own decisions, even if, as Selman states, they might disavow their comments after the scene is over.

The other attempt to find a dramatic form in which character action provokes audience response deals with a similarly important topic, that of visits from friends and family outside. According to Selman, 'The Visit' scene consistently provoked the strongest response: 'It was the first scene the cons took over and told us how to do.' The scene normally came relatively early in the show; the actors found that 'it was the most direct way to get very personal after the system stuff.'

The typescript version of 'The Visit' involves Mike and his wife Gina, but in institutions with younger populations, it would focus on Jim and his family. The structure is simple. Gina has come on one of her regular visits, after having missed the previous week. The conversation is tense, and ends in bitterness. Mike is on edge and suspicious because of Gina's missed visit; Gina is nervous because she has been offered a promotion in another town. The visit ends angrily:

GINA
I can't come down next week.
MIKE
Why not?
GINA
I gotta work.
MIKE
What the hell's going on.
GINA
It's not convenient, Mike.
MIKE
Not fuckin' convenient. Well I'm sorry I'm not fuckin' convenient for your fuckin' life.
GINA
I gotta go. I've gotta life to live.
MIKE
So do I. That's all right. It's time to go.
GINA
Write to me.
MIKE
Yeah
GINA
Bye.
MIKE
Bye   (f 31)

According to Selman, the scene ended when 'the wife left, the con went out [and said], "that fucking bitch" and just waited. That's the form the animation took: just an emotional outburst.' The inmates tended to support Mike, assuming that Gina is cheating on him, although there was also considerable support for Gina's predicament.

This is the only scene in the play in which the audience response is incorporated in a formal extension of the action. In most scenes the animation leads to discussion and a replay of the scene. In 'The Visit' the audience responses are incorporated in the form of improvised 'letters.' The format of the letters sequence is included in the typescript:

Mike-Gina – letters after the visit.
Animation: Mike draws out – kinds of stress couples are under when one is in prison.
– the ways helpful to maintaining relationships while inside. Letter: Each speak the letters they would write to another right after the visit.
The format is:
[paragraph] 1. Salutations and When/Where/Situation/ I've come to some conclusions.
         2. What I need.
         3. What I realize about you.
         4. Conclusion re: – relationship future
                          – issues from scene (money + job decisions)
        Sign off.
The letters are intercut:
Mike Par. 1.
Gina Par 1
Mike Para 2
Gina Para 2
etc.
Content is determined by nature of the audience's input. They challenge attitudes, make the situation real and complex again, provide more clear info. Mike includes what he has learned from animation.
Gina presents a different view.   (f 56)

This technique enables the actors to integrate the audiences' comments into the scene, but more importantly, it gives weight to the woman's point of view. The scene does not attempt to resolve the issues it presents. In most cases, Mike would try to keep Gina, and Gina would contradict that by deciding to accept the job.

The framing technique of the intercut letters is, for Selman, the means of introducing 'the wider view' in the scene by placing the action in a critical context. In 'Mocked Turtle' the actors came to a new understanding of the value of literary devices; in 'The Visit' they came to a similar understanding of the principle of montage. The use of the intercut letters is similar to that of the letter scene in *Buchans*. In *Buchans*, however, the letter scene uses montage as an expository device; here the montage fulfils a more critical function by countering Mike's decisions – which are based on audience response – with Gina's independent will. Hence the dramatic conflict of the scene is unresolved. By giving equal weight to both characters, the scene and the letter sequence that follows acknowledge that the issue of relations with persons outside is one over which inmates have limited control. In his letter to Gina, Mike can explain his decisions and attempt to persuade Gina to accept his point of view, but he has no means of enforcing his will. The device of the intercut letters embodies this frustration.

For the male inmate audience, it is Mike and not Gina who is the central character of the scene, despite the equal weighting in the action. The letter sequence is designed to build on that identification by placing it in a wider dramatic context. This is an effect that neither Boal nor Moreno can achieve with their respective methods. In their techniques as in *Stand Up for Your Rights*, and indeed most of the scenes in *It's About Time*, the typical scene places a representative character in conflict with essentially two-dimensional characters whose motives are schematic rather than wilful. These ancillary characters (Moreno's 'auxilary egos') facilitate or frustrate the central character's objectives according to the needs of the scene. In 'The Visit,' the representative character is placed in a realistic relation with a fully realized character. Gina's actions, no less than Mike's, must conform to the reality that the inmate audiences perceive, even though she is literally on the other side of the fence.

In the 'Obligation/Alter Ego' and 'Visit' scenes, the presentational techniques of documentary theatre are combined with the form of mimetic drama. In the plays discussed previously in this study, the narrative demands of the documentary require a rejection of mimetic drama; when dramatic techniques – in the sense of conflicting characters in action – are used, they are contained in larger scene units in which they function as a form of narrative gesture. This may be seen most clearly in *Paper Wheat*, but it also holds true of *Buchans*, in which techniques derived from mimetic drama – dialogue between invented characters – authenticates the material. *It's About Time* takes narrative technique almost to the point where it is no longer art, but at the same time, of all the plays in this study, it is the one that relies most heavily on character action. This apparent contradiction is resolved by the active role of the audience. Without audience intervention, 'The Visit' is merely a mimetic playlet notable only for its realism; with the intervention, it is a different order of theatre.

When we speak of characters in action, we must necessarily speak of plot, the very thing that documentary theatre repudiates. The concept of 'docudrama' has been applied chiefly to a form of chronicle play, and it rests upon the assumption that audiences can easily reconcile the paradox of an objective account depicted by means of invented detail. This paradox is only reconciled if the play expresses an interpretive ideology accepted by the audience. In the idea of documentary drama, the authenticity of the material is reinforced by the realism of the character action. The documentary and the fable are perceived as one.

It's About Time raises this same question of the relation of documentary and fable, for it partakes of both. The dialogue scenes which represent characters in conflict are contained in a presentational structure that 'foregrounds' the authenticity of the material through the monologues.

It's About Time depicts characters in action, but it has no more of a plot than *Ten Lost Years* or *Buchans*. In mimetic drama the logic of the plot manifests the idea of the play, and its polemical significance, if any, is inherent in the basic conception of the action imitated. In documentary theatre, that unity is provided by the topicality of the subject, the methodology of the research and the rhetorical structures of the performance – which may include characterization. Characterization becomes plot when the characters are invested with freedom of action, when they are placed in a situation that requires them to make choices and abide by the consequences. This is antithetical to the idea of documentary, and yet it is what we find in *It's About Time*.

The solution to this paradox lies in the workshop nature of the play. In mimetic drama the significance of each scene refers to the unfolding significance of the action as a whole. In *It's About Time*, each scene is a self-contained whole, and although Mike, Cindy, and Jim are fully realized dramatic characters, they have no active through-line in the play. They are created anew in each scene; continuity is supplied not by the action of a plot but by the personalities of the actors. The fact that the specifics of each character change according to the place of performance argues that the dramatic elements of the play are essentially rhetorical gestures comparable to the improvised banter in *Buchans*. In form, the dramatic scenes in *It's About Time* appear to belong to the tradition of mimetic drama, but in fact they do not.

It is clear that *It's About Time* represents a different order of documentary than the other plays discussed in this study, but because it is unique it lacks established criteria by which it may be evaluated. For Catalyst, those criteria are pragmatic. If the play creates a situation in which the issues it raises are discussed, then it is by definition successful. In this sense, *It's About Time* must be understood as a workshop project as well as a play. The prison audiences seem to have accepted it as a successful combination of both. The review cited earlier indicates that the prisoners enjoyed the play for its entertainment value. A letter written by an inmate of Drumheller testifies to its success as a workshop forum:

ITS ABOUT TIME is an honest portrail of prison life. Past present, and future questions were asked an neither party pulled any punches. We pushed and pulled, And strained out brains We exercised our imagination, and were forsed to face some harsh realities about ourselves. Together we arrived at some facts. The facts that inmstes could have a chance to discuss some issues that were important to us. THE fact that we were able to come out from behind our masks and express ourselvd is really quite extraordinary ... [sic][30]

This enthusiasm was not universal, and it must be balanced by the recognition that some of the inmates thought the project a waste of time. According to Jane Heather:

There were a couple of women I worked with that to the very end were still saying, 'I have nothing to say to other cons whatsoever. I still don't know why we're doing this.' – after they had seen the show.[31]

In a play such as *It's About Time* the criteria for evaluation are necessarily complex, and they must refer to standards that are external to the theatre. More than any other play in this study, *It's About Time* can only be assessed in terms of its target audience. The prison audience, because of its engagement in the issues of the play, is an active participant in the creation of the performance text.

That an appreciation of *It's About Time* as theatrical entertainment as well as political workshop is dependent on a close involvement with the subject matter can be inferred from Keith Ashwell's review of the show in the *Edmonton Journal*. In January 1983, Catalyst invited interested theatre professionals to a performance of the play at Northern Light Theatre, before an audience of half-way house residents. Ashwell's review reveals inadvertently the transformation that occurred when the play was removed from its context:

[There] were scenes that became dangerously lethargic, because the actors didn't know which route to take next and their 'instructors' were not about to help them.

The production is almost totally sympathetic to the con's view of the world. Whether it can find a convincing handle on a compassionate social response, I don't know, but I think it will because the actors produced some fascinating, intuitive and finely-focussed portraits of prisoners, likenesses that were sincerely applauded.[32]

Attempting to evaluate the play as a public performance – a response Catalyst invited by performing in a theatre – Ashwell brought to it standards and expectations derived from more traditional performance forms. The 'dangerous lethargy' he criticized was an important part of the interactive process (a process hindered by the presence of outsiders), and the matter of a 'compassionate social response' had no bearing on the play. The perceived inadequacies of the play as drama may in fact have been its strengths as interactive theatre.

The argument that the detached observer brings aesthetic experiences to the play which obscure or alter its values can be supported by looking at the nationally broadcast derivative of *It's About Time*, part of CBC's 'Catalyst Television' series. Taped before an audience of inmates, *Incarceration* uses material from *It's About Time* but with different actors under the direction of David Barnet.[33]

Although the broadcast differs from its theatrical parent by stressing information (especially for the uninformed viewers) rather than intervention, the fundamental relation of dramatic material and audience involvement is apparent. Lacking first-hand knowledge of the subject, the disinterested viewer cannot fully understand the qualities of imitation, dramatic logic, and language the inmates understand as entertainment. In effect, the television audience responds to a show about inmates analysing a show about their reality. Boal's defence of a 'poetics of the oppressed' finds some support in the fact that in its aesthetic principles, as well as in its subject matter, *It's About Time* addresses the sensibilities of a special audience.

It is too soon to speculate whether *It's About Time* represents a new direction for documentary theatre in Canada. At the very least it has redefined the boundaries of political peformance. Some immediate influences can be traced: since the project began, Catalyst has led workshops in intervention techniques at three festivals of popular theatre (Bread and Circuses, Thunder Bay, 1981; Bread and Roses, Edmonton, 1983; Bread and Dreams, Winnipeg, 1985; Standin' the Gaff, Sydney, 1987). The growing interest in interactive political theatre (inspired by both Boal and Catalyst) in Canada suggests that the localist documentary (even in its activist form, as developed by Chris Brookes) has given way to a more analytical approach which emphasizes problem solving rather than community sentiment. These interactive performances reinforce the argument that 'documentary' does not just signify a specific theatrical or dramatic form but rather an active relationship existing between the performance and the audience that accepts it as a factual, non-fiction treatment of actuality. In the Canadian context, *It's About Time* expands the scope of what documentary means, challenging established definitions and suggesting new possibilities.

Conclusion

Canadian Documentary Theatre in Context

The six plays examined in this study represent the major directions documentary theatre has followed in Canada. Together they reveal the formal and thematic characteristics that identify the Canadian documentary as a development of documentry theatre in general. By way of conclusion I wish to define these characteristics and consider their place in the context of modern Canadian theatre as a whole, and their effect on contemporary Canadian drama.

The most notable common features of these plays are their emphasis on collective creation and the transformation of historical or community experience into art. These features are not unique to the documentary; nor are they unique to Canada, although they may be more closely identified with the Canadian documentary than with comparable genres elsewhere. The interest in collective creation that made its way to Canada in the late 1960s coincided with a revival of nationalist (and by extension, regionalist) sentiment, and it provided a generation of theatre workers with the artistic method to explore local themes in the absence of an appropriate dramatic literature. In Britain, continental Europe, and the United States, the documentary developed as a genre of political theatre which embodied an implicit critique of established dramatic forms. In Canada, however, the documentary theatre evolved parallel to, and in some cases as part of, an emerging dramatic literature. The traits which distinguish it from comparable genres in Europe and the United States are those which characterize the Canadian alternative theatre as a whole.

The Canadian documentary has been an inextricable part of the search for a theatre that would be both indigenous and popular. All the plays in this book were created as 'popular theatre,' and, with the arguable exception of *Ten Lost Years*, all were intended originally for audiences who had a special interest in the subject but little familiarity with the theatre. In most cases, the original audience brought their own experience to an understanding of the performance.

The Clinton audience knew of Les Jervis and may have visited his animal sanctuary; the miners of Buchans had only recently finished the strike documented on the stage; the farmers who applauded *Paper Wheat* and *No. 1 Hard* had built the grain co-ops; the inmates who participated in *It's About Time* knew more than the actors ever could about the realities of prison life.

Unlike the Piscatorian tradition of documentary, with its emphasis on polemic, the typical Canadian documentry does not examine the value of actuality as evidence. It authenticates experience rather than ideology or polemical inquiry. It is for this reason that the plays in this book rely heavily on first-person monologues. The Canadian documentary has tended to be anti-ideological; it does not try to explain the significance of the matter it documents in an intellectual scheme, but rather suggests the significance of a shared historical or community experience by transforming it into art. In all the plays in this study, the fact of that transformation is as important as the textual content of the performance. This preference for community affirmation over ideology suggests that the Canadian documentary is ultimately a moralistic genre.

If the documentary is one expression of the alternative theatre's attempt to discover indigenous dramatic forms in Canada, it is nevertheless a distinct tradition. On the most simple level, the number of performances in the last twenty years of plays which have relied wholly or in large part on the presentation and authenticaton of actuality argues that the documentary must be considered a genre in its own right. Most of those plays originated in theatres that were committed to new Canadian plays and which directed most of their energies to non-documentary works; the documentary was for most of them one of several dramatic strategies for exploring local material. Of the groups represented in this book, only the Mummers Troupe maintained an almost exclusive interest in documentary (and even so, most of its plays combined documentary material with improvised satire). In many cases, the documentary production developed within the context of an ongoing body of work in several theatrical idioms. This is the case of *The Farm Show*, *Ten Lost Years*, and *It's About Time*. In other cases, it was a significant departure from the normal work of the theatre, as it was for the Globe with its documentary trilogy.

When considering the scope of the documentary as a genre, it is useful to question the extent and means of cross-fertilization between theatres. In Canada the theatrical community is quite small, but it is spread out across great distances. As a result, it is extremely difficult to establish direct lines of influence, or to decide whether similar experiments at opposite ends of the country were coincidental or related. Certain lines of influence can be defined in the development of the documentary theatre, such as those that connect

Littlewood to Luscombe, Cheeseman to Kramer, and Thompson to such companies as 25th Street Theatre and Theatre Network in Edmonton. Chris Brookes may have decided upon a community documentary at the same time as Thompson, but his approach to *Buchans* owed much to *The Farm Show*. Brookes had seen several of Thompson's shows in Toronto and, perhaps more importantly, had worked with actors who had worked with Thompson. Of the *Buchans* cast, for example, Howie Cooper had the year before worked with Thompson on *Oil*, a collective documentary on the history of the Ontario town of Petrolia. The importance of migrating actors, second-hand reports, and rumour may be difficult to assess, but all three are necessary to an understanding of why theatres separated by vast distances with little or no contact should conform to common patterns.

These common patterns have deeper sources; they are inscribed in the historical and linguistic contours of Canadian culture. As such they are the means by which we recognize that culture for what it is. When we compare the contemporary Canadian theatre with the emerging theatres in Latin America, Africa, and Australasia, certain parallels are apparent. There seems to be a necessary stage of post-colonial consolidation in the theatre, when playwrights and collectives seek and define images, thematic patterns, metaphors, and performance techniques that can express cultural realities overlooked or repudiated by the received colonial traditions. The search for indigenous forms must be to some degree artificial and self-conscious; of the numerous possible artistic forms available in a culture, certain ones will better express particular traits of a society at a particular point in its development. In that sense, the documentary plays of today are no more 'Canadian' than were the patriotic, imperialist verse tragedies of a century ago; the definition of what indigenous means is itself subject to historical change. At the same time, it is obvious that if a conscious attempt to establish indigenous cultural forms leads to widespread adoption of the techniques discovered there is a case to be made for a deeply rooted cultural need that the forms fulfil. The success of the Canadian documentary in that sense has validated its implicit critique of Canadian culture as the expression of a colonized mentality. The process of rejecting colonial standards may involve the self-conscious attempt to prescribe indigenous replacements but as the Canadian example has shown, that self-consciousness may be a necessary step in the evolution of a post-colonial culture.

The Canadian documentary developed as a vehicle to explore local subjects, but its characteristic emphasis on collective creation developed for separate reasons. The vogue of collective creation that developed in the 1960s to challenge the hierarchical structures of traditional theatrical creation gave artists the techniques and theatrical vocabulary to explore their vision of an indigenous theatre. It may be that there is a common basis in the alternative theatre's nationalism and its collectivist populism, that the tide of Canadian nationalism that made its mark in the 1960s was related to the anti-establishment liberationist sentiment that swept through western society. Although such a relationship cannot be proven, it would do much to explain the Canadian documentary's emphasis on shared experience and its inclusion of the research process into the performance text.

The Canadian documentary defines culture in terms of community and it defines community in terms of shared experience. Collective creation, with its improvisational element and its emphasis on the actors as authors, embodies that concept of community; it shows shared experience as a creative process. When combined with the populist desire to define local subjects, collective creation became more than a passing theatrical fad; it was the key which for the first time enabled Canadian artists to define indigenous theatre in terms of a popular audience rather than an educated elite. That is why collective creation has not been restricted just to the localist documentary in Canada, but has been applied to a whole range of dramatic genres, of which the most important have been comedy (as in the work of Newfoundland's Codco) and historical drama. In all cases, collective creation recreates traditional literary genres as genres of performance.

If, then, the Canadian documentary is a genre of performance that can be characterized by its use of collective creation to explore local themes and the authentication of actuality in the performance itself, it originated with Paul Thompson's decision to create *The Farm Show* in 1972. As with any genre, there are a number of exceptions to the norm; *The Trial of Louis Riel, Ten Lost Years*, and *No. 1 Hard* are notable examples. In each case, documentary forms developed in other countries have consciously been adopted and applied to Canadian subjects.

The place of the documentary in the larger context of modern Canadian drama is obscured by the fact that the documentary is a genre of performance rather than dramatic literature. The few documentary plays that have been published occupy an important but minor page in the canons of Canadian drama; they are usually included with polemic historical dramas in a hybrid genre of 'docudrama.' Considered solely in terms of dramatic literature, the documentary's validity as a genre is not easily demonstrated. It is only when considered in terms of theatrical performance and the large number of unpublished performance texts (many of which survive only in second-hand reports) that the contours of the genre are visible.

Although it is still too soon to determine the influence the documentary theatre has had on the development of Canadian playwriting, there are indications that its effect has been important. Its contribution may be suggested in two areas: the widespread adoption of collective creation as a playwriting technique, and the popular use of presentational performance techniques in literary drama.

Fifteen years after Paul Thompson began experimenting with collective creation, it is still widely practised in Canada, but following Thompson's own lead (in such plays as *The West Show* and *Torontonians*) it is no longer identified with community documentaries. Rather it has become for many companies a more efficient way of writing a play. A group of skilled actors can improvise a play in six weeks while a single playwright might take several years. The difference is not only in the fact that the collective play will lack the deeply intuitive structures and patterns of a written drama. As the product of several minds synthesizing their responses to the subject, the collective play tends towards involved performance structures rather than verbal complexity or poetic structure. As Thompson discovered, collective creation lends itself towards a theatre of physical and visual metaphor. For that reason it has become a common technique among avant-garde theatres. There may be fewer collective plays produced today than there were ten years ago, but they cover a wider range of interests and styles.

The presentational theatricality that characterizes most Canadian documentaries has become a familiar feature of other genres as well, especially in historical drama. In the documentary the actors present the performance as a collective report of their experiences; in literary drama presentational techniques commonly appear as metaphorical devices which challenge the illusionistic conventions that audiences normally expect in the theatre. The ensemble performances of James Reaney's *Donnelly Trilogy*, the history-as-hockey metaphor of Rick Salutin's *Les Canadians* and Sharon Pollock's ringmaster-narrator of *The Komagatu Maru Incident* are typical of the ways playwrights have assimilated presentational techniques into their individual styles. These presentational devices were not the invention of the documentary theatre; in the early 1960s Canadian playwrights such as John Coulter and Reaney were exploring ways of foregrounding performance as a formal innovation in the drama. The documentary theatre popularized the idea of presentational performance and trained a new generation of actors and playwrights in its use.

There is a third and more important area in which the documentary theatre has made a lasting contribution to Canadian drama and theatre, and that is in the evolution of a new acting style. In the late 1970s, the generation of actors who trained in the presentational techniques of documentary theatre began to attract notice for their performances in new dramatic plays. Actors such as Eric Peterson, Linda Griffiths, and David Fox may be better known today for their recent performances in new plays than for their pioneering work in collective companies. As their generation of actors graduate to major roles in the classics as well as new plays, they bring with them a style that combines intimate realism with a delight in broad gesture, and replaces the traditional British-trained diction with recognizable Canadian accents.

At this point it is impossible to assess the significance of this development, but it is likely that this style has had an effect on recent playwriting. As playwrights increasingly write with particular actors in mind, those actors in turn influence the author's dramatic techniques. As well, several of the actors who pioneered this new style have themselves become playwrights, of whom Linda Griffiths (*Maggie and Pierre, O.D. on Paradise*) and Ted Johns (*Naked on the North Shore, Garrison's Garage*) may be the best known.

It is perhaps because the documentary theatre has been above all an actors' theatre that it appears to have moved beyond a first phase of development. Since the late 1970s there has been a notable decline in the number of documentary plays performed in Canada. This may be explained in part by the natural evolution of the genre, as actors and directors refine their art and move on to experiment with other forms, and by a waning interest in the ideas of populism and localism that fuelled the alternative theatre of the 1970s. There are more material reasons as well. The documentary theatre played a considerable role in the formation of new theatre companies in the 1970s. Many of them no longer exist, often for reasons inherent in the companies themselves (such as splits within a collective), but more usually because they did not qualify for increases in public funding. Actors who a decade ago thought little of working for subsistence wages find as they grow older that they can no longer afford to work for non-Equity companies.

Of the theatres discussed in this book, the Mummers Troupe no longer exists; Theatre Passe Muraille and 25th Street Theatre have largely abandoned collective creation in favour of scripted plays, and Toronto Workshop Productions and Globe Theatre produce occasional historical documentaries. Only Catalyst has continued using the documentary as an integral part of its socially active theatre. The example of these theatres suggests that if the documentary is no longer as popular – or as necessary – as it was a decade ago, it survives as an increasingly specialized genre.

In the 1970s the documentary was part of a nationalist movement which explored localism as the basis of an independent culture; in the 1980s there appears to be a tendency for it to document social or political issues rather than community experince. The examination of archival documents in *Medicare!* and the interactive techniques of *It's About Time* suggest two directions the Canadian documentary may take in the future. As well, there has been a notable resurgence of agitprop documentary among women's groups across Canada. Increasingly, the documentary has become a technique of 'popular theatre' as the term is used by the Canadian Popular Theatre Alliance, an organization formed in 1981 to promote socially active theatre. The dozen or so member companies of the CPTA (the exact number varies from year to year) show an ongoing commitment to documentary and collective creation. Significantly, most of those companies work outside the major urban centres; for them the documentary remains a useful strategy for reaching local audiences who share a strong sense of community.

It may be impossible to define with any certainty the significance of the documentary to modern theatre and drama in Canada. Many of the manuscripts and documents which might contribute to such an assessment have been lost or are not yet available. But it is clear that the documentary has been an important force in the establishment of an indigenous Canadian theatre. It has produced some of the most popular productions in the history of Canadian theatre, and it has trained a generation of actors and playwrights in the techiques of collective creation and presentational performance. Its widespread popularity, which coincided with the revival of nationalist sentiment, suggests that it has proven its premise that Canadian audiences welcome theatre that speaks in their idiom about the communal issues of their lives. The documentary theatre has been a major expression of independent culture in Canada, and remains as one of its most visible signs.

Notes

CHAPTER 1 The Evolution of Documentary Theatre in Canada

1 Dorothy Livesay, 'The Documentary Poem: A Canadian Genre,' *Contexts of Canadian Criticism*, ed. Eli Mandel (Toronto: University of Toronto Press 1971), 269
2 Ibid, 267
3 Rick Salutin, 'The Culture Vulture,' *This Magazine* 10, nos 5 & 6 (1976): 26
4 Ted Johns, 'An Interview with Paul Thompson,' *Performing Arts in Canada* 10, no 4 (1973): 30
5 Charles Mair, *Tecumseh: A Drama and Canadian Poems* (Toronto: William Briggs 1901), 3
6 James Bovell Mackenzie, *Thayendanegea: An Historico-Military Drama* (Toronto: William Briggs 1898), iii. Mackenzie's deliberate attempt to outdo Mair's *Tecumseh*, published twelve years earlier, extended even to his attitude to factual verification. His play has twenty-one pages of explanatory notes, compared to Mair's twenty.
7 Cited by Augustus Bridle, *Toronto Star*, 3 January 1942
8 John Coulter, 'Mr Churchill of England,' typescript, 1942, John Coulter Archive, Mills Memorial Library, McMaster University, Hamilton, Ont.
9 Geraldine Anthony, *John Coulter* (Boston: Twayne 1976), 70
10 Desmond Morton, ed., *The Queen v Louis Riel* (Toronto: University of Toronto Press 1974), 205–6
11 John Coulter, *Riel* (Hamilton: Cromlech Press 1972), 97–8
12 John Coulter, *The Trial of Louis Riel* (Ottawa: Oberon Press 1968), 36
13 Geraldine Anthony, ed., *Stages Voices* (Toronto: Doubleday 1978), 16–17
14 John Willet, *The Theatre of Erwin Piscator* (London: Eyre Methuen 1978), 186
15 Karl Kraus, *The Last Days of Mankind*, ed. and trans. Frederick Ungar (New York: Frederick Ungar 1974), 3
16 Peter Cheeseman, introduction, *The Knotty* (London: Methuen 1970), xiv

17 Theatre Ontario program note, Theatre Conference II, Theatre Ontario papers, Archives of Ontario

18 Thompson had 'a few conversations' with Cheeseman during the visit and saw Cheeseman's film of his process, but took exception to Cheeseman's rigorous adherence to primary source material. 'I disagreed with his rules – I couldn't buy that.' Thompson was impressed, however, by the fact that Cheeseman's working method was 'a mess – anarchy.' In this Thompson did not differ. Interview with Paul Thompson, 17 May 1983

19 Martin Kinch, 'Canadian Theatre: In for the Long Haul,' *This Magazine* 10, nos 5 & 6 (1976): 5

20 Bernard K. Sandwell, 'Our Adjunct Theatre,' *Canadian Club Addresses* (Toronto: The Canadian Club of Toronto 1913), 103

21 Archibald Key, 'The Theatre on Wheels,' *Canadian Forum* 13, 156 (1933): 7

22 Diane Bessai, 'The Regionalism of Canadian Drama,' *Canadian Literature* 85 (1980): 30

23 Ibid, 11

CHAPTER 2 Documentary and Collective Creation: *The Farm Show*

1 Urjo Kareda, 'Theatre Passe Muraille,' publicity release, n.d., Theatre Passe Muraille archives

2 Robert Wallace, 'Holding the Focus: Paul Thompson at Theatre Passe Muraille: Ten Years Later,' *Canadian Drama* 8, no 1 (1982): 57

3 Ted Johns, 'An Interview with Paul Thompson,' *Performing Arts in Canada* 10, no 4 (1973): 31

4 Linda West, 'Passing Comment on Theatre Passe Muraille,' *That's Showbusiness*, 20 September 1974

5 Wallace, 'Holding the Focus,' 57

6 Johns, 'Interview,' 30

7 Tom Shandel, 'Ted Johns' *Naked on the North Shore,' Georgia Straight*, 24 February – 3 March 1977

8 Theatre Passe Muraille, *The West Show*, in *Showing West: Three Prairie Docudramas*, ed. Diane Bessai and Don Kerr (Edmonton: NeWest Press 1982), 25

9 Rick Salutin, '*1837: Diary of a Canadian Play,' This Magazine* 7, no 1 (1973): 11

10 R.D. Mackenzie, 'Theatre Passe Muraille, Paul Thompson,' *Alive* 39 (1974): 8

11 Urjo Kareda, 'Collective Theatre: You Write Your Part or You Walk on,' *Toronto Star*, 21 September 1974

12 Liza Williams, 'Passe Muraille: Learning from the Rural Folk,' *Clinton News Record*, n.d., Theatre Passe Muraille archives

13 Paul Wilson, 'Blyth Spirit,' *Books in Canada*, April 1983, 12

14 Wallace, 'Holding the Focus,' 58

15 Robert Wallace, 'Paul Thompson at Theatre Passe Muraille: Bits and Pieces,' *Open Letter* 2nd ser., 7 (1974): 54
16 Theatre Passe Muraille, *The Farm Show* (Toronto: The Coach House Press 1976), 7
17 *The Farm Show*, 19
18 Theatre Passe Muraille, *I Love You, Baby Blue* (Toronto: Press Porcepic 1977), 55–6
19 Urjo Kareda, 'Home Truths,' *Canadian Forum* 57 (1977): 35
20 Mary Jane Miller, 'The Documentary Drama of Paul Thompson,' *Saturday Night* 89, no 7 (August 1974): 37
21 Robert Wallace, 'Growing Pains: Toronto Theatre in the 1970s,' *Canadian Literature* 85 (1980): 70–1
22 Wallace, 'Paul Thompson,' 52
23 Theatre Passe Muraille, *Doukhobors* (Toronto: Playwrights Co-op 1973), 2
24 Urjo Kareda, 'New play *Doukhobors* a praiseworthy effort,' *Toronto Star*, 3 April 1971
25 Herbert Whittaker, 'Sexless Stripping a Useful Artifice in *Doukhobors*,' Toronto *Globe and Mail*, 3 April 1971
26 Candace Bullard, '*I Love You, Baby Blue*: Two Inside Views,' *York Theatre Journal* 5, no 2 (1976): 29
27 The best example of the Québécois documentary theatre may be Le Grand Cirque Ordinaire's *T'en rappelles-tu, Pibrac?*, a 'socio-poétique' agitprop created in three days in 1971. Although such community-based plays have been common in Quebec, they are best discussed in terms of agitprop rather than documentary as such. For a discussion of the political aspects of Québécois theatre, see 'Dossier théâtre populaire, théâtre militant: le Grand Cirque Ordinaire et le Théâtre d'la Shop,' *Stratégie: lutte idéologique* 9 (1974). The theatrical context of the Quebec movement is discussed by Fernand Villemure in 'Aspects de la création collective au Québec,' *Jeu* 3 (1977).
28 West, 'Passing Comment,' 5
29 Janice Keys, 'Chance Remark Started Show,' *Winnipeg Free Press*, 27 March 1974
30 This is also the conclusion of Robert Nunn, who has developed it into a sophisticated analysis of the play. See 'The Meeting of Actuality and Theatricality in *The Farm Show*,' *Canadian Drama* 8, no 1 (1982): 43–54
31 *The Farm Show*, 23. All subsequent quotations are documented by page numbers in parentheses after the text.
32 Paul Thompson, personal interview, 17 May 1983
33 Wallace, 'Holding the Focus,' 57
34 Liza Williams, 'Clinton Area Opening Left Audience Agog, Talking,' *Goderich Signal*, 17 August 1972
35 Wallace, 'Paul Thompson,' 53

36 Johns, 'Interview,' 32
37 For an example of criticism that questions *The Farm Show*'s avoidance of economic and political issues, see Robin Endres, 'Many Actors Make a Play,' Toronto *Globe and Mail*, 14 March 1975, TV Ontario supplement.
38 Thompson, interview
39 Thompson, interview

CHAPTER 3 Documentary and Popular History: *Ten Lost Years*

1 Ted Johns, 'An Interview with Paul Thompson,' *Performing Arts in Canada* 10, no 4 (1973): 30
2 Herbert Whittaker, 'Luscombe, *Ten Lost Years* Both Still on the Go,' Toronto *Globe and Mail*, 23 August 1975
3 Mira Friedlander, 'Survivor: George Luscombe at Toronto Workshop Productions,' *Canadian Theatre Review* 38 (1983): 45
4 Robert Fulford, 'Luscombe Is Top Banana – Again,' *Saturday Night* 43, no 6 (July/August 1978): 5
5 Peoples' Repertory Theatre file, Metropolitan Toronto Library, Theatre Department
6 Howard Goorney, *The Theatre Workshop Story* (London: Eyre Methuen 1981), 26
7 Ibid, 161
8 Quoted in ibid, 45–6
9 Nathan Cohen, 'Much to Admire in *Mechanic*, Nothing to Feel,' *Toronto Star*, 16 October 1965
10 Jack Winter, 'An Experience of Group Theatre,' *Toronto Star*, 27 January 1962
11 George Luscombe, personal interview, 18 December 1984
12 Renate Usmiani, *Second Stage: The Alternative Theatre Movement in Canada* (Vancouver: University of British Columbia Press 1983), 30
13 Luscombe, interview
14 Friedlander, 'Survivor,' 45
15 Luscombe, interview
16 Friedlander, 'Survivor,' 45
17 Anthony Ferry, 'Ten Good People and an Idea,' *Toronto Star*, 15 December 1959
18 Ferry, 'Ten Good People'
19 'Workshop Heads for Resort Area with Tractor, Trailor and Three Plays,' Toronto *Globe and Mail*, 2 July 1960
20 Nathan Cohen, *Toronto Star*, 11 February 1961
21 Cohen, 'Much to Admire in *Mechanic*'
22 Don Rubin, 'Creeping Towards a Culture: Canadian Theatre since 1945,' *Canadian Theatre Review* 1 (1974): 17
23 Cohen, 'A Look at Theatre in Toronto: The Pacesetters Fall Behind,' *Toronto Star*, 5 December 1970

24 Herbert Whittaker, '*Chicago '70*: A Winner Wooed,' Toronto *Globe and Mail*, 4 April 1970

25 Paul Levine, 'Theatre Chronicle: *Chicago '70*,' *Canadian Forum* 50 (July/August 1970): 175

26 Whittaker, '*Chicago '70*'

27 Whittaker, '*Chicago '70*'

28 Robert Hatch, 'New York,' *The Nation*, 15 June 1970, 734

29 Levine, 'Theatre Chronicle,' 176

30 David Brillington, 'CBC Has a Winner with *Ten Lost Years*,' *Calgary Herald*, 1 February 1975

31 Barry Broadfoot, *Ten Lost Years, 1929-1939* (Toronto: Doubleday 1973), vi

32 Joseph Erdelyi, 'Actors Are Reviving Those *Ten Lost Years*,' *Ottawa Citizen*, 21 September 1974

33 'Author Rides Depression Wave,' *Toronto Star*, 2 February 1974

34 Ibid

35 Luscombe, interview

36 James H. Gray, *The Winter Years: The Depression on the Prairies* (Toronto: Macmillan 1966) Michiel Horn, ed., *The Dirty Thirties: Canada in the Great Depression* (Toronto: Copp Clark 1972)

37 Erdelyi, 'Actors Are Reviving Those *Ten Lost Years*'

38 Luscombe, interview

39 Brian Boru [Brian Arnott], 'Ideology, the Breakfast of Champions,' *That's Showbusiness*, 14 October 1974

40 Ibid

41 Toronto Workshop Productions, *Ten Lost Years*, dramatized by Jack Winter and Cedric Smith, *Canadian Theatre Review* 38 (1983). All subsequent quotations are from this edition and the page numbers are given in parentheses following the text.

42 Broadfoot, *Ten Lost Years*, 44

43 Northern Light Theatre, *Ten Lost Years*, dramatized by Scott Swan, typescript, 1977

44 Northern Light Theatre, *Ten Lost Years* program

45 Luscombe, interview

46 Horn, *Dirty Thirties*, 122

47 Gray, *Winter Years*, 42–5

48 Boru, 'Ideology'

CHAPTER 4 Documentary and Regionalism: *No. 1 Hard* and *Paper Wheat*

1 Rex Deverell, 'A Tribute: Sue Kramer,' *Canadian Theatre Review* 21 (1979): 57

2 Globe Theatre, *Annual Report, 1979–1980*, 4

3 Ibid, 10

4 Rex Deverell, personal interviw, 14 June 1983
5 Ibid
6 Ken Kramer, personal interview, 14 June 1983
7 Ibid
8 Rex Deverell, 'Medicare! As a One-Man Collective,' introduction to Medicare!, in Showing West: Three Prairie Docudramas, 176
9 Deverell, 'Medicare!'; Kramer, interview
10 Deverell, interview
11 Globe Theatre, No. 1 Hard, typescript, 21–2. Two corrupt versions of the play exist in typescript, one from 1978 and one from 1979, each of which contains some but not all of the revisions made after the first performance. All quotations are from the first revised version; page numbers are given in parentheses in the text. Song lyrics appear in an unpaginated appendix.
12 Kramer, interview
13 Rex Deverell, 'On the Making of No. 1 Hard,' Canadian Council on Social Development, Perception 1, no 6 (July/August 1978): 12
14 Don Kerr, 'Paper Wheat: Epic Theatre in Saskatchewan,' in Paper Wheat: The Book, ed. Don Kerr (Saskatoon: Western Producer Prairie Books 1982), 19
15 Bob Bott, 'Prairie Song,' Canadian Magazine, 15 Sept. 1979, 1
16 Bob Bainborough, 'Recollections of the Making of Paper Wheat,' Paper Wheat: The Book, 33
17 Andras Tahn, personal interview, 30 June 1983
18 Ibid
19 Kerr, 'Paper Wheat,' 17
20 Guy Sprung, personal interview, 28 August 1984
21 Ibid
22 25th Street Theatre, Paper Wheat typescript, 1978, 1. All subsequent quotations from the Tahn version are taken from this typescript, which is a transcription of the Saskatoon performance at the end of the first tour; page references are given in parentheses following the quotation.
23 Bainborough, 'Recollections,' 33
24 Bob Jeffcott, 'Paper Wheat,' Next Year Country 4, no 4 (1977): 30
25 Tahn, interview
26 Tahn, interview; Sprung, interview
27 Minnie Harvey Williams, The Romance of Canada: An Historical Pageant (Toronto: Ryerson 1923), 27
28 Paper Wheat: The Book, 38. Unless specified otherwise, all subsequent quotations are taken from this edition; page references are given in parentheses in the text.
29 25th Street Theatre, Paper Wheat, Canadian Theatre Review 18 (1978): 75. Tahn

rewrote the opening lines of the Partridge speech for his edition (*Paper Wheat: The Book*, 62).

30 *Paper Wheat, Canadian Theatre Review*, 86
31 Martin Knelman, 'Moral Uplift on the Prairies,' *Saturday Night* 44 (1979): 60–1
32 Jean-Paul Daoust, '*Paper Wheat*,' *Jeu* 12 (1979): 200

CHAPTER 5 The Political Documentary: *Buchans: A Mining Town*

1 Urjo Kareda, 'Mummers Troupe Shuns Risks,' *Toronto Star*, 18 June 1975
2 Chris Brookes, 'History of the Mummers Troupe,' untitled typescript 1983, 'Conception,' 6. Each chapter of the typescript is paginated separately.
3 Brookes, 'History: Conception,' 6
4 Chris Brookes, 'Popular Theatre in Newfoundland,' typescript, 1981
5 Brookes, 'History: The Mummers Play,' 26
6 Dudley Cox, 'Theatre Newfoundland – The Professional Theatre in Newfoundland,' brief to the Canada Council, 16 September 1973, Mummers Troupe archive, Petty Harbour, Newfoundland
7 Keith Turnbull, 'Report to the Canada Council,' 6 May 1974, Mummers Troupe archive. On the basis of Turnbull's report, the council did in fact require that the three companies join together for grant purposes for the 1975–6 season. The merger proved to be of no benefit and was abandoned.
8 Quoted by Brookes in 'History: Anarchist, Agit-prop, Political Warfare ... ' 7
9 Quoted by Brookes in 'History: Anarchist ... ,' 5
10 Mummers Troupe, 'Manifesto,' 26 July 1976, Mummers Troupe archive
11 Brookes, 'History: Evolutions,' 5
12 Brookes, 'History: The History Play,' 11
13 Mummers Troupe, *Newfoundland Night*, typescript, 1973, 20
14 Brookes, 'History: The History Play,' 11
15 Chris Brookes, 'Useful Theatre in Sally's Cove,' *This Magazine* 8, no 2 (June 1974): 6
16 Ibid, 3
17 Ibid, 4
18 Ibid, 6
19 Mummers Troupe, *Gros Mourn*, typescript, 1973, 10
20 *Gros Mourn*, 7
21 'Demonstrators' Threats Fail to Stop Gros Morne,' *Corner Brook Western Star*, 14 August 1973
22 Brookes, 'Useful Theatre,' 6
23 Ibid, 6
24 Ibid, 3

25 Brookes, 'History: *Company Town*,' 4
26 Brookes, letter to Steven Bush, spring 1975, n.d., Mummers Troupe archive
27 Brookes, 'History: *Company Town*,' 4–5
28 Brookes, Buchans rehearsal diary MS, 17 July 1974
29 Ibid, 4 August 1974
30 Ibid, 29 July 1974
31 Brookes, 'History: *Company Town*,' 9
32 Brookes, diary, 21 July 1974
33 Brookes, letter to the author, 30 January 1984
34 Brookes, diary, 5 August 1974
35 Mummers Troupe, *Buchans: A Mining Town*, typescript, 1974, 1. All subsequent quotations are taken from this typescript, and page references are given in parentheses in the text.
36 Allen Booth, letter to Chris Brookes, 12 February 1975, Mummers Troupe archive
37 Sandra Heindsmann, '*Company Town*,' *Mayday* 1, no 1 (1975): 36
38 Brookes, letter to the author, 30 January 1984.
39 Urjo Kareda, 'Mummers Troupe Show Risks,' *Toronto Star*, 18 June 1975
40 Brookes, 'History: *Company Town*,' 8
41 David Billington, 'Mummers Re-enact Miners' Woes,' *Montreal Star*, 25 October 1974
42 Mummers Troupe, *Company Town* audiotape, 19 June 1975
43 Brookes, personal interview, 19 July 1983
44 Brookes, personal interview, 10 March 1979

CHAPTER 6 Documentary and Audience Intervention: *It's About Time*

1 David Barnet, personal interview, 22 June 1983
2 *Catalyst Courier* 1 (December 1981): 1
3 Paulo Freire, *Pedagogy of the Oppressed*, trans. Myra Bergamn Ramos (New York: Herder and Herder 1970), 67
4 Ibid, 100
5 Ibid, 52
6 Jane Heather, '*Stand Up for Your Rights*,' *Catalyst Courier* 1 (December 1981): 3
7 *Stand Up for Your Rights*, prod. Jack Emack, Catalyst Television, CBC-TV, 1981
8 Barnet, interview
9 Heather, '*Stand Up for Your Rights*'
10 Augusto Boal, *Theatre of the Oppressed*, trans. Charles A. McBride and Maria-Odillia Leah McBride (New York: Urizen 1977), 47
11 Ibid, 122
12 Ibid, 182

13 *Pour le meilleur ou pour la pire*, Théâtre sans Détour performance, Edmonton, 20 June 1983
14 Edgar Quiles and George Schuttler, 'Theatre for a World in Transition: Excerpts from an Interview with Augusto Boal,' *Theatrework* 3, no 5 (1983): 19
15 J.L. Moreno, *Psychodrama*, 4th ed. (New York: Beacon House 1977), 352
16 Ibid, 357
17 Ibid, xii
18 Ibid, 6
19 Ibid, 4
10 Ibid, 353
21 Ibid, 360
22 Ibid, 369
23 Ibid, 354
24 Catalyst Theatre, *It's About Time*, typescript, [1983?], 3. The typescript is incomplete and unpaginated. All subsequent references are identified by folio page numbers in parentheses following the quotations.
25 Jan Selman, '*It's About Time*,' public seminar, Bread and Roses Festival of Popular Theatre, Edmonton, 23 June 1983
26 Jan Selman, personal interview, 28 June 1983. All subsequent quotations of Selman are from this interview unless otherwise noted.
27 Selman, seminar
28 'Catalyst Theatre Delivers *It's About Time*,' Drumheller Institution inmates' newsletter, n.d., Catalyst Theatre files
29 Selman, seminar
30 Anonymous inmate, letter to Catalyst Theatre, n.d., Catalyst Theatre files
31 Jane Heather, '*It's About Time*,' public seminar, Bread and Roses Festival of Popular Theatre, Edmonton, 23 June 1983
32 Keith Ashwell, 'Cons earn accolades,' *Edmonton Journal*, 2 January 1983
33 *Incarceration*, prod. Jack Emack, 'Catalyst Television,' CBC-TV, 1983

Bibliography

This bibliography is in two parts. Part A lists material pertaining specifically to the plays and theatres or companies discussed in detail. Part B is a general listing of pertinent books and articles.

Part A is divided into the following seven sections: John Coulter and *The Trial of Louis Riel*; Theatre Passe Muraille and *The Farm Show*; Toronto Workshop Productions and *Ten Lost Years*; Globe Theatre and *No. 1 Hard*; 25th Street Theatre and *Paper Wheat*; Mummers Troupe and *Buchans: A Mining Town*; and Catalyst Theatre and *It's About Time*. The material in each of these sections is arranged in the following subsections as appropriate: Texts, History and Criticism, Archives, and Audiovisual. Unpublished letters, reports, publicity releases, and clippings are not listed individually; rather, they are included in the archives of files of the particular theatre. Interviews are not listed in the bibliography but are cited in the notes.

PART A

1 John Coulter and *The Trial of Louis Riel*

Texts
Coulter, John. *The Crime of Louis Riel*. Toronto: Playwrights Co-op 1976
– *Mr Churchill of England*. Typescript, 1942, John Coulter Archive, Mills Memorial Library, McMaster University, Hamilton
– *Riel*. Hamilton: Cromlech 1972
– *The Trial of Louis Riel*. Ottawa: Oberon 1968

History and Criticism
Anthony, Geraldine. *John Coulter*. Boston: Twayne 1976
– 'John Coulter.' In *Stage Voices*, edited by Geraldine Anthony, 1–26. Toronto: Doubleday 1978
Bridle, Augustus. 'Drama on Churchill written in Toronto.' *Toronto Star*, 3 January 1942
Morton, Desmond. *The Queen v Louis Riel*. Toronto: University of Toronto Press 1974

Osachoff, Margaret Gail. 'Riel on Stage.' *Canadian Drama* 8, no 2 (1982): 129–43

2 Theatre Passe Muraille and *The Farm Show*

Texts
Salutin, Rick, and Theatre Passe Muraille. *1837: The Farmers' Revolt.* In *Canadian Theatre Review* 6 (1975)
Theatre Passe Muraille. *Doukhobors.* Playwrights Co-op 1973
– *The Farm Show.* Toronto: The Coach House Press 1976
– *I Love You, Baby Blue.* Erin, Ont.: Press Porcepic 1977
– *The West Show.* In *Showing West: Three Prairie Docu-dramas,* edited by Diane Bessai and Don Kerr. Edmonton: NeWest 1982
Wiebe, Rudy, and Theatre Passe Muraille. *Far as the Eye Can See.* Edmonton: NeWest 1977

History and Criticism
Bullard, Candace. '*I Love You, Baby Blue*: Two Inside Views." *York Theatre Journal* 5, no 2 (1976): 27–31
Johns, Ted. 'An Interview with Paul Thompson.' *Performing Arts in Canada* 10, no 4 (1973): 31–3
Johnson, Chris. 'Theatrical Scrapbook' (review of *The Farm Show*). *Canadian Literature* 85 (1980): 131–6
Kareda, Urjo. 'Collective Theatre: You Write Your Part or You Walk On.' *Toronto Star,* 21 September 1974
– '*The Farm Show*: A Rich Theatrical Experience.' *Toronto Star,* 22 September 1972
– 'Home Truths' (review of *The Farm Show*). *Canadian Forum* 57 (1977): 55
– 'New Play *Doukhobors* a Praiseworthy Effort.' *Toronto Star,* 3 April 1977
– 'Theatre Passe Muraille.' Publicity release, Passe Muraille archives
Keys, Janice. 'Chance Remark Started Show.' *Winnipeg Free Press,* 27 March 1974
Knelman, Martin. 'Ondaatje's Inside View of *The Farm Show*.' Toronto *Globe and Mail,* 1 May 1975
Mackenzie, R.D. 'Theatre Passe Muraille, Paul Thompson.' *Alive* 39 (1974): 8
Martin, Robert. '*The Farm Show*: Snippets from Life Form Effective Picture.' Toronto *Globe and Mail,* 22 September 1972
Miller, Mary Jane. 'The Documentary Drama of Paul Thompson.' *Saturday Night* 78, no 7 (1974): 35–7
Nunn, Robert. 'The Meeting of Actuality and Theatricality in *The Farm Show*.' *Canadian Drama* 8, no 1 (1982): 43– 54
Salutin, Rick. '*1837*: Diary of a Canadian Play.' *This Magazine* 7 (May/June 1973): 11–15
Shandel, Tom. 'Ted Johns' *Naked on the North Shore*.' *Georgia Straight,* 24 February 1977
Wallace, Robert. 'Holding the Focus: Paul Thompson at Theatre Passe Muraille Ten Years Later.' *Canadian Drama* 8, no 1 (1982): 55–65
– 'Paul Thompson at Theatre Passe Muraille: Bits and Pieces.' *Open Letter* 2nd ser., 7 (1974): 49–71
West, Linda. 'Passing Comment on Theatre Passe Muraille.' *That's Showbusiness,* 20 September 1974

Williams, Liza. 'Clinton Area Opening Left Audience Agog, Talking' (review of *The Farm Show*). *Goderich Signal*, 17 August 1972
Whittaker, Herbert. 'Sexless Stripping a Useful Device in Doukhobors.' Toronto *Globe and Mail*, 3 April 1971

Archives
Passe Muraille archives. Theatre Passe Muraille, Toronto
Passe Muraille file. Metropolitan Toronto Library, Theatre Department

Audiovisual
The Clinton Special. Director Michael Ondaatje. Mongrel Films 1974
The Farm Show. Producer Ron Meraska. CBC-TV *Performance* 1972

3 Toronto Workshop Productions and *Ten Lost Years*

Texts
Northern Light Theatre. *Ten Lost Years*. Typescript, [1977]. Adapted by Scott Swan. Northern Light Theatre files, Edmonton
Toronto Workshop Productions. *Ten Lost Years*. Dramatized by Jack Winter and Cedric Smith. *Canadian Theatre Review* 38 (1983).

History and Criticism
Ashley, Audrey. 'Moving Account of Lost Years.' *Ottawa Citizen*, 9 September 1974.
'Author Rides Depression Wave.' *Toronto Star*, 2 February 1974
Billington, David. 'CBC Has a Winner with *Ten Lost Years*.' *Calgary Herald*, 1 February 1975
– 'Play Revives Depression's "Lost Years."' *Windsor Star*, 26 September 1974
Boru, Brian [Brian Arnott]. 'Ideology, the Breakfast of Champions' (review of *Ten Lost Years*). *That's Showbusiness*, 14 October 1974
Brissenden, Constance. 'Collective Creativity: Toronto Workshop Productions.' *White Pelican* 2, no 1 (1971): 35–52
Cohen, Nathan. 'A Look at Theatre in Toronto: The Pacesetters Fall Behind.' *Toronto Star*, 5 December 1970
– 'Much to Admire in *Mechanic*, Nothing to Feel.' *Toronto Star*, 16 October 1965
Erdelyi, Joseph. 'Actors Are Revising Those *Ten Lost Years*.' *Ottawa Citizen*, 21 September 1974
Ferry, Anthony. 'Ten Good People and an Idea.' *Toronto Star*, 15 December 1959
Friedlander, Mira. 'Survivor: George Luscombe at Toronto Workshop Productions.' *Canadian Theatre Review* 38 (1983): 44–52
Fulford, Robert. 'Luscombe Is Top Banana – Again.' *Saturday Night* 43, no 6 (1978): 5
Hatch, Robert. 'New York' (review of *Chicago '70*). *The Nation*, 15 June 1970, 734
Jackson, B.W. '*Ten Lost Years*: A Stark Portrait of Stark Times.' *Hamilton Spectator*, 5 March 1974
Kareda, Urjo. '*Ten Lost Years* Beautiful Theatre.' *Toronto Star*, 7 February 1974
Knelman, Martin. 'How the Stage Makes Epics of Our Lives.' *Saturday Night* 90, no 6 (1975): 89
Levine, Paul. 'Theatre Chronicle: *Chicago '70*.' *Canadian Forum* 50 (July/ August 1970): 174–6

Whittaker, Herbert. '*Chicago '70*: A Winner Wooed.' Toronto *Globe and Mail*, 4
    April 1970
– 'Lost Years: Making the Past Vivid.' Toronto *Globe and Mail*, 7 February 1974
– 'Luscombe, *Ten Lost Years* Both Still on the Go.' Toronto *Globe and Mail*, 23
    August 1975
– 'Return of *Ten Lost Years* and TWP Both Stirring Events.' Toronto *Globe and Mail*,
    13 December 1974
Winter, Jack. 'An Experience of Group Theatre.' *Toronto Star*, 27 January 1962
'Workshop Heads for Resort Area with Tractor, Trailor and Three Plays.' Toronto
    Globe and Mail, 2 July 1960

Archives
Jack Winter Archive, Mills Memorial Library, McMaster University, Hamilton
TWP file, Metropolitan Toronto Library, Theatre Department
TWP files, Toronto Workshop Productions

Audiovisual
Ten Lost Years. Producer Robert Allen. CBC-TV 1974
Smith, Cedric, and Terry Jones. *Ten Lost Years and Then Some*. Rumour Records 1976

4 Globe Theatre and *No. 1 Hard*

Texts
Bolt, Carol. *Next Year Country*. Typescript, 1971. Globe Theatre files
Deverell, Rex. *Black Powder: Estevan 1931*. Moose Jaw, Sask.: Coteau Books 1982
– *Medicare! Showing West: Three Prairie Docudramas*, edited by Dianne Bessai and
    Don Kerr. Edmonton: NeWest 1982
Globe Theatre. *No. 1 Hard*. Typescript, 1978, 1979. Globe Theatre files

History and Criticism
Ball, Denise. 'Globe to Take Play About Grain on Tour of Rural Communities.' *Regina
    Leader Post*, 1 March 1978
Cosbey, Bob. 'Number One Hard.' *Next Year Country* 5, no 3 (1978): 30–1
Deverell, Rex. 'On the Making of *No. 1 Hard*.' *Perception* [Canadian Council on Social
    Development] 1, no 6 (1978): 12– 13
– 'A Tribute: Sue Kramer.' *Canadian Theatre Review* 21 (1979): 57–9
Glauser, L. 'Prairie Portraits: Globe Theatre, Regina.' *Canadian Theatre Review* 21
    (1979): 53–6
'Globe play to look at grain industry.' *Regina Leader Post*, 23 February 1978
'*Next Year Country*: Revue As Poignant As Blown Topsoil.' *Brandon Sun*, 3 March
    1971
Portman, Jamie. 'Travelling Troupe Really Socks It to Trudeau and Friends.' *Edmon-
    ton Journal*, 8 November 1978
Robertson, Lloyd. '"Hard" Times in the Country.' *Briarpatch*, April 1978, 15–18
Shields, Alex. 'Globe Theatre Revue Presents View on Farm Life.' *Regina Leader Post*,
    1 March 1978
Silvester, Reg. 'The Globe.' *Canadian Theatre Review* 11 (1976): 127–8

Archives
Globe Theatre files. Globe Theatre, Regina

Globe Theatre file. Metropolitan Toronto Library, Theatre Department

Audiovisual
Ursell, Geoffrey. *Number One Hard.* Caragana Records, TCC 7902, 1979

5 25th Street Theatre and *Paper Wheat*

Texts
25th Street Theatre, *Paper Wheat.* Typescript, [1977]. 25th Street Theatre files
– *Paper Wheat. Canadian Theatre Review* 17 (1978)
– *Paper Wheat: The Book.* Saskatoon: Western Producer Prairie Books 1982

History and Criticism
Adams, James. 'Ovation in Sintaluta Launched *Paper Wheat.' Edmonton Journal,* 7 May 1982
Aswell, Keith. 'Prairie Roots Plumbed.' *Edmonton Journal,* 4 July 1979
Bott, Bob. 'Prairie Song.' *Canadian Magazine,* 15 September 1979, 8–10
Conlogue, Ray. '*Paper Wheat* Is the Toast from Coast to Coast.' Toronto *Globe and Mail,* 24 November 1979
– 'Dazzling *Paper Wheat* Inventive and Delightful.' Toronto *Globe and Mail,* 22 November 1979
Cuthbertson, Ken. '*Paper Wheat* Has Something to Please Almost Everyone.' *Regina Leader Post,* 29 November 1977
Daoust, Jean-Paul. '*Paper Wheat.' Jeu* 12 (1979): 199– 201
Eamer, Clair. 'Saskatoon's 25th Street House.' *Canadian Theatre Review* 23 (1977): 111–13
Enright, Robert. 'New Wheat Crossbred from History and Farce.' *Maclean's* 92, no 39 (24 September 1979): 44b–d
Garebian, Keith. '*Paper Wheat.' Scene Changes* 6, no 10 (1978): 27–9
Jeffcott, Bob. '*Paper Wheat.' Next Year Country* 4, no 4 (1977): 28–30
Knelman, Martin. 'Moral Uplift on the Prairies.' *Saturday Night* 44 (1979): 60–1
Lisac, Mark. 'Prairie Play Triumph for Regional Theatre.' *Ottawa Citizen,* 18 August 1979
Macpherson, Jean. '*Paper Wheat*: A Review.' *Saskatoon Star-Phoenix,* 30 March 1977
Mallet, Gina. 'Farm Play's Bright Cast Unable to Fulfill Promise.' *Toronto Star,* 21 April 1980
Perkins, Don. '*Paper Wheat* as Theatre Centre.' *Saskatoon Star-Phoenix,* 14 August 1979
Portman, Jamie. '*Paper Wheat* Ripe for Harvest.' *Edmonton Journal,* 20 June 1979
– 'Popular Historical Farm Stage Production Making Own History in Rural Saskatchewan.' *Calgary Herald,* 3 December 1977
Schoonover, Jason. 'Prairie Portraits: 25th Street House Theatre, Saskatoon.' *Canadian Theatre Review* 21 (1979): 48–51

Archives
25th Street Theatre file. Metropolitan Toronto Library, Theatre Department
25th Street Theatre files. 25th Street Theatre, Saskatoon

Audiovisual
Paper Wheat. Producer Robert Allen. CBC-TV 1980
Paper Wheat. Director Albert Kish. National Film Board of Canada 1979

6 Mummers Troupe and *Buchans: A Mining Town*

Texts
Mummers Troupe: *Buchans: A Mining Town.* Typescript. Mummers Troupe files
– *Gros Mourn.* Typescript. Mummers Troupe files
– *Newfoundland Night.* Typescript. Mummers Troupe files

History and Criticism
Billington, David. 'Mummers Re-enact Miners' Woes.' *Montreal Star*, 25 October 1974
Brookes, Chris. 'History of the Mummers Troupe.' Transcript 1983
– 'Popular Theatre in Newfoundland.' Paper delivered to the Association for Canadian Theatre History Conference, Halifax, 1981
– 'Useful Theatre in Sally's Cove.' *This Magazine* 8, no 2 (1974): 3–7
– Rehearsal Diary, *Buchans: A Mining Town.* Manuscript
'Chris Brookes, Founder of the Mummers, Feels That Theatre Should Be "Useful."' *Newfoundland Herald* TV *Week*, 14 December 1977
Cooke, Michael. '*Buchans – A Mining Town.*' *St. John's Evening Telegram*, 16 September 1974
'Demonstrator's Threats Fail to Stop Gros Morne.' *Corner Brook Western Star*, 14 August 1973
Heindsmann, Sandra. '*Company Town.*' *Mayday* 1, no 1 (1975): 30–9
Kareda, Urjo. 'Concerned Theatre from the Maritimes.' *Toronto Star*, 9 June 1975
– 'Mummers Troupe Shuns Risks.' *Toronto Star*, 18 June 1975
Mallet, Gina. 'Baby Seals Don't Club Baby People, Do They?' *Toronto Star*, 2 March 1978
McVicar, William. 'Mummers' Mining Town Tale Unfolds As Both Drama and Documentary.' Toronto *Globe and Mail*, 12 June 1975
Sherk, Susan. 'One Man's Vision Created the Mummers of Nfld. Now, All He Needs Is Money.' *Atlantic Insight*, May 1979, 54– 5
Souchotte, Sandra. 'Newfoundland's Mummers troupe – from One Controversy to Another.' *Scene Changes* 3, no 7 (July 1975): 7–8

Archives
Mummers Troupe files. Chris Brookes, Petty Harbour, Newfoundland

Audiovisual
Buchans: A Mining Town. Videotape. Mummers Troupe files
Gros Mourn. Videotape. Mummers Troupe files
Newfoundland Night. Videotape. Mummers Troupe files
You Know You're Downtown. [*East End Story*]. Director John Doyle. Film East 1975

7 Catalyst Theatre and *It's About Time*

Texts
Catalyst Theatre. *It's About Time.* Typescript, [1983]. Catalyst Theatre files

History and Criticism
Ashwell, Keith. 'Cons Earn Accolades.' *Edmonton Journal*, 2 January 1983
Bosley, Vivian. 'Catalyst: A Theatre of Commitment.' *Canadian Theatre Review* 27 (1980): 121–4
Catalyst Theatre. *The Catalytic Converter* 1 (December 1981)
– *Catalyst Courier* 2, no 1 (August 1982)
Francis, Lesley. 'Theatre Delights Children with Social Action.' *Edmonton Journal*, 11 July 1980
'Legal Rights for Handicapped Play's Focus.' *Edmonton Journal*, 26 March 1980
Ross, Beverly. 'Rebel Theatre.' *Edmonton Magazine*, January 1981, 41–2
Selman, Jan, and Jane Heather, '*It's About Time.*' Public seminar, Bread and Roses Festival of Popular Theatre, Edmonton, 23 June 1983
Sheppard, Allan. 'Good Theatre for a Change.' *Interface*, January 1983, 38
Silvester, Reg. '"All the world's a stage" and Catalyst Theatre Portrays It.' *Alberta Magazine*, September 1980, 29–30
Willocks, Terry. 'Actors Portray Effects of Alcoholism.' *Lethbridge Herald*, 25 August 1977

Archives
Catalyst Theatre files, Catalyst Theatre, Edmonton

Audiovisual
Incarceration. Producer Jack Emack. CBC-TV 'Catalyst Television' 1983
Stand Up for Your Rights. Producer Jack Emack. CBC-TV 'Catalyst Television' 1981

PART B

Bessai, Diane. 'Documentary into Drama: Reaney's *Donnelly Trilogy.*' *Essays on Canadian Writing* 24–5 (1982–3): 186– 208
– 'Documentary Theatre in Canada: An Inquiry into Questions and Backgrounds.' *Canadian Drama* 6, no 1 (1980): 9–21
– 'The Regionalism of Canadian Drama.' *Canadian Literature* 85 (1980): 7–20
Boal, Augusto. *Theatre of the Oppressed.* Translated by Charles A. McBride and Maria-Odilia McBride. New York: Urizen 1979
Cheeseman, Peter. *The Knotty.* London: Methuen 1977
– *Fight for Shelton Bar.* London: Methuen 1977
Filewod, Alan. 'The Changing Definition of Canadian Political Theatre.' *Theaterwork* 3, no 3 (1983): 47–54
– 'Collective Creation: Process, Politics and Poetics.' *Canadian Theatre Review* 34 (1982), 46–58
Freire, Paulo. *Pedagogy of the Oppressed.* Translated by Myra Bergman Ramos. New York: Herder & Herder 1970
Goorney, Howard. *The Theatre Workshop Story.* London: Eyre Methuen 1981
Halpert, Herbert, and George Story, *Christmas Mumming in Newfoundland.* Toronto: University of Toronto Press 1968
Key, Archibald. 'The Theatre on Wheels.' *Canadian Forum* 13 (September 1933): 462–3

Kinch, Martin. 'Canadian Theatre: In for the Long Haul.' *This Magazine* 10, nos 5 & 6 (1976): 3–8

Livesay, Dorothy. 'The Documentary Poem: A Canadian Genre.' In *Contexts of Canadian Criticism*, edited by Eli Mandel. Toronto: University of Toronto Press 1971

Mackenzie, James Bovell. *Thayendanegea: An Historico-Military Drama*. Toronto: William Briggs 1898

Mair, Charles. *Tecumseh: A Drama and Canadian Poems*. Toronto: William Briggs 1901

Nunn, Robert. 'Performing Fact: Canadian Documentary Theatre.' *Canadian Literature* 103 (winter 1984): 51–62

Quiles, Edgar, and George Schuttler. 'Theatre for a World in Transition: Excerpts from an Interview with Augusto Boal.' *Theaterwork* 3, no 5 (1983): 13–21

Ridout, Denzil. *United to Serve*. Toronto: The United Church of Canada 1927

Rubin, Don. 'Creeping towards a Culture: The Theatre in Canada since 1945.' *Canadian Theatre Review* 1 (1974): 6–21

Ryan, Toby Gordon. *Stage Left: Canadian Theatre in the Thirties*. Toronto: CTR Publications 1981

Salutin, Rick. '*Front Page Challenge* and the Curse of Canadian Culture.' *This Magazine* 10, no 5 & 6 (1976): 26– 7

– 'More on Documentaries.' *This Magazine* 11, no 4 (1977): 23–4

Usmiani, Renate. *Second Stage: The Alternative Theatre Movement in Canada*. Vancouver: University of British Columbia Press 1983

Villemure, Fernand. 'Aspects de la création collective au Québec.' *Jeu* 4 (1977): 57–71

Wallace, Robert. 'Growing Pains: Toronto Theatre in the 1970s.' *Canadian Literature* 85 (1980): 71–85

– and Cynthia Zimmerman. *The Work: Conversations with English Canadian Playwrights*. Toronto: The Coach House Press 1982

Wright, Richard, and Robin Endres. *Eight Men Speak and Other Plays from the Canadian Worker's Theatre*. Toronto: New Hogtown Press 1976

Index